Effectual Entrepreneurship

What are you waiting for?

Whether you're dreaming about starting a business, learning about entrepreneurship, or on the brink of creating a new opportunity right now, don't wait. Open this book. Inside you will find everything you need.

This book contains:

- A vivid new way to learn about and to practice entrepreneurship.
- Practical exercises, questions and activities for each step in your process.
- Specific principles derived from the heuristics of expert entrepreneurs.
- 70+ case briefs of entrepreneurs across industries, geographies and time.
- Applications to social entrepreneurship as well as the creation of opportunities in large enterprises.
- Data that will challenge assumptions you might have about entrepreneurship.
- A broader perspective about the science of entrepreneurship and implications for how individuals can shape their own situation.

You will find these ideas presented in a concise, modular, graphical form, perfect for those learning to be entrepreneurs or already in the thick of things.

If you want to learn about entrepreneurship in a way that emphasizes action, this book is for you. If you have already launched your entrepreneurial career and are looking for new perspectives, this book is for you. Even if you are someone who feels your day job is no longer creating anything novel or valuable, and wonders how to change it, this book is for you. Anyone using entrepreneurship to create the change they want to see in the world will find a wealth of thought-provoking material, expert advice, and practical techniques inside.

So what are you waiting for?

Stuart Read is a Professor of Marketing at IMD.

Saras Sarasvathy is the Isadore Horween Research Associate Professor at The Darden School, University of Virginia.

Nick Dew is an Associate Professor of Strategic Management in the Graduate School of Business and Public Policy at the Naval Postgraduate School.

Robert Wiltbank is an Associate Professor of Strategic Management at the Atkinson School of Management, Willamette University.

Anne-Valérie Ohlsson is an independent writer, researcher, and creator.

Effectual Entrepreneurship

Stuart Read,
Saras Sarasvathy,
Nick Dew,
Robert Wiltbank and
Anne-Valérie Ohlsson

 Routledge
Taylor & Francis Group

LONDON AND NEW YORK

First published 2011
by Routledge
2 Park Square, Milton Park, Abingdon, Oxon OX14 4RN

Simultaneously published in the USA and Canada
by Routledge
711 Third Avenue, New York, NY 10017

Routledge is an imprint of the Taylor & Francis Group, an Informa business

Typeset in Minion and Frutiger by
Florence Production Ltd, Stoodleigh, Devon

British Library Cataloguing in Publication Data
A catalogue record for this book is available from the British Library

Library of Congress Cataloging in Publication Data
Effectual entrepreneurship/Stuart Read . . . [et al.].
        p. cm.
    Includes bibliographical references and index.
    1. Entrepreneurship.   2. New business enterprises.   3. Success in business.
    I. Read, Stuart.
    HB615.E453 2011
    658.1′1—dc22   2010022448

ISBN13: 978–0–415–58643–6 (hbk)
ISBN13: 978–0–415–58644–3 (pbk)
ISBN13: 978–0–203–83690–3 (ebk)

Contents

Acknowledgments

Writing any textbook is an effort which extends well beyond a team of authors. And writing one about effectuation involves an enormous network of self-selected stakeholders, many of whom we would like to recognize here. First, we would like to thank our families for their enduring patience as we talk endlessly about this topic and then disappear endlessly to write about it. Second, we recognize the entrepreneurs. As you read through this book and enjoy the uniqueness and color of each of the stories, please appreciate that this was enabled by individuals willing to share their time in teaching us. Third, we have had many useful inputs from individuals active in new venture financing, and we would like to call to special attention Artie Buerk and Andy Dale of Montlake Capital for their access and patience in exploring ideas around new ventures. Fourth, we would like to express gratitude to our institutions. Willamette University, Darden, NPS and IMD have offered us the freedom, funding and encouragement to pursue big projects, and we are deeply grateful. And finally, though not least, our writing collaborators. In addition to Beverley Lennox spending tireless hours trying to turn our Word documents into English, Catherine Egli and Emma Brown accumulating permissions for all the interesting art in the book, with Amy Wiltbank working for countless revisions to create a cover that communicates the idea of an opportunity that's made, together with Terry Clague and Elisabet Sinkie and the team at Taylor & Francis who co-created something novel and hopefully valuable with us, there is a greater cast of editors and reviewers within the academic system who, over many years, have provided us with challenging questions and great suggestions for our academic papers that have significantly refined the ideas in this book. That said, all errors and omissions are completely our responsibility, and as entrepreneurs we will use these unexpected surprises to inform and improve the next revision. Effectually yours, the author team.

Image acknowledgments

The authors and publisher would like to thank the following, for permission to reproduce their images in this book.

'New chart' (p. v) © Rob Bouwman – Fotolia.com; 'Start' (p. viii) Tetra Images/Getty Images; 'Old map' (p. 1) © Alex Staroseltsev – Fotolia.com; 'Bears in stream' (p. 2) © Red – Fotolia.com; 'Old sailing ship' (p. 2) © Carina Hansen – Fotolia.com; 'Pet Rock image' (p.7) Courtesy of http://montaraventures.com/blog; 'Earth' (p. 8) NASA/courtesy of nasaimages.org; 'Light bulb' (p. 10) Epoxydude/Getty Images; 'Waste plastic' (p. 12) © Roberto Fasoli – Fotolia.com; 'Loft bed' (p. 15) Photo courtesy of CollegeBedLofts.com; 'Key lime pie' (p. 15) Photo courtesy of Kenny's Great Pies; 'Dinner at Unsicht-Bar' (p. 16) Photo courtesy of Unsicht-Bar; 'Mark Moore' (p. 17) Photo courtesy of Mark Moore; 'Skiier' (p. 20) © Ludwig Berchtold – Fotolia.com; 'Mouse with Helmet' (p. 21) Courtesy of Boeri; 'U-Haul truck' (p. 28) Photo courtesy of U-Haul; 'Empty pockets' (p. 30) © Vitaliy Pakhnyushchyy – Fotolia.com; 'Coffin couch' (p. 34) Photo courtesy of 1–800-Autopsy; 'Fortune teller' (p. 36) Tom Le Goff/Getty Images; 'Satellite image' (p. 39) Courtesy of the Office fédéral de météorologie et de climatologie MétéoSuisse; 'Beatles' (p. 40) © Corbis; 'Sinking ship' (p. 40) © Corbis; 'Sigg bottle' (p. 41) Photo courtesy of Sigg AG; 'Freitag bags' (p. 42) Photo courtesy of Freitag AG; 'Swimming man' (p. 44) Floresco Productions/Getty Images; 'Sears poster' (p. 45) Courtesy of Sears Advertising Archives; 'Drawing from Boing-Boing book' (p. 47) Courtesy of Can of Worms Enterprises; 'Ark cartoon' (p. 51) © Off the Mark Cartoons; 'Goodkaarma soap' (p. 53) Photo courtesy of GoodKaarma; 'Dougal Sharp' (p. 55) Photo courtesy Innis & Gunn; 'Lemonade/bottled water cartoon' (p. 56) © Mike Baldwin – www.cartoonstock.com; 'Wavebob rig' (p. 57) Photo courtesy of Wavebob; 'Padmasree Harish and a rickshaw' (p. 59) Photo courtesy of EasyAuto; 'Failure/success signpost' (p. 61) © jaddingt – Fotolia.com; 'Bratz' (p. 63) Photo courtesy of MGA Entertainment; 'HERSHEY'S® chocolate bar' (p. 65) Provided courtesy of HERSHEY'S®; 'Ice Cold Lemonade cartoon' (p. 65) © Vahan Shirvanian –

www.cartoonstock.com; 'Bird losing fish' (p.67) © Doug Harrington Photography; 'Graveyard cartoon' (p. 69) Courtesy of Business around the Globe © 2006 Michiel Jonker; 'Sunset sailing' (p. 71) © Stefan 2003 – Fotolia.com; 'Open refrigerator' (p. 72) © bshphotography – Fotolia.com; 'AquaStasis pH level indicator' (p. 76) Photo courtesy of AquaStasis; 'EcoEnvelopes logo' (p. 77) Image courtesy of EcoEnvelopes; 'Esher drawing' (p. 83) © 2010 The M.C. Escher Company – Holland. All rights reserved. www.mcescher.com; 'Manon chocolates' (p. 86) Courtesy Manon Chocolates; 'Manon chocolates' (p.87) Courtesy Manon Chocolates; 'Waste paper' (p. 88) © cs-photo – Fotolia.com; 'Powerkiss table' (p. 90) Photo courtesy of Powerkiss; 'Scales' (p. 91) © istock: http://www.istockphoto.com; 'Crop harvest' (p. 92) Photo courtesy of Novozymes; 'Building the world' (p. 94) © Stephen Coburn – Fotolia.com; 'Fortune Newspapers cartoon' (p. 96) © Clive Goddard – www.cartoonstock.com; 'Risk cartoon' (p. 99) © Patrick Hardin – www.cartoonstock.com; 'Newspapers' (p. 100) © Robert Harding Picture Library/SuperStock; 'Flowers' (p. 101) © Otmar Smit – Fotolia.com; 'Calvin and Hobbes cartoon' (p. 102) © 1995 Watterson. Reprinted by permission of Universal Uclick. All rights reserved; 'Boots' (p. 105) © Warren Millar – Fotolia.com; 'Stacy's Pita Chips' (p. 111) Photo provided courtesy of Frito–Lay North America, Inc; 'Solution image' (p. 113) © Roman Milert – Fotolia.com; 'Quilt' (p.113) © R_R – Fotolia.com; 'Fifty–fifty split cartoon' (p.114) © Patrick Hardin – www.cartoonstock.com; 'Expanding cycle of resources' (p. 117) © Accent Alaska.com. All rights reserved; 'ICEHOTEL' (p. 118) Photo courtesy of ICEHOTEL; 'ICEHOTEL' (p. 119) Photo courtesy of ICEHOTEL; 'Electric vehicle' (p. 122) © AlcelVision – Fotolia.com; 'Pilots' (p. 125) © Ian Andrews – Fotolia.com; 'Congratulations cartoon' (p. 129) © John Morris – www.cartoonstock.com; 'Dog cookies' (p. 130) Photo courtesy of Castor & Pollux; 'The yellow sari' (p. 135) © Jeremy Richards – Fotolia.com; 'Apple' (p. 138) © vikiri – Fotolia.com; 'Surprised man' (p. 140) © MAXFX – Fotolia.com; 'Silly putty' (p. 142) Photo provided courtesy of Crayola LLC, used with permission. © 2010 Crayola. (Silly Putty® is a registered trademark of

Crayola LLC); 'Surprise signpost' (p. 143) Joseph Sohm–Visions of America/Getty Images; 'Sun art' (p. 146) © napi – Fotolia.com; 'Elephants' (p. 148) Photo provided courtesy of Wilderness Lodges; 'Business plan placards cartoon' (p. 151) © Mike Baldwin – www.cartoonstock.com; 'Rubik's Cube®' (p. 154) used by permission of Seven Towns Ltd – www.rubiks.com; 'Children in gDiapers' (p. 156) Photos provided courtesy of gDiapers; 'Baby' (p. 157) © Monika Adamczyk – Fotolia.com; 'Rocket' (p. 159) © AlexanderGordeev – Fotolia.com; 'Wind turbine' (p. 160) Photo provided courtesy of Ecotricity; '"If not now" cartoon' (p. 162) © Marek – Fotolia.com; 'Red man' (p. 163) © istock: http://www.istockphoto.com; 'Company logo cartoon' (p. 164) © Tim Cordell – www.cartoonstock.com; 'Quixote knight' (p. 166) © hava – Fotolia.com; 'Coffee beans' (p. 167) Image courtesy of Lyell Read; 'Panera Bread logo' (p. 167) Photo courtesy of Panera Bread; 'Ducati images' (pp. 169–70) Provided courtesy of Ducati; 'Future signpost' (p. 173) © Joe Gough – Fotolia.com; 'Ken Lay's future cartoon' (p. 180) © Harley Schwadron – www.cartoonstock.com; 'Soldier' (p. 181) Photo provided courtesy of Hydration Technologies, Inc; 'Dominoes' (p. 182) © Grasko – Fotolia.com; 'Red Hat logo' (p. 185) Photo provided courtesy of Red Hat; 'Men at sea' (p. 186) © Ralph Hagen – www.cartoonstock.com; 'Racing boat' (p. 187) © Darren Baker – Fotolia.com; 'Grow' (p. 189) JGI/Getty Images; 'Fortune teller' (p. 191) © Pete Saloutos – Fotolia.com; 'Spice' (p. 192) © felix – Fotolia.com; 'Gore–Tex membrane' (p. 195) Photo courtesy of GORE–TEX®; 'Grameen Bank money' (p. 200) © Photononstop/SuperStock; 'Hospital bed image' (p. 202) © Jonathan Torgovnik – photo provided courtesy of the Institute for OneWorld Health; 'Ashoka image' (p. 205) Photo provided courtesy of Ashoka; 'Image of space' (p. 208) Photo provided courtesy of NASA/nasaimages.org.

Every effort has been made to contact copyright holders for their permission to reprint images in this book. The publishers would be grateful to hear from any copyright holder who is not here acknowledged and will undertake to rectify any errors or omissions in future editions of this book.

Introduction

DEAR READER,

Whether you come to this book as an entrepreneurship student, a corporate manager, or a seasoned creator of new ventures, you already know that entrepreneurship is becoming the de facto engine of growth, innovation, and that most delicious of personal freedoms—financial self-reliance.

What you will discover in this book is that there is a science to entrepreneurship—a common logic we have observed in expert entrepreneurs across industries, geographies, and time. The underlying principles are the same ones that enabled Josiah Wedgwood in the eighteenth century to transform a pottery business into an enduring brand, helped Earl Bakken, founder of Medtronic, to transform his college job into a company that has become a global leader in medical technology, and allowed Mohammed Yunus to transform the lives of millions of women in Bangladesh. As you begin the book, you will come face-to-face with some of the common misconceptions about entrepreneurship, as well as some of the fears faced by every entrepreneur. In the heart of the book, you will find four core principles plus a fifth overarching view that expert entrepreneurs have learned in the process of creating new ventures, products, and markets. Each of these will be explained through cases, stories, thought exercises, and a variety of practical applications. Though simple and easy to put into action, these principles challenge and even invert traditional logic used in mature organizations:

1. **Start with your means**. Don't wait for the perfect opportunity. Start taking action, based on what you have readily available: who you are, what you know, and who you know.
2. **Set affordable loss.** Evaluate opportunities based on whether the downside is acceptable, rather than on the attractiveness of the predicted upside.
3. **Leverage contingencies.** Embrace surprises that arise from uncertain situations, remaining flexible rather than tethered to existing goals.
4. **Form partnerships.** Form partnerships with people and organizations willing to make a real commitment to jointly creating the future—product,

firm, market—with you. Don't worry so much about competitive analyses and strategic planning.

5. **Create opportunities.** When you can make the future happen by working with things within your control and people who want to help co-create it, you don't need to worry about predicting the future, determining the perfect timing, or finding the optimal opportunity.

Throughout the book you will find examples of consumer and business-to-business ventures, technical and non-technical, in as many industries and geographies as we could find. As you reach the conclusion of the book, you will find applications of these principles to issues that range from social entrepreneurship to large firms. And you will understand the challenges entrepreneurs face as lovingly created ventures become mature businesses.

When you start a new venture—for-profit or not, individually or within existing organizations—you are not only trying to make a good living, you are engaged in expanding the horizon of valuable new economic opportunities. This book is designed to help you do that from start to finish. And, in form and content, the book embodies the expert entrepreneurs' logic—bold, systematic, pragmatic, and at all times full of energy, mischief, and fun.

How to use this book

We carefully designed this to be much more than a textbook. Certainly, it can accompany you through a course in entrepreneurship, and we hope it will.

But it is also prepared to venture outside the academic environment into the uncertain world of start-up creation.

As much as the sequence of the book is intended to tell a logical and sequential story, every one of the chapters is also designed to stand on its own. So whether you start at the beginning and read through, or jump to the chapter (13) on partnerships in the moments before a meeting with a prospective stakeholder, we intend that the book be your partner in creating new opportunities.

Practically speaking

In every chapter you will find brief stories of new ventures. Every one of the more than 60 stories about entrepreneurs illustrates at least one of the principles described in this book. You will find stories matched with topics in each chapter. But if you choose to focus on just the "practically speaking" stories, you can skip from one to the next, and quite literally tour the entrepreneurial world. Alternatively, you can select specific stories as we have created a directory connecting stories with effectual principles, industry, or geography.

Research roots

There is an enormous body of academic research on entrepreneurship; far too much for us to include in a book you could actually carry in your laptop case. So we searched for foundational research that has shaped thinking over the years, and contemporary research that reflects current knowledge to date. In the context of a chapter, we summarize the key points of a research stream in "research roots" to give you an idea of what other scholars are working on and to offer directions for further reading if you have interest in a specific topic.

Roadmap

Let's face it, entrepreneurs like to do things. So at the end of each and every chapter we have prepared a series of actionable things you can do to put the ideas in the chapter into practise. Like everything else in the book, these are designed to accompany the sequential story or to stand alone. So create your roadmap as you read, or feel free to review the entire inventory of roadmaps to get a feel for what a complete new-venture journey might look like.

Explained:

The word effectuation is not one that you might have used every day—before you read this book, that is. And a handful of other terms and ideas need a bit of background. So the first time we use a word that makes people in the classroom give us that quizzical look, we highlight it in a box within the text. Not in a glossary where you have to flip to it, but right there in anticipation of your question.

So what?

Impatient? Eager? Want the bottom line? We have tried to summarize the one idea we hope you will take away from each chapter in "So what?" The goal is not to encourage you to skip the chapter. Quite the contrary. If you are wondering whether a chapter is worth your time, skip to the "So what?" If the idea seems relevant to the challenge of starting a new venture, know that you will find a whole lot more detail in the chapter.

Bigger questions

Between them, the authors of this book have more than ten new ventures under their belts. So we understand the need for practical, immediate, and relevant material. At the same time, we have provided space to consider some of the larger topics entrepreneurship opens up: the more intellectual questions that you may not find appealing in the moment when you have to close a financing round, but you might appreciate on a long contemplative hike with your partner during the weekend. We keep these for the very end of each chapter so as not to distract from the business of getting a venture going. But we hope you will enjoy taking the time to step back every once in a while and consider the broader implications of what you are accomplishing.

I want to be an entrepreneur but . . .

PART I

The eight chapters that compose the first part of the book present the four most common misconceptions about entrepreneurship, and the associated and pragmatic questions that hold individuals back from starting a new venture—namely, "I don't have an idea, money, entrepreneurial skills—and I'm afraid to fail." These fears arise from misconceptions that are similar to those ascribed to those pioneering explorers who set sail onto the open seas. History has stylized early adventurers as visionary heroes, possessing superhuman abilities and extraordinary luck. In fact, the process of drawing the map of the world is similar to the process an entrepreneur employs in starting a new venture. Both do what they can with the things they have available. Both embrace surprise as an asset. And both create new maps that define our world for generations to come. We encourage you to look past the glamorous retelling of entrepreneurial lore and instead focus on the systematic principles that experts learn, principles that you can apply yourself as you create your own map.

CHAPTER 1

Many opportunities are created, not discovered.

Myth: Entrepreneurs are visionaries

■ ■ ■

I**F YOU ARE** reading this, you are most probably looking for a roadmap to success. You are, of course, not alone. Most human beings who have their basic needs satisfied share this quest with you. Each may define success differently: For some it may be a happy family, for others it may be power and fame, and for yet others it might simply be independence, dignity, and the opportunity to achieve the creative potential within—and of course make oodles of money doing it! There are probably as many ways to define and achieve success as there are human beings. However you define success, entrepreneurship is an exciting, important, and useful way to achieve it—for entrepreneurship is about the very creation of new roadmaps, not only for you, but also for a subset of humanity around you.

This book is about roadmaps: not only about finding existing ones that work well, but also about fabricating new ones that forge new paths and even help reshape the terrain and perhaps even make new worlds altogether. So, fasten your seatbelts—here come mind-bending possibilities rooted in street-smart realities, all culled from rigorous academic research.

THE LEGENDARY ROADMAP TO SUCCESS

Let's begin with one standard roadmap to success—the kind that Bellman's crew might laugh at, but one that a lot of people think is the most typical one used by entrepreneurs:

1. "Entrepreneur" searches for "new" and "high-potential" opportunity.
2. Light bulb goes on.
3. Writes business plan.
4. Goes out fund-raising—especially from venture capitalists (VCs).
5. Hires great team.
6. Builds product.
7. Orchestrates big launch.
8. Achieves steady or hockey stick growth.
9. Sells or launches initial public offering.
10. Retires to Bahamas.

However, there is a problem with this roadmap. When we look at the start-up histories of companies and the biographies of the entrepreneurs who founded them, this roadmap has no bearing on their actual course. One study found that only 28 percent of a sample of Inc. 500 firms had completed a formal classic business plan (Bhidé, 2000). And less than 27 percent of IPOs are funded by VCs (Gompers and Lerner, 2001: 145).

So how do expert entrepreneurs really create enduring companies? For the past 12 years or so, we, along with collaborators around the world, have been engaged in research to answer this question and describe specific techniques based on the answers we uncovered. The results of our investigations point to clear principles detailed in this book. The results challenge us to rethink several key issues concerning what people believe about how great entrepreneurship actually happens.

THE MYTHICAL VISIONARY

Entrepreneurs are the heroes of our times: Jeff Bezos, Stelios Haji-Ioannou, and Richard Branson are the daring visionaries of our common corporate cultures—conquering new markets, thriving on risk and pursuing opportunities that others simply could not see. Their map of the world, unlike that of Lewis Carroll's Bellman, seems to hold direct leads to the treasure. Or so it seems.

The portrait of the visionary entrepreneur is very much in line with the dominant belief in economics and entrepreneurial research today—that new opportunities are discovered through the exploration of a given set of existing markets and the identification of the most promising opportunity—the search and select approach. A promising opportunity is one expected to yield the highest

> The Bellman himself they all praised to the skies—
> Such a carriage, such ease and such grace!
> Such solemnity, too! One could see he was wise,
> The moment one looked in his face!
>
> He had bought a large map representing the sea,
> Without the least vestige of land:
> And the crew were much pleased when they found it to be
> A map they could all understand.
>
> "What's the good of Mercator's North Poles and Equators,
> Tropics, Zones, and Meridian Lines?"
> So the Bellman would cry: and the crew would reply
> "They are merely conventional signs!"
>
> "Other maps are such shapes, with their islands and capes!
> But we've got our brave Bellman to thank"
> (So the crew would protest) "that he's bought us the best—
> A perfect and absolute blank!"
>
> Lewis Carroll, *The Hunting of the Snark* (1874)

returns after adjusting for potential risks.

But let's see how it can possibly work. For example, who could predict the returns, before anyone else had tried it, of investing in an expedition looking for a route to India in 1649? Of creating a low-cost airline targeted at customers who pay for their own tickets in 1980? Of putting a bookstore online in 1990?

With the benefit of hindsight, the search and select approach seems to make a lot of sense. Clearly, discerning European palates wanted exotic spices by the boatload. Of course there was a market for low-cost airlines! Naturally, people would want to buy their books online, where they can choose from an almost infinite selection and do not have to stand in a queue! All an entrepreneur does is identify the opportunity and exploit it, in the same way the bears pictured at the start of the chapter have identified the ideal time and place for lunch. But this assumes that the decision to create a new market can be backed by perfect, or near perfect, information that can be acquired prior to starting the venture and that will remain valid once the venture is started.

To see both sides, imagine investing your own personal retirement funds. Based on past patterns of how people buy items at garage sales, would you have bought into Auctionweb's expected return projections in 1995? If you had, you would be a very wealthy shareholder in eBay now. But then, using very similar historical information on pet product purchases, you would also have trusted the insight behind the spectacular failure that awaited Pets.com. The visionary entrepreneur, just like the bears in our picture, turns out to be unusual indeed.

ARE OPPORTUNITIES FOUND OR MADE?

If the search and select view cannot explain some of the successes or

failures of new ventures, what is the alternative? Do opportunities exist, or do they not? Is historical information useful as a basis for decision-making, or is it not? And how does this help someone interested in starting a business?

There is no right or wrong answer to the question of whether opportunities

Explained:

Create and transform

Transformation logic suggests that entrepreneurs generate new opportunities without searching and selecting from existing "markets." Instead, entrepreneurs are observed using an "effectual logic," whereby they start with who they are, what they have, and who they know (we outline the principles of effectuation in Chapter 7 and detail them in Part II).

An important part of the process lies in the role of self-selected stakeholders who choose to become part of the new market creation process. The entrepreneur and committed stakeholders together transform their means into new goods and services. Often, the final product/service is neither anticipated at the start of the venture nor even imagined as an objective or goal to be reached.

Explained:

Search and select

The basic idea is that a market already exists in some form and that companies enter that market via technology innovations, better offerings, or seizing opportunities that emerge from what buyers implicitly or explicitly ask for (an unmet need). In each of these cases it is possible to estimate the potential of the market based on population segments and past demand. We call this a causal process. Causal venture creation begins with exploration resulting in the identification, recognition, or discovery of an opportunity, followed by a series of tasks necessary to exploit the opportunity. The search and select view goes hand in hand with the supply and demand theory of classical economics.

are found or made. The search and select approach (opportunities found) is useful in explaining the success of new ventures in predictable environments. We know people listen to music on the move and we know the Internet provides broader access to music libraries. So we search and select the software and a device, add some design, and we have the MP3 player. However, this does not explain the Walkman. There was no market and no historical data to guide its creation. The idea that possibilities are transformed into opportunities (opportunities are made) is an alternative view that is useful in exactly those situations where the past cannot help predict the future. As such, which view dominates depends on how the entrepreneur chooses to see the situation.

Opportunities are found

Entrepreneurs operating under the search and select worldview start by looking at traditional growth areas of a market and the largest unserved segments of the population in that market. This information will help them select the best possible opportunity. Once the opportunity is chosen, entrepreneurs develop business plans based on extensive market research and detailed competitive analysis. He or she then looks to acquire the resources and stakeholders that will help implement the plan. Over time, entrepreneurs adapt the venture to the environment, in an attempt to create and sustain a competitive edge.

The "found" view assumes that the budding venture is sufficiently similar to an existing business so that historical information will inform decisions in the new venture, and the environment is sufficiently stable so that outcomes from the past will be relevant to the current situation and the future.

Opportunities are made

Under the made approach, the information available to the entrepreneur at the start of a venture is both incomplete and overwhelming. The market cannot be defined. Consumers are not aware of their future preferences. New technologies may emerge. Available data are confusing and conflicting. That implies that entrepreneurs do more than simply recombine existing resources or transfer them from their current use to one that yields better returns. In reality, he or she *creates* or *transforms*, thereby generating new opportunities from mere possibilities.

Because new ventures are uncertain, effectual logic often prevails

Surprising as it may seem to aspiring entrepreneurs, the "made" view and associated effectual logic often prevails in the world of expert entrepreneurs. Many of the firms we admire started out doing nothing close to what they do today. Opportunities were made over time and through interactions with customers, partners, and employees. The following practical example gives us two alternative routes of how to pursue the same possibility. One alternative is "found," the other is "made."

PRACTICALLY SPEAKING: CURRY IN A HURRY

Imagine an entrepreneur who wants to start an Indian restaurant. Using a search and select approach, she would start by doing some market research in the restaurant industry in the city of her choice. Based on the market research, she would then select a location very carefully, segment the market in a meaningful way, select target segments based on estimates of potential return, design a restaurant to appeal to her target segments, raise the required funding, bring her team together, and, finally, implement specific marketing strategies and manage daily operations to make her restaurant a success.

Research roots

Joseph Schumpeter (1934) theorized that demand could be created, proposing that innovations took the form of "new combinations" that involved employing existing things in new ways (transformations). These transformations could result in new markets, new production processes, new products, new ways of organizing, and new methods of distribution. Schumpeter defined "the carrying out of new combinations" as the essence of entrepreneurship.

CONTRASTING VIEWS ON THE SOURCE OF OPPORTUNITY

The difference between:	The market	The logic	The process
Search and select (causation)	Search and select normally assumes, either explicitly or implicitly, a conscious intent to capture a new, underserved, or latent market. In the literature on entrepreneurship, this normally takes the form of visionary individuals searching for and exploiting market opportunities.	In the search logic, the entrepreneur has a finite set of possibilities that he/she can look into, generally at the local level. The logic does not say how such a search is actually conducted, only that it leads to a given set of possibilities.	Because the goal is predetermined at the start of the venture, the search and select process is a static process that does not evolve over the course of the venture. Surprises are seen as bad.
Creation and transformation (effectuation)	In the concept of transformation, the creation of a new market need not be intentional or even the result of foresight or imagination of possible new markets. It could simply be one way to fulfill an individual's motivations and/or an unanticipated consequence of people just doing things they think are possible and worth doing.	Transformation also begins with very local possibilities. However, rather than looking to select these, entrepreneurial action is seen as involving the transformation of possibilities into opportunities.	Transformation is dynamic and interactive—it is the actions and interactions with committed stakeholders who self-select into the entrepreneurial process that leads to particular transformations that may or may not lead to new markets. Surprises are good.

Using a more creative and trans-formative approach, what actually happens would depend on who our entrepreneur is, what she knows, and who she knows. For the sake of understanding the process here, let us say she is a good Indian chef who is considering starting an inde-pendent business. Assuming she has very little money of her own, what are some of the ways she can bring her idea to market? She might partner with an existing restaurant, participate in food fairs, set up a catering service, and so on. Let us say that the actual course of action she decides to pursue is to persuade friends who work downtown to allow her to bring lunch for their office colleagues to sample. Then some customers sign up for a lunch service, and she begins preparing the lunches at home and delivering them personally. Eventually, she could save up enough money to rent a location and start a restaurant.

It is equally plausible that the lunch business does not take off beyond the first few customers. However, using a creative and transformative logic, our entrepreneur could co-create other enterprises depending on whatever her customers are actually interested in, besides her cooking. For example, maybe it is her personality that is interesting; she could then produce a cooking video or maybe start a cooking school. Contingent on who is interested in what, our entrepreneur could go into any one of several different businesses. To cite but a few possibilities, her eventual successful enterprise could turn out to be in any one or all of the following industries —entertainment, education, travel, manufacturing and packaging, retail, interior decoration, or even self-help and motivation!

Explained:

Causation

The focus is on achieving a desired goal through a specific set of given means. Causation invokes search and select tactics and underlies most good management theories.

Effectuation

The focus is on using a set of evolving means to achieve new and different goals. Effectuation evokes creative and transformative tactics. Effectual logic is the name given to heuristics used by expert entrepreneurs in new venture creation.

THE PRINCIPLES OF EFFECTUAL KNOWLEDGE

The "curry in a hurry" example illustrates two principles of the effectual logic. The first is that opportunities can be made. The second is that the creation of a new market may be the result of an accident, good old Murphy's Law or serendipity. Not only that, but the new market is viewed as residual, in some ways a "side effect" of lots of different people doing things they think are worthwhile. In the process, they produce a new market, even though they may not have consciously intended that in

Practically speaking

Making a market out of a joke

Gary Dahl was out one evening having a few drinks with his buddies when the conversation turned to pets. Dahl, a California advertising man, joined in by claiming he had a pet rock—an ideal pet with a great personality that was easy and cheap. His friends laughed at the idea. Little did they know that a pop-culture fad was about to be born.

It was April 1975, and Dahl's initial idea was to write a book—*The Care and Training of Your Pet Rock*—a step-by-step guide to having a happy relationship with your geological pet. He spent the next few weeks writing the book, which included instructions on training the Pet Rock to do tricks, such as roll over (best taught on a hillside) and play dead (which the rocks love to practice on their own). As the book took shape, Dahl decided to add some props—an actual rock nestled in some excelsior and packaged in a little carrying case, equipped with breathing holes. Dahl found his Pet Rock in a builder's supply store in San Jose. It was the most expensive rock in the place at a penny apiece.

After introducing the Pet Rock at the San Francisco gift show in August, and then later in New York, Neiman-Marcus placed an order for 500. Then, based on a homemade news release that showed a picture of Dahl surrounded by his Pet Rocks in their carrying cases, Dahl was able to attract some great publicity, including a half-page story in *Newsweek*. He was also invited to be a guest on *The Tonight Show* twice. By the end of October he was shipping 10,000 Pet Rocks a day, and by Christmas, when 2.5 tons of rocks had been sold, three-quarters of all the daily newspapers in the US had run Pet Rock stories.

Just a few months after unleashing his Pet Rock, he had sold more than one million units at US$3.95 apiece. Dahl—who, from the very beginning, had decided to make at least one dollar from every rock—had become an instant millionaire.

Served by http://montaraventures.com/blog/

the beginning, let alone articulated it or explicitly adopted it as a goal. The goals of the venture are just as likely to be created in the process of doing as they are to be preconceived a priori. While Columbus had the goal of discovering India, his mission was transformed when he was surprised by a new continent.

The Pet Rock is a particularly amusing example of a market that could not have been anticipated or preconceived. Read the example nearby and consider whether Dahl was serving an apparent unmet need for pet rocks. Remember that there was no historical data on "non-living or geological pets" at the time; the venture began more or less as a joke between an entrepreneur and his friends, with no intention of making money.

This in turn highlights another important aspect of effectual logic:

Success or failure does not hinge on how accurate the original vision turns out to be and how well the strategies crafted to deliver that vision are executed. Success is individually defined and it may change as the venture changes. The relationships formed in the process of venture creation also influence what the venture looks like and how success is defined.

CREATE YOUR OWN OPPORTUNITIES

Casual readers of history often see heroes, visionaries, and explorers as possessing super-human qualities. This impression is reinforced by the larger-than-life descriptions of successful entrepreneurs we read about in the news. In this chapter, we have started separating myth from reality. Our first finding is that entrepreneurs are not necessarily visionaries who are

better/faster/smarter than others at seizing and exploiting opportunities that no one else can see. Instead, in many cases, they make their own opportunities using mundane means. While entrepreneurs have traditionally been thought of as discoverers, we view them also as creators—terra-forming as well as map making.

TAKEAWAY: IT'S UP TO YOU

What does that mean for you? Basically, it means that you do not need to sit and wait for a unique opportunity to come hurtling at you from the sky. On the contrary, it is up to you to create that opportunity. This calls for a much more active role on your part and for you to feel comfortable with a blank map that you will fill in based on your tastes, abilities and means, what you know, and who you know. This is the situation our early explorers (and the Bellman) were in. Entrepreneurship is what happens when the co-creation of opportunity does not need to rely on luck.

In the next chapter we talk about one of the big implications of created entrepreneurial opportunities versus discovered. If entrepreneurial opportunities are discovered, having a great idea is the key. If they are co-created with partners, that great idea is not the critical ingredient.

> Twenty years from now, you will be more disappointed by the things you didn't do than by the ones you did do.
>
> So throw off the bowlines. Sail away from the safe harbor. Catch the trade winds in your sails.
>
> Explore. Dream. Discover.
>
> Mark Twain (1835–1910)

Roadmap

You have seen two different approaches to how markets come into existence. For insight into your own venture:

- ■ Look at your favorite companies and think about whether they made or found opportunities.

- ■ If you imagine they were made, what were the ingredients?

- ■ How do you "make" an opportunity?

- ■ Is there anyone in your environment you can co-create with?

So what?

The transformation approach systematically results in more variety and is strongly preferred by expert entrepreneurs as a means of creating new markets and new businesses.

Bigger questions

Beyond the immediate topic of this chapter, think about the following questions:

- ■ What is the purpose of entrepreneurship?

- ■ Is there a dark side to entrepreneurship—no map, no rules?

- ■ Is there anything that cannot be created?

CHAPTER 2

Most people who want to start a venture say they haven't yet because they don't have a good idea.

The fact is that good ideas are cheap and plentiful.

It's what you do with them that matters.

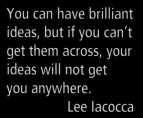

You can have brilliant ideas, but if you can't get them across, your ideas will not get you anywhere.
Lee Iacocca

I don't have a good idea

BECAUSE PEOPLE are focused on the myth of the visionary entrepreneur, the thing that holds many potential entrepreneurs back is that they have not yet had that eureka moment of pure vision—they don't have a good idea.

One clear fact emerges from research into entrepreneurial expertise and early-stage histories of new ventures —it is not possible a priori to know with any certainty whether an idea will turn out to be a good business opportunity. In fact, successful entrepreneurs and experienced investors state that there is only one way to determine whether a given idea is a good business opportunity: go ahead and implement it creatively with very low levels of investment and either find real customers who are willing to buy the product or service at a reasonable price, or locate partners willing to commit real resources to the venture early on—or, ideally, both.

Understandably, most first-time entrepreneurs, especially those who have good job-market prospects, tend to worry a lot about finding the "right" opportunity. Hence, the angst about waiting for an idea that is "good."

What is a good idea? Where do ideas come from? Who decides what a good idea is? When and how do you recognize that an idea is feasible or not?

As you think about these questions, consider Medtronic. In 1949, inspired by the impact of electricity on life as depicted in the 1931 movie *Frankenstein*, Earl Bakken founded the medical devices firm. But it was a long time until the pacemaker was even conceived. Bakken spent his first eight years operating as a medical equipment repair technician. In 1957, after years of interaction with doctors and the medical industry, the founder began pioneering the pacemaker. Even then, the idea was hardly a vision.

Where do ideas come from?

In theory:

- *Patent Office Gazette*
- Government (NASA, CERN)
- Technology transfer
- Trade shows
- Doctoral dissertations
- Invention expositions
- Brainstorming

In practice:

- Personal satisfaction and dissatisfaction
- Link with prior vocation: market knowledge
- Outgrowth of hobbies
- Ideas thrust on one by others
- Acquisition of company or product already started
- The news
- Ideas rejected by employer or other company
- Very small start, then growth
- Customer generated ideas

Once introduced, a medical industry analyst organization predicted an all-time world market for pacemakers of most 10,000 units. Ironically, though that meant a small market to analysts, Bakken and his team rejoiced—they were selling fewer than 100 at the time! Today, Medtronic is an US$11 billion business and a leader in the medical devices field. So set aside your worries about having a good idea. Opportunities are created by action.

IDEAS ARE A DIME A DOZEN

The simplest way to come up with an idea is to think of things we like and things we don't like, things we wish we had, things we would like to get rid of, things we care about, and so on. In fact, like the queen in *Alice in Wonderland*, most of us can come up with six new venture ideas before breakfast. But we don't necessarily know what to *do* with them. Or even whether we want to do anything with them.

It is important to reiterate here that there is no such thing as a "good" idea upfront—there are only ideas we implement and ones we don't. A good idea can be wasted, just like a bad idea can be turned into an opportunity.

Think of successful ventures you know and where their ideas came from. Throughout this book there are examples of such ventures, most of which started out as mundane, even silly ideas. Yet today they are financial blockbusters like Google and Walmart, or ventures that achieved sweeping social change, like Grameen Bank and the Red Cross. Some, like Agilyx

(see the nearby box), even came from trash. If you still feel you need some kind of validation, we suggest ways of assessing an idea on the following pages. But these are not meant to be "go—no-go tests." They are simply ways for you to think through and choose between multiple ideas in a useful way.

IS IT A GOOD IDEA?

DeWhitt's story is one example of an entrepreneur who went for what mattered to him. Mark Moore's creation of One True Media (detailed

Useful contacts for generating ideas

- Lawyers
- Other entrepreneurs
- Accountants
- Venture capitalists
- Bankers
- R&D people
- Patent attorneys
- Purchasing agents
- Businesspeople
- Salespeople/distributors
- Trade associations
- Executives
- Potential customers (could be any of the above!)

Practically speaking

Another person's treasure

Good ideas for new companies can come from anywhere—from a frustrated customer, a breakthrough invention, or, as Kevin DeWhitt would tell you, from the trash. In 2004 he and his wife founded Agilyx Corporation with the idea of taking plastic waste and turning it into something better than money—crude oil. From a chemical engineering perspective, it makes perfect sense. Plastic is a petroleum product. Why not reverse the process when you're done with the plastic? Simple enough, in theory. In practice, the science turned out to be difficult, but the business even more difficult.

You need customers to generate revenues. You need a product to attract customers. And you need cash to build a product. DeWitt had none of these to start the cycle. The team's solution was to combine angel investment with a customer willing to assist in the development and deployment of a fully operational prototype. By creating with its customer, Agilyx built a complete working system that could be demonstrated to potential new customers, provide real-time environmental data to regulators, and give the team ideas for optimizing the system for full commercial deployment. The reason it worked is that Agilyx and the customer are operationally committed to the success of co-creating an entirely new approach to the problem of plastic waste.

Today, Agilyx's initial client can convert several thousands of pounds of mixed waste plastic into hundreds of gallons of sweet synthetic crude oil each day. While this is exciting, it is utterly dwarfed by the fact that 26 million tons of plastic are sent to landfills annually in the US, and more than three times that amount are disposed of in Europe and China. Having proven the concept, Agilyx now has to figure out how to scale the business up to be able to handle this enormous quantity of fuel.

Starting with trash might not be the most intuitive basis for a new venture, but with the potential to process mixed waste plastic into nearly 250 million barrels of crude oil annually in the US alone, the opportunity could be worth more than US$25 billion. If you are scoffing at this, consider that eBay created a market of more than twice that size for people's unwanted household items (translation: trash) in just over ten years. So if you are looking for a business idea, one of your assets might just be another person's trash.

on p. 17) was a reaction to the frustration his friends had in managing the explosion of photos generated by digital cameras. But how do you assess the feasibility of an idea? With hindsight, it is easy to say it was a good idea, but when you're at the edge and getting ready to jump, how do you know you should?

There are countless frameworks in textbooks, trade books, journal articles, periodicals, and on the web that claim to predict the feasibility and value of new venture ideas. The "Assessing opportunity 'doability'" figure depicts a simple and useful summary of four key concepts that are at the heart of many of these frameworks:

- Is it doable?
- Is it worth doing?
- Can I do it?
- Do I want to do it?

The first two elements have to do with external factors such as the technology of the time and the market environment for the business idea. The last two are internal, depending on the personal circumstances and motivations of the entrepreneur making the decision. We will explore the latter in more detail in Chapter 6.

Following is a list of questions that correspond to each of the four quadrants of the figure. The techniques usually recommended for gaining the answers to these questions include market research based on surveys, focus groups, interviews, demand forecasting, risk evaluation and risk reduction strategies, and financial pro formas with sensitivity analyses. Where you cannot get information, use these questions as a checklist of what you should be thinking about.

Is it doable?

Technological feasibility

- Is the technology for your product already available, or is it still in development?
- If the technology is still in development, what stage is it at and what can go wrong?
- If the technology is available, is anyone else using it to develop the same product/service as you?
- If not, why not?
- If so, who are they and how does that affect your prospects?
- What kind of entry barriers for the future does your technology provide?
- How long would those entry barriers last should your idea prove to be a high-potential opportunity?
- What are your adoption risks? List reasons why the end user

might not want to use your technology even though your product/service might be technologically superior.
- What other nascent technologies might become competition in the future—one year from now, five years from now, a few decades from now?

Market feasibility (product)

- What exactly are you selling?
- Is it a technology looking for a market or vice versa?
- How do you define your niche?
- How is the need being filled now?
- Who/what is the competition?
- What are the advantages/disadvantages of the product/service?
- Why your product (differentiation/uniqueness/proprietary)?

Customer

- Who is your customer (a typical profile)?
- Will the customer pay enough? Can you charge enough?
- What critical factors will lead you most quickly to your customer base?

Market

- Is there a market?
- How large is the market?
- What is its structure?
- How fast is it growing?
- Where could future competition come from?

Economic feasibility

- Are there any obvious roadblocks from the government—both local and national?
- Is the international situation likely to change?

ASSESSING OPPORTUNITY "DOABILITY"

	FEASIBILITY	VALUE
MARKET	**Is it doable?** Technological feasibility Market feasibility Economic feasibility	**Is it worth doing?** Financial feasibility
PERSONAL	**Can I do it?** What will it take to do it? Who else do I need?	**Do I want to do it?** What turns me on about it? Why do I want to do it? Exit strategies

- What are your exit strategies?
- Is your timing ideal?
- Are you in the path of a paradigm shift?
- Are you too far ahead of the times?
- What is the shape and duration of the "window" for this opportunity?

Is it worth doing?

Financial feasibility
- What is the initial outlay of funds required?
- What would convince an investor to contribute those funds?
- If you personally owned those funds, would you invest them in this idea?
- How is the financing connected to the timing issue (breakeven, cash consumption (burn) rate)?
  - Develop a set of financial forecasts.
  - State the primary financial assumptions for your projections.

Can I do it?

What is it going to take?
Every idea is different in terms of exactly what it would take to build it into a business. But some general negative expectations might include:

- long and often unpredictable work hours
- setbacks and disappointments along the way including the possibility of major failures
- an arduous and sometimes awkward learning process with

regard to dealing with people—including hiring and firing
- negotiating tough contracts
- dealing with rejections of various types
- sustaining the best stakeholders through bad times such as cash crunches.

A realistic understanding of some of the negative experiences, combined with a strong positive motivation, is essential for long-term success in entrepreneurship.

Why you?
- What special strengths do you bring to this enterprise?
- What are your relevant weaknesses and how will you overcome or compensate for them?

Do I want to do it?

- Does it excite you?
- Why do you want to do this—really?
- What are your exit strategies?

The importance of commitment

These questions will also help you decide which idea to go for if you have more than one. However, remember that it doesn't matter how good the checklist looks, an idea is not a good idea until you find someone who is willing to support it in one way or another—some form of pre-commitment from partners or customers is essential.

In the end, what really matters is not whether you think it's a good idea but

whether you can get someone to commit to your idea. Otherwise, the idea is not sustainable. Commitment is not only financial—it can come in the form of someone lending you office space, taking the time to serve as

Research roots

Innovation adoption

Everett Rogers (2003) initiated a line of research on new products across products, industries, and time where he has identified five attributes of an innovation that are highly predictive of whether the innovation will be adopted. They include:

- ◻ Relative advantage: Is the innovation perceived as better than what it replaces?

- ◻ Compatibility: Is the innovation consistent with the values, experiences, and needs of potential adopters?

- ◻ Complexity: Is the innovation perceived as difficult to use?

- ◻ Trialability: Is the user able to experiment with the innovation?

- ◻ Observability: Are the results of an innovation visible to users?

Whether or not you like the words, these are good, common-sense tests of whether "the dogs are going to eat the dog food."

a mentor, a company willing to share manufacturing resources, someone who picks up a phone and calls others for you, and so on.

We will look at pre-commitments and partnerships in greater detail in Chapter 13, but there is at least one thing you need to consider at the very outset: If you can't find anyone beyond yourself that thinks it's a good idea, maybe it's not. Finding someone willing to commit to your idea in a tangible manner stops you from going out and investing a lot in something in which people have only expressed polite interest. There is no such thing as tentative commitment.

But how do you know when you should give up? How long do you look for someone to commit before simply dropping the idea? That question depends on how much you can afford to lose (more on this in Chapter 11). Maybe you can afford to wait for years for your idea to come of age. Early investors in video-conferencing technology did so. Sometimes ideas, especially technology-based ideas such as certain kinds of renewable energy today, stew on the back burner for a long time. Affordable loss puts a limit on how much time you commit.

THE IDEA BEHIND THE BUSINESS

PRACTICALLY SPEAKING: TURNING A HOBBY INTO A BUSINESS

When John Vence's son Michael went off to college, his father equipped him

with a loft bed to maximize the tight space in the campus dormitory. Word of mouth soon spread and Vence was delivering loft beds hundreds of miles from his home in Horseheads, New York. Demand got to be so great that Vence investigated what was necessary to ship his beds nationally, and took the hobby to a full time business. Now, College Bed Lofts makes and sells about 5,000 unfinished wood lofts a year to customers coast to coast.

PRACTICALLY SPEAKING: TURNING A PASSION INTO A BUSINESS

Kenny Burts is a man passionate about key lime pie. A connoisseur by the age

of nine, he refined his own key lime pie recipe in the mid-1980s, and nearly everyone who tasted his pies told Burts he should sell them. In 1989 he started Key Lime Inc. as a part-time venture, making about 100 pies per week for individuals and small local restaurants out of his apartment. Now located in Smyrna, Georgia, the firm has gone on to land name brand clients such as California Pizza Kitchen, has hired 20 people, and has the capacity to produce 6,000 pies a day. Not to worry, though. In spite of the success, Burts assures us that the firm, which is now called Kenny's Great Pies and celebrated its 20th anniversary in 2009, is still making key lime pies according to exactly the same recipe and using the same fresh-squeezed key lime juice that earned his early rave reviews.

PRACTICALLY SPEAKING: TURNING A DISABILITY INTO A BUSINESS

Ever been on a blind date? Most people say it's simultaneously scary and exciting, and it's always memorable; which is also what people say about Axel Rudolph's Unsicht-Bar. Unsicht-Bar is a small Cologne eatery run by the blind where patrons enjoy wine, cuisine, and conversation in pitch dark. Even the glow of a mobile phone is not permitted in this establishment. Diners are attended by blind waiter/guides who describe the food both in terms of its preparation and its location on the plate.

Since its opening in 2002, Unsicht-Bar has won acclaim from critics and restaurateurs alike. In addition to the novel yet empathic experience of spending the evening with someone who can't see, eliminating the sense of sight intensifies the rest of the senses so that Unsicht-Bar's simple fare (the chef seasons with only salt, pepper, garlic, onions, and herbs) comes alive in a way that you might never have tasted before.

> **You smell better, you are more receptive to differences in texture, consistency and temperature . . . it's a holistic experience.**
>
> **Axel Rudolph**

Unsicht-Bar's popularity has led Rudolph to open additional locations in Hamburg and Berlin, and has brought an intriguing innovation to the rather old and boring restaurant industry.

Rudolph's venture embodies a powerful insight into success that is visible in innovations in a variety of areas. Take Post-it notes, for example—who would want glue that cannot stick? Blindness is generally considered a liability—a handicap. Rudolph inverts

Characteristics of a good idea

- High margins—able to estimate costs accurately
- "Goodness" ratio: price × performance = two or more
- Relatively low capital—at least to prove business works
- Financeable—time to break even relatively short
- Understandable
- Helps to be "fashionable"
- Growing market or market segment; big enough
- Identifiable market, distribution, reasonable marketing cost
- Where management skill can be leveraged
- Proprietary, patents, trade secret, uncommon knowledge
- Where skills, speed of response, and flexibility are important
- Changing environment—produces opportunities
- Specific market need identified versus a new process/technology looking for applications
- Technical development risks relatively low compared to payoff
- Big enough to be significant
- Initial critical mass not too big

it. Unsicht-Bar makes blindness a point of differentiation and a basis for advantage. He takes a negative and makes it positive.

Inversions are everywhere. Consider violent video games. Criticized for the disruptive psychological effects on minors, games like Full Spectrum Warrior are now the basis for an emerging software market in treating war veterans with post-traumatic stress disorders. Retro styles are an inversion of the idea that clothing goes out of fashion. And celebrities driving inexpensive, compact Toyota Priuses invert the notion that wealth and luxury are embodied in a large car.

The next time you feel you are on a blind date with destiny, look around you. Look for things that evoke a negative response. And think about transforming them into a positive basis for a new venture. For, as experienced entrepreneurs will tell you, opportunities are usually blind dates—simultaneously scary and exciting, yet memorable and, more often than you might think, worth embracing.

THE IDEA-TO-VENTURE FORMULA

So now you know that divine intervention is not the source of opportunities, where do viable ventures come from? They start with an idea. And ideas generally start with a transformation of the means you already have:

But we also know that ideas are plentiful—and commonplace. It is action that turns a mere idea into a valuable opportunity:

> **IDEA = ANYTHING + YOU**

Gathering information does not count as action. Action is proposing a deal with a client. Action is getting a supplier to knock together a prototype.

> **OPPORTUNITY =**
> **IDEA + ACTION**

Action is convincing a co-founder to join the business. Action goes beyond observation and calculation to invoke transformation, manipulation, fabrication—it's a function of interaction with the world:

> **ACTION = FUNCTION**
> **(INTERACTION) on MONEY,**
> **PRODUCT, PARTNERS . . .**

Practically speaking

One True Media

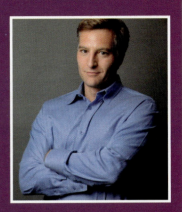

Mark Moore is an expert entrepreneur. With two acquisitions and an IPO behind him, expectations on the venture he founded, One True Media, are high. So where do the ideas come from? How does Mark create that flash of brilliance that gives ignition to a company—a successful company? Mark keeps a list. Not a list of ideas for companies, but a list of problems he sees every day. Call him a technology anthropologist. The problem behind One True Media was that suddenly people everywhere were generating an unmanageable quantity of digital content. Tiny digital cameras, video cameras, and camera phones were filling hard disks with photos and videos at an alarming rate. There was no good way to organize, present, or edit the information. Mark knew he could create something the world needed.

What exactly did amateur photographers want? And how would he translate that into a business model? Mark simply got started. He founded One True Media knowing he would change the business model quickly and continuously. The initial online service let users create a montage—a scrapbook from their photos. One True Media would print it, package it in a photo album, and mail it to the user. From the start, the company began learning and is still learning. It changes the service every two weeks. Employees watch how people use the service, constantly adding and removing features. There is a phone number, an email feedback form, and a live chat for suggestions. Every week Mark reviews all the inputs and sends the top five promising or consistent suggestions to the entire company.

In creating ventures, it's little changes that really matter. One True Media had a terrific holiday season in 2005, but in January 2006 the business went dark. Mark and his team kept changing. At the end of January they had a breakthrough. People wanted to share. One True Media added a simple feature that let users put photos and video onto MySpace, an internet community site. All of a sudden, users were doubling every two weeks. Countless more changes later, One True Media has over a million registered users who have created millions of videos, and the firm just launched a new venture called SpotMixer which enables business users to create their own videos without any software.

Mark is not unique. Successful ventures are rarely a flash of brilliance. An idea is sculpted and sometimes radically changed in conjunction with customers and partners. Mark's philosophy is this: "Think of yourself in a room with many locked doors. Your customer is on the other side of one of the doors. She is yelling at you, saying, 'I'm over here.' Your job is to unlock the right doors. The faster you unlock doors, the sooner you find real opportunity."

Finally, what turns an opportunity into a viable business is commitment. Commitments result in revenue, hiring, and production lines starting up at suppliers:

> **VIABLE VENTURE =
> OPPORTUNITY +
> COMMITMENT**

This formula is dynamic and iterative. Most enduring firms started very differently from where they are at today. Their founders repeatedly implemented the formula to interactively create more valuable opportunities than their original ideas would have allowed them to ever imagine.

TAKEAWAY: EVERYBODY HAS A GOOD IDEA

Eric von Hippel (1994) at MIT examined the sources of successful invention in large corporations. He found that the overwhelming majority of new ideas that turned out to be profitable product lines came not out of research and development departments, but out of customer inputs such as complaints and suggestions piped in through support and service departments. Similarly, most enduring new ventures did not come from the original ideas upon which they were founded. For example, FedEx began with the idea of delivering spare parts, RealNetworks began as an interactive television channel, and it did not initially occur to the founders of Starbucks to brew a cup of the exotic coffee beans and ground coffee they were trying to sell. In fact, most successful entrepreneurs find that they have to abandon the opportunity they first perceived and be willing to change their "vision" in response to external feedback and stakeholder negotiations, both in the early stages and as they grow.

Sticking very closely to who you are, what you know, and who you know tells you not only what to do, but also what not to do. The problem with most novice entrepreneurs is not that they do not have great new ideas for ventures, it is that they have too many.

WHAT BUSINESS PLAN? EXAMPLES OF RADICAL BUSINESS MODEL CHANGE

Company	Where they started	What they do now
Tiffany & Co.	Started as a provider of stationery in 1837.	Not until 1853 did the firm shift over to jewelry.
Colgate	Soap, candles, and starch were the first products.	Though founded in 1806, Colgate did not make toothpaste for nearly 70 years.
Nokia	Since its founding in 1865, Nokia has been in industries from rubber to paper.	Only about 100 years after its founding, in the 1960s, did Nokia start with phones.
Hasbro	Textile remnants were the first offering from the Hassenfield Brothers.	Toys were not offered until 1952, some 30 years after founding.
John Deere	Started as a blacksmith making plows.	It has a full range of farm products, but it is best known for making tractors.

And they don't move any of them to real commitments from other people. They see opportunities everywhere and, if they have the resources, feel tempted to expand product lines too soon, or jump into too many new market segments all at once. Especially if they have some initial success, it is easy to feel prescient (i.e. believe they can clearly predict the future) as well as omnipotent (i.e. believe they can achieve the improbable). But good ideas are often a lot less glamorous than that.

Robert Reiss, founder of R&R, a company that brought games like Trivial Pursuit to the US once said,

People think they shouldn't go into business unless they have a blockbuster idea that's going to change the world. It doesn't really work that way. There are few new blockbuster ideas. There are just mundane kinds of ideas. You do something better than someone else. You take an existing thing and you add a new twist. It is just like Scrabble. You take an existing word, you put one letter on it and you get credit for the whole word—your letter plus the whole word.

Roadmap

As you work toward plunging:

- [ ] List five ideas that you think are really good and five that you think are terrible. What is the difference between them?

- [ ] Think of an idea you love, pick the critical hurdle to making it happen, and think about how you would solve it. This may change the scope and nature of your idea, which does not mean it was a bad idea. Why is that hurdle the hurdle?

- [ ] Consider the extreme case: How about becoming an entrepreneur without having any ideas at all? What would be the first step?

A mediocre idea that generates enthusiasm will go further than a great idea that inspires no one.
Mary Kay Ash

So what?

You need not wait for the blockbuster idea or the multi-billion-dollar opportunity to come your way. You can begin with a simple problem for which you see an implementable solution—or even something that you simply believe would be fun to attempt—and start.

Bigger questions

Beyond the immediate topic of this chapter, think about the following questions:

- [ ] Do we live in societies that encourage innovation?

- [ ] Now that we realize that the magic of entrepreneurship is not in the idea, where is it?

Risking their own time, money and reputations, entrepreneurs are more conservative even than bankers.

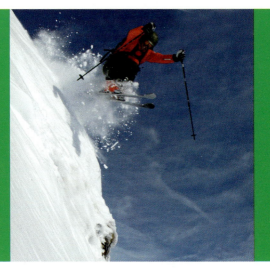

Security is mostly a superstition. It does not exist in nature, nor do the children of men as a whole experience it. Avoiding danger is no safer in the long run than outright exposure. Life is either a daring adventure, or nothing.

Helen Keller

Myth: Entrepreneurs are risk takers

I S RISK TAKING an attribute of people—something they are born with? Or is it something that can be taught and learned? Is risk an inseparable attribute of entrepreneurial ventures, or is it a characteristic of the environment in which entrepreneurship occurs? Are all risks created equal? If not, what metrics can we use to classify different types of risks? Do all people perceive the same "risk" in the same venture? If not, why not?

FACTORS OF PRODUCTION

After reflecting a little on these questions, let us roll up our sleeves and explore a framework through which we can tackle them. For that, we turn to one of the very first and most exciting dissertations in entrepreneur-ship published in 1921 by a doctoral student named Frank Knight.

Take any simple product, say a pen. If you ask yourself, "where does the value or price of this pen come from?", you will get at least three types of answers—these can be mapped onto the three "factors of production" that are listed in every Economics 101 textbook. They are as follows:

- The value of the pen comes from the raw materials that go into it—the factor of production equivalent here is "land" and the price of land is usually termed "rent."

- The value of the pen also comes from the people who actually produced it—their time and effort and skills. This factor is "labor" and the price of labor is usually termed "wages."

- The value of the pen also includes the ideas, creativity, and design of the technologists who invented it and the machinery and business processes that were used to produce it. This is listed under "capital" and the price of capital is usually termed "interest" or "return on investment."

And, if the market is "efficient," argued the classical economists, then these three factors of production cover all the value that goes into the making of the pen—and should cost no more and no less than the prices paid for the three factors. Ergo, "profit" should equal zero in this set—i.e. when demand and supply are in sync with each other in an open and efficient market environment.

THE FOURTH FACTOR OF PRODUCTION: ENTREPRENEURS

It was this utopian view of micro-economics that Knight (1921) assaulted when he argued that human capital (which includes entrepreneurship) is a necessary fourth factor of production, and that "profit" was the price paid for it. While Knight did not say it in these words, this is a simplistic interpretation of his argument.

What do entrepreneurs contribute?

So what do entrepreneurs bring to supply and demand? And why do they appear to keep such a big share of the price of the products and services that, after all, are made up of the raw materials, labor, and investments

belonging to their stakeholders? The answer lies in the simple fact that after the other three factors are paid for, there may or may not be anything left over for the entrepreneur who brought them together to create new value in the world. In other words, before new products or services are produced and sold, there is no guarantee that they can indeed be produced, nor is there any assurance that they will indeed be bought at a price above the cost of production. Someone has to bear the uncertainties involved in bringing new products and services into the market—even creating new markets where none existed before. In other words, demand and supply are not always and cannot always be known before the entrepreneur acts.

Why do entrepreneurs get the lion's share?

Most entrepreneurs have never even heard of Knight—and that's okay. But imagine you started an IT firm that needs to hire a chief technology officer. Most good technical people do

not understand how the price of a product is determined. Not because they are not smart (they can often be smarter and perhaps more sophisticated than founding entrepreneurs), but because good technical people have been spending their time and energy on technical skills. And even the best of technology education frequently does not include exposure to business concepts or the role of entrepreneurship in economics.

Hence, good technologists, even when they perceive the technical "value" of a product (or think they do!), wonder why products are priced so high, or why the marketing person often makes more money than the techie, or even why the founding entrepreneur gets the lion's share of the pie in the first place. Pointing to Knight's (1921) thesis not only makes a credible case to them, but also provides a fun and easy way to approach otherwise delicate issues such as negotiating relevant and just compensation—not to mention the necessity to share in the risk.

Most people, not just technical folks, assume that price, customers, and

markets can be analyzed and outcomes predicted. Or they go to the other extreme and fear vague and undefined "risks" associated with starting a company—based on the oft-repeated bromide "most firms fail." We will tackle this particular combination of misconceptions in later chapters. For now, let us return to Knight for a very useful way to understand problems of risk in the entrepreneurial setting. Because not only did Knight make a very strong case for the relationship between risk taking and profit, he also showed in some detail that not all risks are alike.

A JAR FULL OF RISK

Imagine a game where you win if you pick a red ball. There are three jars in front of you. One has an equal number of red balls and green balls. The second contains balls, but you do not know how many are red. And you have no idea what the third jar contains. Which jar would you choose?

In 1961 Ellsberg (1961: 643–69) did an experiment and found that most people prefer the game with the jar in which they know the proportion is 50/50 and not the one where they do not know the proportion. That seems intuitive enough. But now, ask yourself, "Which of those jars would an entrepreneur choose?" Researchers speculated that entrepreneurs might prefer the unknown to the known, i.e. they are risk takers and hence would pick the second jar.

But all those years ago Knight had already argued that entrepreneurs, by definition of operating in the unknowable, implicitly would choose the third jar; that there are so many dimensions to the entrepreneurial problem and each of these dimensions is likely to vary in so many different ways as to make the prediction problem impossible to even attempt, let alone solve. Knight (1921) also argued that entrepreneurs should be entitled to profits above what might be economically normal in exchange for managing what

has since come to be known as "true" uncertainty or "Knightian" uncertainty.

To put this into context, few business situations are represented by the first jar. Nothing is cleanly predictable. Educators believe that most business situations fall into the second jar. All the forecasting, prediction, and scenario analysis tools that are taught in school are approaches for determining the distribution contained in the second jar. But when you understand that entrepreneurs are drawing from a completely different jar, it's easy to understand why a set of completely different principles apply to how they learn to make decisions.

Without arguing whether expert entrepreneurs actually view the world through the lens of Knightian uncertainty, let us simply ask ourselves what some good examples of the three types of jars would be. Once we describe, understand, and play with this notion enough, we can begin talking about how to make decisions and act in the face of true uncertainty—in fact, a substantial portion of this book is devoted to strategies and tactics to play the game in Knight's third jar.

PREDICTION, RISK, AND UNCERTAINTY: WHERE'S THE MAP?

We will be using the terms prediction, risk, and uncertainty to identify the types of problems that the three jars represent. It is important to understand the difference between the three concepts because each calls for a different approach. When the future

Research roots

Frank Knight

Frank Knight was born in 1885 in McLean County, Illinois. The son of Christian farmers, he never completed high school, but went on anyway to American University in Tennessee in 1905. By 1916 he had completed his doctoral studies in economics with a dissertation entitled "Cost, Value, and Profit."

This was the start of brilliant academic career. In addition to teaching many of the Nobel Laureates of the current era (Milton Friedman, Kenneth Arrow, and Herbert Simon among them), Knight was a prolific publisher. Within his contributions, he creates the notion of entrepreneurship as the fourth factor of production; that in addition to land, labor, and capital, the entrepreneur manages uncertainty and in exchange is justified a profit.

is predictable (i.e. we know the distribution of balls within the jar), we can use our knowledge of the past to predict future occurrences and common recurring patterns. When the future is risky (i.e. when we are dealing with an unknown distribution), we can still use the past and our instincts about the future, but we also need to test the waters as we go, learn new patterns, and find ways to adapt to the new patterns wherever possible, as well as hedging our bets any way we can.

But when the future is truly uncertain (i.e. when the distribution is unknowable or nonexistent or not yet in existence), what do we do?

Prediction: The static map

Classical economists (and most business schools) teach us that markets exist and are predictable, to a greater or lesser degree, and that sooner or later every market reaches a point of perfect equilibrium where supply and demand intersect.

Since Adam Smith (1759) introduced the notion of the invisible hand of the market that helps allocate scarce resources to the best possible use through individuals making decisions based on their self-interest, countless academics and managers have found ways to predict the behavior of that invisible hand. Underlying virtually every management tool today, from the sales forecast to expected value calculations to real options analyses, is the belief that Adam Smith's insight can be estimated from historical information of one sort or another.

Research roots

Adam Smith

Adam Smith was a key figure in the intellectual movement known as the Scottish Enlightenment. He gained international attention when his examination of societal ethics—*The Theory of Moral Sentiments*—was published in 1759. But it was his book entitled *An Inquiry into the Nature and Causes of the Wealth of Nations* (1776) that secured his fame and went on to beome a classic of modern economics. Widely acknowledged as the "father of economics," Smith is known for his explanation of how rational self-interest and competition can lead to economic well-being and prosperity. He also coined the metaphor, "invisible hand of the market," which is a term economists use to describe the self-regulating nature of the marketplace. His work helped to create the modern academic discipline of economics and provided one of the best-known rationales for free trade and capitalism. It was his writings on supply and demand that encouraged academics and businesspeople to believe that many economic activities could be modeled and predicted.

In recent times there has been a larger appreciation of the fact that not all elements of the market are known or even knowable in any meaningful manner. Our models, therefore, cannot rely on prediction alone but have to allow for risk—the idea that not all the actors would necessarily behave in a predetermined manner nor would everyone even have access to the information necessary to make good decisions. Notions such as risk and imperfect information, therefore, have

Explained:

Prediction

Prediction is the ability to determine future events based on past recurring patterns.

become more common in economic analysis today.

Risk: The dynamic map

Unlike problems of prediction, which only require extrapolation, problems of risk call for the estimation of likely changes under multiple scenarios over time. Decision-making under risk involves calculating the odds of a specific outcome, based not only on existing information, but also on trial and error as we gain more information. In other words, while prediction only allows defensive tactics, risk can be *managed* through more proactive measures.

Countries assess risk—for example in the Cold War the super powers attempted to use scenario planning to assess a range of possible outcomes. This approach was picked up and

Risk taking: Comparing entrepreneurs and bankers

Which, would you say, is the most risk averse profession? Until the financial crisis of 2008, most of us would probably answer "bankers" (while secretly thinking, they had better be, after all, they are managing my account). We decided to test that hypothesis. A group of bankers and entrepreneurs were given a series of problems to solve, all in the context of managing a manufacturing plant. The problems included financial risk, risk to human life and health, and risk of a natural disaster. For each problem, we looked for similarities and differences in the ways bankers and entrepreneurs reacted.

When it came to purely financial problems (investing in a new product), the entrepreneurs and bankers seemed to have very different perceptions of what could be controlled: The entrepreneurs seemed to accept risk as a given—as a result, they worked on controlling the returns rather than the risk. Their approach was to pick an acceptable level of risk and then push for larger profits, selecting the project with the best worst-case scenario. They also expressed confidence that they could make the reality better than the worst-case probability. In contrast, bankers suggested many ways of controlling risk and practically no measures to increase returns. They seemed to believe that they could generate the highest possible returns and somehow work on minimizing the risks.

The next set of problems involved decisions around human life and health. The context was the following: The factory's industrial hygiene consultant has recommended an investment of US$3 million to put a hood and special ventilation apparatus over the production area. The consultant concluded that a rupture of a pipe could spill an extremely toxic chemical, endangering the workers. When questioned closely, the consultant expected the pipe would rupture less often than once every ten years, that a rupture could cause the death of eight workers, and that putting up the hood and ventilation system would mean that only four workers would die if a pipe ruptured. A second option would require a US$10 million investment to put in special pipes and enclose the area so there would be a much lower chance of a pipe bursting, and there would be no worker exposure if the pipe did rupture.

In this situation, where the trade-off was between a US$3 million option that only reduced the risk to the workers' lives due to a pipe burst but did not eliminate it, and a US$10 million option that eliminated it but could not be afforded by the firm, all the entrepreneurs rejected the US$3 million option outright and came up with creative suggestions to pay for the US$10 million option. Besides possible technical suggestions, they also considered asking for volunteers and giving up equity, selling to a larger company, or cooperating with competitors to increase price.

None of the bankers made a decision—their suggestions were doubtful and evasive. All of them said they would invest the US$3 million because that was better than doing nothing. They did not make creative suggestions for raising the US$10 million. Their reactions focused on trying to delay the decision, suggesting that more information was needed, or hoping that they would not have to make the decision. The way both groups saw their decision spaces can be schematized, as illustrated in the figure "Differential approach to risk between entrepreneurs and bankers."

continued . . .

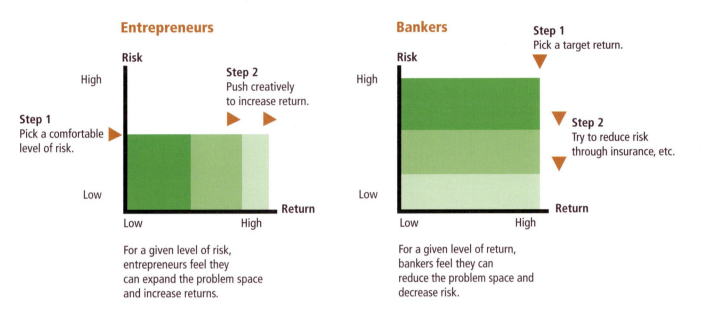

DIFFERENTIAL APPROACH TO RISK BETWEEN ENTREPRENEURS AND BANKERS

For a given level of risk, entrepreneurs feel they can expand the problem space and increase returns.

For a given level of return, bankers feel they can reduce the problem space and decrease risk.

. . . continued

In the first figure the light green square represents the initial problem space of the entrepreneurs. They seemed to pick a relatively low level of risk that they felt comfortable with, and then came up with suggestions as to how they would increase returns at the same given level of risk. They expressed ways to expand the original problem space (the light green square) into the darker rectangles along the X-axis.

The second figure shows how the bankers used their problem space. They picked a level of return that they aspired to (the light green square) and came up with ideas to reduce the risk involved at that level. So they proceeded to collapse the original problem space (the light green square) into the darker rectangles along the Y-axis.

What we see is that entrepreneurs accept risk as a given and focus on controlling outcomes at any given level of risk; they also frame their problem space with personal values and consequently assume greater personal responsibility for influencing outcomes. Bankers use target outcomes as reference points and attempt to control risk within the existing structure of the problem space, avoiding situations where they risk higher levels of personal responsibility. In short, their approaches to risk are different—the bankers try to predict risk while the entrepreneurs try to control risk and are willing to accept uncertain outcomes over unacceptable outcomes.

improved upon by companies such as Shell, who used scenario planning to determine the risks associated with fluctuations in oil production and prices. It then made its way to financial derivatives (options, futures, and the like) before being generalized as a tool for decision-making.

Uncertainty: The blank map

Uncertainty refers to a situation in which no historical data exists to help the decision maker. Uncertainty cannot be modeled or predicted. It is a future that is not only unknown but also unknowable.

Uncertainty is a situation that is not new to academic research. Influential business writers such as Clayton Christensen (1997) and Chan Kim and Renée Mauborgne (2005) have looked at uncertainty in the context of innovation and new markets. Christensen focused primarily on how to help managers who were the "victims" of uncertainty, while Kim and Mauborgne looked at how managers could turn the existing environment upside down, in effect creating uncertainty for others. While both of these approaches help us consider uncertainty as a given of the business environment, they do not provide an overall perspective on how to work with uncertainty as an opportunity for creation.

Uncertainty exists with any new product, new market, or new technology that one chooses to go into and it can happen at any level—from the macro (global warming, the end of fossil fuels) all the way to the micro (the CEO has a heart attack). Who can predict the future of stem cell research today? Or that of bio fuels? When the price of oil dropped below US$10 per barrel in December 1998 it seemed unimaginable—barring any major damage to production or distribution capacity—that by the summer of 2004 the price would jump to over US$50 and keep going to reach a peak

Research roots

Disruptive innovation

Disruptive technologies are one source of externally driven uncertainty. A disruptive technology or innovation has the impact of "disrupting" an existing market. Because it overturns dominant products or services, a disruptive technology imposes uncertainty on customers, firms, and entire industries.

The term disruptive technology was coined by Clayton Christensen and Joseph Bower in their article "Disruptive technologies: catching the wave" (Christensen and Bower, 1995). In that article and in Christensen's subsequent book, *The Innovators' Dilemma*, they show how each new generation of disruptive technologies in the disk drive industry successively wiped out the existing players who were over-serving existing customers and introduced a whole new wave of firms and partners using the new technology.

Research roots

Research roots: Blue ocean strategy

Blue ocean strategies offer one example of internally driven uncertainty. The metaphor of red and blue oceans describes the market universe. Red oceans are industries in existence today—the known market space. In the red oceans, industry boundaries are defined and accepted, and the competitive rules of the game are known. Blue oceans, in contrast, denote all the industries not in existence today—the unknown market space, untainted by standards, expectations, and competition. In blue oceans, demand is created rather than fought over. There is ample opportunity for growth that is both profitable and rapid. In blue oceans, competition is irrelevant because the rules of the game are waiting to be set. Blue ocean strategies are about playing a different game—with the the aim of creating blue oceans. These strategies generate uncertainty for the environment rather than attempt to react to uncertainty imposed by the environment, as is the case with disruptive technologies. The term blue ocean strategy was coined by Kim and Mauborgne (2005) in their book *Blue Ocean Strategy*.

Explained:

Uncertainty

Uncertainty is a situation in which no historical data exists to help the decision-maker. Uncertainty cannot be modeled or predicted. It is a future that is not only unknown but also unknowable.

THE DIFFERENCES BETWEEN PREDICTION, RISK, AND UNCERTAINTY

The difference between prediction, risk and uncertainty	Prediction (known)	Risk (unknown)	Uncertainty (unknowable)
What matters	Data, the past	Variance and possibility	Expertise, influence, and control
How you move ahead	Refine prior efforts—strive for perfect business plan	Robustness, preparedness—scenarios	Co-creation and affordable loss
Dealing with surprises	Quality checking (must have been my mistake)	Weather the storm, work to stay on track/on plan	Embrace and rethink: it provides new opportunities
Measuring success	Actual versus plan, execution	Actual versus plan, closeness to the vision, within margin	Valued novelty, are we somewhere that has potential

of US$100 a barrel in November 2007. Nor could anyone have predicted that Steve Jobs, the iconic founder of Apple, would be fired by his board in May 1985, only to come back in December 1997, nor the impact that both moves would have on the company.

Keeping these examples in mind, it is clear that uncertainty is not confined to start-ups in budding industries. Consider the implications of the fact that one of every four firms on the Fortune 500 list simply did not exist 30 years ago. That means that every 88 days, a new firm is created that will replace one of the existing Fortune 500. What new competitors, products, and business models that have yet to be imagined will burst onto the landscape without advance notice?

PRACTICALLY SPEAKING: U-HAUL, OR TRANSFORMING UNCERTAINTY INTO SUCCESS

In 1945, newly married and with barely US$5,000 in his pocket, Leonard Samuel (L.S.) Shoen and his wife Anna Mary Carty Shoen set out on the journey that led to their partnership in the founding and creation of U-Haul.

Four years later, U-Haul made it possible to rent a trailer one-way from city to city throughout most of the United States. When we examine Shoen's journey, we find that this feat could not have been accomplished by using prediction. In fact, when students today set out to write a business plan for this venture (using the typical causal process), they invariably conclude that the plan is financially infeasible, and even psychologically infeasible, since it requires a large and risky capital outlay, most of which gets locked up in relatively worthless assets such as trucks and rental locations. Moreover, the logistics of starting the business on a much smaller scale and growing it as fast as Shoen did overwhelms the analytical prowess of the best of causal thinkers. The complete lack of any entry barriers to imitators with deep pockets is seen as another insurmountable obstacle to success.

Shoen, however, did not do elaborate market research or detailed forecasting and fundraising in the sense in which we use the terms today. Instead, using effectual means (who he was, what he knew, and whom he knew), he plunged into action, creating the market as he grew the business, working from the observation that people kept coming to his father-in-law's garage asking whether they could borrow the truck that was parked in the back. In his own words:

Since my fortune was just about enough to make the down payment on a home and furnish it, and knowing that if I did this we would be sunk, we started the life of nomads by putting our belongings in a trailer and living between in-laws and parents for the next six months. I barbered part time and bought the kind of trailers I thought we needed to rent from anybody who happened to have one at a price I thought was right. By the fall of 1945 I was so deep into the trailer rental deal economically that it was either make it or lose the whole thing.

Shoen moved with his wife and their young child to the Carty ranch in Ridgefield, Washington. There, with the help of the Carty family, the Shoens built the first trailers in the fall of 1945. They painted them in striking orange with the evocative name U-Haul on the sides, and they used the the ranch's automobile garage (and milk house) as the first manufacturing plant. Shoen often gave renters discounts on their trailer rentals if they would find a reputable gas station that would agree to rent U-Haul trailers in the cities they moved to. In the 1950s the company established a fleet ownership program that enabled investors (which included dealers and eventually employees) to purchase trailers for the U-Haul fleet, in return for future dividends. Shoen established a dealer network by partnering with service stations across the country. U-Haul provided the trailers (trucks were added in 1959), and the gas station provided the unused land and labor to service the U-Haul customers. U-Haul benefited from new business, and the service station owner benefited from a second source of income.

Together, this vast network of stakeholders formed a substantial entry barrier to any imitator who would have to risk a large capital outlay to compete. Advertising was entirely limited to the Yellow Pages and to the sudden and startling sight of growing numbers of distinctively painted vans being driven along the freeways of the country.

At any given moment U-Haul could have failed, but the resulting financial fall-out would not have been a disaster since the investments were spread across so many stakeholders.

Looking at the story of U-Haul's creation, we see that Shoen dealt with uncertainty step by step, using effectual principles—his means, partnerships, and setting a limit on the potential downside loss. Of course, we could rewrite history and suggest that he could have done market research, found out about the migration of populations in the US in the late 1940s, borrowed money from investors to set up locations, and so on. But as demonstrated by students' attempts at creating feasible business plans around the idea, this approach would probably have killed the venture. Instead, because he could not and would not measure the risk, he managed the uncertainty as best he could.

EXPERT ENTREPRENEURS DEAL WITH UNCERTAINTY, NOT RISK

Entrepreneurs face uncertainty. But what have they learned through the accumulation of their expertise in this unique setting that is teachable and learnable?

To better understand, we not only studied experts themselves as described in the "Risk taking" section, but also conducted follow-on studies with business novices, and managers with expertise in large multinational corporations. We describe these studies in more detail later in the book. Here we will only very briefly summarize what we found.

The most important difference between the expert entrepreneurs and the other two groups lay at the foundation of their decision-making strategies. The novices and the expert managers wanted desperately to predict. Clearly, expert entrepreneurs did not try to predict. But they were also not merely shooting from the hip or exhibiting any divine insight into the future. Instead, they had developed workable and sometimes even winning strategies for the game embodied in Knight's third jar. In terms of that jar, experts had learned something like the following: work with the first few things you draw from the jar and ignore the rest of what's in it; or add red balls into the jar so you are more likely to win; or rebuild the jar from

what you have and convince others to play a different game altogether.

In sum, expert entrepreneurs appear to have developed a set of techniques that effectively answers the question, "How do I control a future I cannot predict?" This expert pattern of decision-making behavior is what we call effectuation. Throughout the second section of the book we explore each component of effectuation and understand how each works within different stages of the lifecycle of new ventures as well as in a variety of other settings such as large corporations and the social sector.

TAKEAWAY: YOU CAN TRANSFORM UNCERTAINTY INTO OPPORTUNITY BY CONTROLLING YOUR ENVIRONMENT

All actors in the economic system seek to make good decisions. And whether in new ventures, old markets, or in life in general, prediction can help. But as we have seen, prediction problems are only one of at least three types of problems in life. Risk management techniques provide some improvement over mere extrapolation, but they are not the best way to deal with uncertainty. Yet uncertainty is at the heart of real value in entrepreneurial opportunity.

As you consider stepping into the unknowable, think about the following:

- You can either control your environment or be controlled by it.
- You can select your environment, choosing predictability or uncertainty.
- You should match your strategy to the environment.

If you choose uncertainty, the effectuation principles will provide you with a unique set of heuristics which you can use to transform uncertainty into opportunity.

So what?

Remember that you can try to control virtually any situation, but that you can only predict the predictable.

Roadmap

Think about the following:

- [ ] Interview five entrepreneurs. Ask them what they were willing to risk when they started their ventures.

- [ ] What would you be willing to risk?

- [ ] Choose your favorite new product. Is its market risky, predictable, or uncertain?

- [ ] Think about ten situations you experienced as uncertain. What made them uncertain? How did you respond? What aspects could you control? Not control?

- [ ] Consider your current job—how much time do you spend trying to predict versus trying to control. Is that mix of prediction and control a good match for the environment in which you are operating?

- [ ] Think about the last market research report you read. How useful would it have been for a company in that environment? How predictable or uncertain was that company's environment?

- [ ] How might you use a market research report to facilitate an approach focused on controlling uncertainty?

Bigger questions

- [ ] How does one quantify the degree of unknowable? That is, how do I know I'm in the unknowable?

- [ ] Should governments fund entrepreneurs once they realize they are putting money into something that cannot be predicted?

CHAPTER 4

Starting without money is more challenging than starting with money, which is exactly why starting with little money generates strong new ventures.

I don't have enough money

■ ■ ■

OF ALL THE REASONS that wannabe entrepreneurs give for why they haven't already started their ventures, the most common is the lack of adequate start-up capital. So how much money is enough to get started?

WHEN US$90 MILLION IS NOT ENOUGH . . .

One of the most promising start-ups of all time in Silicon Valley was a company called Zaplet. In early 1999 Brian Axe and David Roberts created the concept of Zaplets—dynamic, updateable, web-like messages and applications delivered through email. Zaplet's history followed the textbook path for high-tech ventures—from two techies in a garage to pitching venture capitalists in the Valley systematic market research leading to the perfect plan focused entirely on delivering a financial homerun—the proverbial hockey stick that every new entrepreneur naively dreams about and every investor secretly hopes for.

Zaplet did everything right. Venture capitalists fell in love with the product. Silicon Valley buzzed with the market

How much does it take to start a business?

- Dell computer—launched in 1984 with US$1,000.

- According to *Inc. Magazine*'s October 2002 survey of 500 fastest growing, 14 percent had opened the venture with less than US$1,000 (Bartlett, 2002).

- *The Wells Fargo/National Federation of Independent Businesses* report shows that 70 percent of small business owners started with less than US$20,000 (Dennis, 1998).

- Ninety-eight percent of new US businesses start with no venture capital or angel funding.

possibilities for Zaplet. Wall Street could not get enough of the story. By July 2000 Zaplet had hired 27 product managers and 30 developers were writing code for six independent, potentially revenue-generating areas.

Before it began its descent into oblivion in 2001, Zaplet had raised a total of US$90 million in venture funding!

. . . YET US$5,000 IS PLENTY

Around the same time, in Bozeman, Montana (population around 27,000), Greg Gianforte built Rightnow Technologies starting with a software product that helped companies respond to their customers' emails quickly and effectively. Starting with a goal of creating 2,000 jobs in his beloved Bozeman, Gianforte invested US$5,000 of his own money and booked about US$20,000 in revenue in the first year of his business.

Working alone, coding a bare-bones product whose specs were derived from a series of cold calls to customers, Gianforte began booking sales, often taking price out of the equation by offering bargain-basement deals such as a few thousand dollars for a two-year lease. He could even afford to give the product away for free in return for actual early adoption and detailed real time feedback-in-use.

Once he had about 40 adoptions, Gianforte hired five employees—all of them salespeople. Gianforte does not believe cold calling is disreputable work, nor does he believe fundraising

or even product building has to precede sales. Instead, he waxes poetic about selling. For example, he told Professor William Sahlman and Research Associate Dan Heath of the Harvard Business School:

> Some entrepreneurs don't like sales very much. They do it only because they have to, and as soon as they can, they hire someone else to do the selling. They may even feel that there's something a little bit sleazy about calling up strangers for money. Yes, sales can be hard work. No one likes making cold calls. But sleazy? On the contrary, I think sales is actually the noblest part of business. It's the part that brings the solution together with the customer's need.

When Rightnow finally hired its chief financial officer in 1999, she had to put in financial systems almost from scratch and implement a host of accounting and procedural logistics while getting ready for an IPO. It had taken four years, but the little venture had grown from an investment of

> I really believe that sales is the only job that has to be done well in building a business. To this day, I keep a sign on my desk in my office that says, "Nothing happens until somebody sells something."
>
> **Greg Gianforte, Founder, Rightnow Technologies**

US$5,000 and sales of US$20,000 in its first year to revenues of over US$35 million and a post-money valuation of US$100 million in the year 2000.

MONEY MATCHING: CASH IN AND CASH OUT

In order to stay in business, the simple fact is that every venture (profit and non-profit alike) must take in at least as much cash as it spends, and in the case of for-profit ventures, ideally a bit more. And as much as the old adage rings true that "it takes money to make money," taking investment money at the outset starts a new venture off in a deficit position. As far as the venture is concerned, any money it does not generate through sales is money it owes to another—even if the "other" is you.

This chapter is all about bringing that cash deficit as close to zero as possible or maybe even into the positive. This is in stark contrast to the venture capital approach to start-ups, where step one is "raise US$5 million." Here we encourage you to try to think about "not having money" as an asset in itself—an asset that challenges you to build a more robust business, forces you to be more creative in how you deal with customers and partners, and allows you to maintain more control over your venture.

Money matching: Accountants and entrepreneurs

Accounting works to extend the money matching principle over time. For example, while it costs US$500,000 to buy a new machine, we don't charge the entire amount to expenses in that year. Instead, we spread it out over the number of years the machine will be producing product revenue, say ten years. We match the expenses and the revenues through depreciation.

How can this possibly matter to an entrepreneur? Depreciation happens only on paper. Entrepreneurs make it happen in fact. Whereas accountants are okay with actually paying out the US$500,000 in full for the machine, and then writing it off on paper over ten years, entrepreneurs seek to find ways to pay out only one tenth of the cash upfront for the same machine—and work hard to match funding to actual use in each time period.

This difference in matching mirrors the difference in Zaplet and Rightnow. It is the difference between matching funding to a predicted vision and matching it to actual implementation. Or it is the difference between selecting courses of action based on five-year projections of expected return fueled by imagined uses for technical prowess and focusing on the immediate, next step at hand, completely underwritten by actual commitments from real stakeholders.

From a matching standpoint, ask yourself questions like these:

- How much output do I need right now?
- Are there ways to get the impact of that output without producing it in advance?
- How can I delay cash outflows or accelerate cash inflows?
- Can a customer pay half upfront?
- Will suppliers give me net 60-day terms instead of net 30? How can I make it worthwhile for them at net 90 days?
- Can I focus on the non-cash intensive part of the business model first, and have funding happen on my terms later?

One of the most common ways to do this is to convert fixed costs into variable costs. Instead of buying the machine, you might find someone else who owns a similar machine and is willing to sell you units from that machine. You may have to pay a premium for this option, but even that is likely to be dramatically better than trying to raise US$500,000 to own the machine (which you would likely under-utilize anyway). Additionally, creative thinking along these lines often leads to the discovery of slack resources (i.e. resources lying around unutilized, such as nighttime hours in a factory or a bagel shop) that you may be able to get access to for very little, getting a discount rather than paying a premium, or even for free on a trial basis.

Move from asking yourself, "Can I make US$500,000 in revenue to pay for the new machine?" to asking, "How can I make the US$500,000 without actually buying the machine at all?" or at least ". . . without incurring the fixed cost of buying the machine?" reduces your cash needs.

But there is an "if." If I made all of my fixed costs variable, my costs could be too big for me to make the profit I want in this business; in fact, it could make me vulnerable to another lower-cost provider. Or, if I don't buy this particular asset outright, and it turns out to be the cornerstone of the business, will the owner of that asset have me over a barrel? The answer is yes. Early in the life of a venture, the greatest threat is survival. Time and money run out as entrepreneurs develop value propositions and relationships that really attract buyers, develop systems that enable them to do things effectively, and develop capabilities that enable them to do this repeatedly. When time and money run out . . . the venture dies.

Research roots

Wealth unrelated to starting a firm

It is easy to read the stories of new ventures that secure millions in venture funding and assume that lots of cash is a necessary prerequisite for starting a company. But in a study published in 2004 Erik Hurst and Annamaria Lusardi showed that wealth is not important for starting a business. The median amount of capital used by households founding their own business was US$22,700, and nearly a quarter were started with less than US$5,000. These results are consistent with Bhidé (2000), who found that of firms in *Inc. Magazine's* 500 fastest growing list, most started with little capital, and 26 percent started with less than US$5,000 in up-front capital.

The real cost of capital

Creative ideas around financing slow this down . . . at a cost. That cost is your real cost of capital. Cost of capital is not just your debt interest rate, or the rate of return your investors require from you as you learn in finance. The cost of capital also includes:

- Premium variable price (for example, paying top rental rates for a factory) in order to avoid a major fixed cost investment (for example, by building your own factory).
- Exposure to renegotiated terms if you turn out to be really successful. If you contract with someone to use their facilities and things really take off, they may well try to increase their price or some other costs because they know you can pay it.
- Exposure, if you don't control the parts of your business that are most competitively valuable. Upfront, it's not always clear what will end up being your competitive advantage.

We describe this as a cost of capital issue because entrepreneurs often make two mistakes:

- They walk away from an opportunity to convert a fixed cost into a variable cost because it might have a premium price, only to turn around and sell a large percent of their firm to an investor (a variable cost with a premium price).
- They only consider the cost of one type of capital versus another type of capital, overlooking the cost of capital versus the cost of NOT capital.

To the first point, the questions of premium prices and competitive advantage (or disadvantage) associated with matching in all of its forms can be more effectively evaluated when treated simply as different forms of capital costs. Investors and lenders have similar premium pricing factors, and even have interesting implications for competitive advantage and strategic choice that can impact the future success of a venture every bit as much as the variable costs or control issues.

The cost (benefit) of NOT capital

To the second point, we have yet to see the cost of capital kill a new venture. Optimizing/reducing the cost of capital at the expense of having enough capital is akin to reducing your expenses by focusing on your petty cash fund and not your rent, travel, or payroll expenses. The simple fact is that the market for lending and investing surrounding new ventures is far from easily accessible. Even if you effectively evaluate the true costs of your sources of capital (per the first point), and let's say that venture capital comes out as the most cost effective source, the reality of making that happen is another thing entirely. It may be very expensive in terms of the time you spend and all the venture-building you do not do (the customers you do not talk to, the suppliers you do not negotiate with, and the employees you do not inspire and build long-term relationships with)

because you are out chasing venture capitalists. You may spend all of the next six months chasing that cost effective capital source unsuccessfully, leaving you without time and capital, which results in death. The cost of capital, even well managed, is much higher than the cost of NOT capital as ventures develop.

In the event of continued growth and success, priorities may change; the cost of NOT capital goes down significantly, and the importance of optimizing the cost of capital becomes more valuable. As a result, setting up milestones for addressing those issues, "alternatives" contracts, even pre-negotiated changes that are different for "good" versus "bad" situations, can be an important part of your effort to use those creative sources of capital. Beware, of course, that you don't let your predictions of the future take over in these moments. For example, your predictions of the assets that you think are most strategic (and those that you don't) can lead you to seek narrow control rights over those assets, rather than continue to be effectual with those potential partners.

BOOTSTRAPPING BENEFITS

In a book devoted to the topic named *Bootstrapping Your Business—* Gianforte and Gibson (2007) make the case that starting with nothing is a good idea. We agree, and summarize the highlights:

- **You can start now.** Instead of waiting for a prospective funder to come along, be inspired by your business, and write you a

Practically speaking

Bringing a career back from the dead

At first glance, Vidal Herrera seems just like any other person trying to make his way in the world. He lives in Los Angeles, drives a white SUV, and his firm sponsors local baseball and polo teams. Average enough, except that the baseball team he sponsors is named "The Stiffs" because Herrera is the founder of an entrepreneurial business named 1–800-Autopsy. Of course, with the advent of the internet, he has added a ".com" to the name, but Herrera still offers the same thanatology services to private clients as he did when he started the firm 21 years ago.

Autopsy on demand is not the first idea that comes to most people when they start on their entrepreneurial careers. And it did not occur to Herrera either until he became disabled and unemployed as a result of lifting a 5'2" 284-pound female corpse in 1984. After he lost his job as a field deputy coroner investigator (CSI) in Los Angeles County, try as he might, no one wanted to employ him. Necessity being the mother of invention, he started doing contract work to make ends meet, retrieving tissue for Veterans Administration WLA researchers.

As part of the job, Herrera visited local funeral homes and met grieving families anxious to understand the fates of their loved ones. People wanted to answer questions ranging from the cause of their relative's death to solving paternity mysteries, and had no viable ways of obtaining this knowledge. Based on his interactions with "next of kin," Herrera began to form the basis of a service offering. He launched 1–800-Autopsy in 1988 using nothing more than a meager retirement income, as banks refused to lend him money.

Unwilling to invest his cash in advance in a new business, Herrera has since opened franchise locations in Orlando, Florida, Northern California, and Las Vegas, Nevada. So instead of investing his money into expansion, he gets paid when someone else takes the risk to expand. The business continues to grow even in the current financial crisis, and it seems likely to expand further as the baby boomer generation ages. As Herrera puts it, "Death is a recession-proof business."

It is the sheer unlikeliness of this story that offers an interesting insight—who would have thought that there is in fact a market for private autopsy services? If Herrera had not started 1–800-Autopsy, would the independent thanatology market exist at all? In fact, 1–800-Autopsy gives us a rare glimpse at how markets and firms are conceived. We tend to assume that the entrepreneur's job is to track down economically inevitable opportunities that are hidden in the sand through careful sifting and prophet-like prescience. Reality often points the other way. Herrera's story shows us the reality that new firms and new markets are created when entrepreneurs, driven by all kinds of motivations (needing income being a primary one, though not the only one) and the peculiarity of their individual circumstances, begin interactions with potential customers and other stakeholders, and end up creating something novel and valuable. And almost always the ventures they begin spring from things they already have or already know.

Of course, Herrera's story is far from finished. Ever the entrepreneur, Herrera is both negotiating with new potential franchisees of 1–800-Autopsy, and has also kicked off two new ventures. The first, named CoffinCouches.com, was created when someone asked him to construct a piece of furniture from a casket. Herrera now acquires defective or rejected coffins and transforms them into unique sofas, adding legs and custom upholstery. As a collector of antique morgue and mortuary equipment, Herrera was also approached by stagehands in entertainment (another "only in LA" story, of course) to rent his gear to studios filming morgue scenes. With the unmistakable moniker MorguePropRentals.com, this business provides equipment ranging from embalming tables to body crypts for television shows and movies that include *CSI* and *Law and Order*. Clearly, that's an opportunity to die for.

check, there is nothing holding you back from starting your dream today.

- **You can start learning now.** Most ventures we know and love were created through interaction with suppliers, customers, partners, and employees. Cash can encourage you to ignore those inputs, and not learn as quickly.
- **Cut your waste.** When you have money, it is easy to waste it on speculative ideas. But if you have none, its hard to throw it out the window.
- **Limit your downside.** If you do not have a huge amount of cash invested in the venture, the mistakes you will inevitably make will likely be proportionately less huge as well.
- **Increase your upside.** Taking investment generally means selling equity. And the more you sell, the less you have when it comes time to realize the value created in your venture.
- **Increase your creativity.** Studies show that constraints increase creativity. When you have money, the first answer is always to spend it. When you don't, you add a constraint that makes you more creative.

TAKEAWAY: HAVING NOTHING IS A GOOD THING

The reality is that most firms in the world operate without any outside funding, instead making decisions with an eye to affordable loss/acceptable downside. This is because they place a high priority on staying in business and being cognizant of keeping downside risks acceptable.

Starting without invested capital means that you get the feedback and the cash you need from customers, in order to refine your idea, as well as new and productive partnerships with people whose slack resources you put to valuable new use. Starting without invested capital also forces you to go out to try to make a sale, which is when you will learn whether you really have a business, or not. You can't make a big mistake (fail cheap and early) and you don't have to give away a lot of equity/control. Perhaps having nothing is a good thing after all?

Roadmap

Take stock of your monthly expenses and ask yourself how many of those you can do without, and how many you could fund through slack resources that belong to other people. For example, do you really need that watch on your wrist?

So what?

Given that starting without external investment is beneficial, there have to be some inputs that give some substance to the venture. These come from you, your means: who you are, what you know, and who you know.

Bigger questions

- What would happen if a rich uncle died and left you a couple of million dollars? Would you still want to start this new venture?
- Where does money get its value?

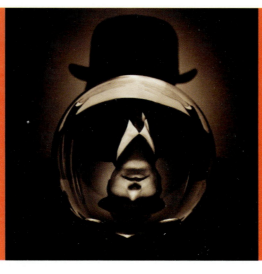

CHAPTER 5

In the uncertain new venture setting, prediction is irrelevant.

Instead, entrepreneurs work to control those elements of the situation that are shapeable.

He who asks fortune-tellers the future unwittingly forfeits an inner intimation of coming events that is a thousand times more exact than anything they may say. He is impelled by inertia, rather than curiosity, and nothing is more unlike the submissive apathy with which he hears his fate revealed than the alert dexterity with which the man of courage lays hands on the future.
Walter Benjamin

Myth: Entrepreneurs are extraordinary forecasters

■ ■ ■

IN THIS CHAPTER:

THERE ARE different perceptions about how much control one has over the environment. Some societies believe that everything is under the individual's control, while others believe that we are victims of fate. One way to rationalize randomness is to try and predict what will happen next. Yet as Nassim Taleb argues in his book *The Black Swan* (2007), even major events such as world wars were not predictable ex ante. If you look at the value of bonds prior to World War One, there was nothing to indicate that anyone had an inkling the war was about to happen.

This observation applies to market research, forecasting, stock market analysis, weather presenters, fortune-tellers, and astrologists. They are all in the business of offering control through prediction. But are they successful?

Philip Tetlock, a professor of organizational behavior at the University of California, Berkeley, has mapped 82,000 forecasts of almost 300 expert forecasters against real world outcomes over the last 25 years. The results: Even the experts barely beat a random forecast generator, and they did no better than reasonably well-informed non-experts. More famous experts did slightly worse than the average of the experts (Tetlock, 2006).

One of the undying myths about entrepreneurs is that they are experts at predicting trends in the economy, products, and services. But entrepreneurs have an especially uneasy relationship with prediction. This has been explained at various times as overconfidence (Busenitz and Barney, 1997) or as high risk propensity (Begley and Boyd, 1987). But we have shown that risk and failure are not good explanations of what happens in new ventures. In the first chapters, we looked at how entrepreneurs create rather than find their opportunities and deal with uncertainty rather than prediction.

While we question the idea that entrepreneurs succeed due to their ability to predict better, we do so because we now know that they attempt to create, shape, and transform their environment. In other words, they exercise control.

Clearly, certain situations allow for larger or smaller degrees of control. Uncertainty can be forced on you, or generated by you. When it is forced on you, your degree of control is not null, but it is less. In situations where you create uncertainty for the environment, your degree of control is higher. Although you can never completely influence how the market and your competitors are going to react to a new product or service, you can still work as much as possible with those things that are within your control to influence them to co-create the future with you.

In this chapter we will look at control and how entrepreneurs shape their environment so prediction becomes unimportant.

ACHIEVING CONTROL WITHOUT PREDICTABILITY

The thousands of books about strategy suggest two levers that enable decision-making. The first lever is prediction. If the future can be predicted, the decision-maker can steer the company toward a position where it will have an advantage. The second lever is control. In this case, the business leader needs to create an environment that gives it an advantage over the competition. These levers are not alternatives, but rather tools that managers can apply to improve the chances of making a good decision. The diagram entitled "Strategies with respect to prediction and control" shows how companies can be positioned in different quadrants depending on which combination of levers they choose to use. In each of the quadrants, companies compete using different rules.

In the planning and adaptation quadrants on the left-hand side, strategic thinking suggests that companies have to either plan more (predict better) or be more flexible and faster in responding to changes in their environment (adapt better). Both approaches rely on the firm's ability to sense and make sense out of the environment, either in the longer term (planning) or in the shorter term (adapting).

In a mature, stable environment, planning, as the source of strategy making, can be effective. Planning assumes that information—particularly

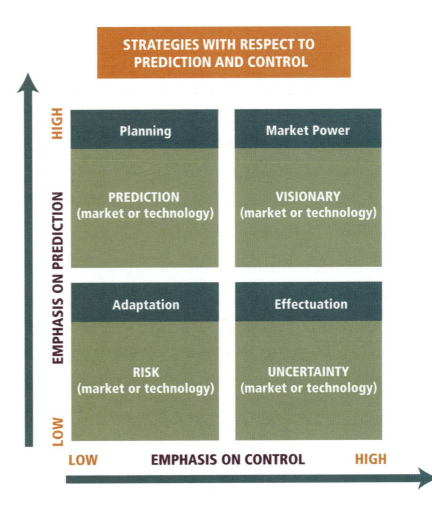

STRATEGIES WITH RESPECT TO PREDICTION AND CONTROL

EMPHASIS ON PREDICTION (HIGH / LOW)

EMPHASIS ON CONTROL (LOW / HIGH)

Planning	Market Power
PREDICTION (market or technology)	VISIONARY (market or technology)
Adaptation	Effectuation
RISK (market or technology)	UNCERTAINTY (market or technology)

historical information from the environment—is reliable enough to provide a base for your strategy (prediction is possible).

In an environment where dynamic capabilities are key, adapting and learning, with a view to outpacing the competition, may be the preferred strategic approach. Adaptation assumes you are faster at responding to changes than your competitors (you are in the risk quadrant, outpacing others).

The visionary (market power) and effectuation quadrants on the right-hand side call for a more proactive approach to the environment. If a company has market power (government-regulated markets or quasi monopolistic status such as that achieved by Microsoft), it can try to dictate what will happen in that environment, imposing its view (visionary) on the landscape and ensuring the position of the organization within that environment. Visionary or market power assumes you have enough power to impose a solution on the environment (a unique monopolistic situation).

The effectuation quadrant, the one we are concerned with, calls for a different approach. Because the company does not have market power, it will need to co-create (with partners, customers, suppliers, and so on) its environment, developing a new product, firm, or market from which all the players will benefit. Effectuation assumes you can put together partnerships that will successfully create a new situation (uncertainty calling for creation).

Some may argue that managing uncertainty must surely be possible through a combination of predicting better and adapting faster. Because they were working on predicting better, Coca-Cola and Pepsi missed the opportunity that allowed RedBull to create a new category and define a new group of customers—those who connect a high-caffeine beverage with sports. And trying to adapt to market research led, for example, to the failure and subsequent costly termination of New Coke.

It is also true that with time, most companies move from the effectual to the planning/adaptation quadrants, as

Theory in practice: KEEP180

Imagine a popular independent radio station, KEEP180, that plays a wide range of new music from country and western to French rap. The station broadcasts locally and has a growing online audience. The station is funded by donations from listeners and is facing a strategic decision about where to invest its limited resources. Let's think about how the radio station would evolve in each of these environments:

- *Planning*. The station might carry out market research and predict an explosion in a new genre of French music. It could then invest in bringing that music to its audience and consequently capitalize on higher ratings.

- *Market power.* Alternatively, the producer at KEEP180 may simply love the French language and may build a format exclusively on French rap and other novel French music, knowing s/he will own the category if s/he can establish it.

- *Adaptation.* Given the high rate of change in technology and customer demand, the station might devote its efforts to watching other independent stations and talking with customers, ready to move quickly as new trends are identified.

- *Effectuation.* Finally, the station might partner with a French recording label and a current American music icon to create an explosion in French rap music, selling music online, where all of them profit from the new environment they create together.

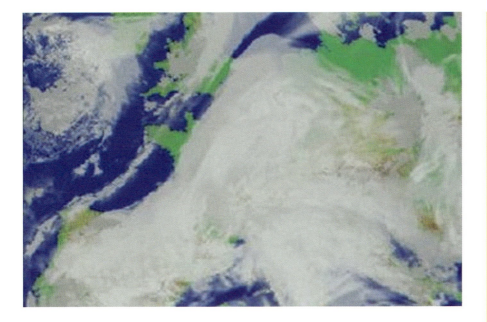

Research roots

The future that's already happened

Highlighting an area where prediction is reasonably accurate, management guru Peter Drucker (1985) showed the reliability of demography predictions over the last 650 years, terming it the future that's already happened.

The challenge to the entrepreneur? Take demographic information (or any other reliable predictive information) and use it to create the basis for opportunity!

You can't predict who will change the world

The American system of trial and error produces doers: Black Swan-hunting, dream-chasing entrepreneurs, with a tolerance for a certain class of risk taking and for making plenty of small errors on the road to success or knowledge . . . It is high time to recognize that we humans are far better at doing than understanding, and better at tinkering than inventing. But we don't know it. We truly live under the illusion of order believing that planning and forecasting are possible. We are scared of the random, yet we live from its fruits. We are so scared of the random that we create disciplines that try to make sense of the past—but we ultimately fail to understand it, just as we fail to see the future.

Nassim Nicholas Taleb
(2007)

their product, technology, or market takes off and becomes a mature business. This assumes that they have been able to turn uncertainty into an actionable opportunity. As such, the choice to use prediction or control is driven to some extent by what stage the company is in—during the early stage, the start-up phase, there is very little that is predictable; as the company grows, venture capitalists and other sources of capital may ask for a business plan and some degree of prediction.

Finally, as the company reaches a more mature, larger stage, it often predicts too much; when this happens, it must then try to introduce innovation and the accompanying uncertainty back into its environment.

DEBUNKING PREDICTION

We all know great stories of failed predictions. There are countless websites dedicated to failed predictions and end-of-world stories, the most famous one being the millenium hype prior to the shift from the last century to this one. Some other examples include:

> That idea is so damn nonsensical that I'm willing to stand on the bridge of a battleship while that nitwit tries to hit it from the air.
> Newton Baker, Secretary of War, 1910, responding to the suggestion that airplanes might sink battleships by dropping bombs on them

> We don't like their sound. Groups of guitars are on the way out.
> Mike Smith, Decca Recording Co. executive, turning down The Beatles in 1962

> With over 50 foreign cars already on sale here, the Japanese auto industry isn't likely to carve out a big slice of the US market for itself.
> *Business Week*, August 2, 1968

These are all good examples of why you would not want to predict in an uncertain environment. Look at some of the predictions you made in your own environment. How many of these came true? What did you lose when they didn't come true? Did they apply to uncertain environments?

The stories are funny only insofar as you haven't put any money, time, or effort into a business that is based on prediction.

 **PRACTICALLY SPEAKING: THE STORY OF GREEN AND ME**

Do trends create opportunities, or do opportunities create trends? Two of the biggest trends today, trends that seem to even weather economic downturns, are the interest in environmental friendliness and the appeal of personalized consumer goods. Both have emerged over the last few years, and to understand how they relate to entrepreneurial opportunity we look at two trendy Swiss firms.

The saga of Sigg

For more than 100 years Sigg has been crafting a variety of aluminum

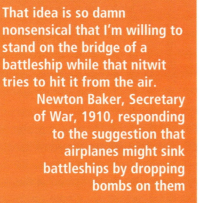

products including drinking bottles in Biel, Switzerland. For about 90 of those years, the Sigg bottle existed in relative obscurity, a boutique reusable container in a disposable world. But during the 1990s recycling finally gained traction and the Sigg bottle was declared an environmentalist status symbol. It represents a handheld rejection of the 60 billion tons of plastic waste created each year. Demand soared. Sigg responded by not only increasing manufacturing capacity, but also by adding manufacturing flexibility. The original single color drinking bottle could now sport a variety of individual designs that Sigg could alter based on interest. Today, consumers can choose from 48 different bottle designs and 20 different caps, generating over a thousand possible unique and personalized combinations.

The fable of Freitag

Not far from Biel, in Zurich, Switzerland, Markus and Daniel Freitag started thinking about a new business from their apartment overlooking the main Zurich truck route at Hardbrücke. Dissatisfied with the durability of available bicycle messenger bags, the pair wanted to create a heavy-duty, water-repellent product. So in 1993 they started up manufacturing at Freitag AG. But instead of sourcing the latest high-tech materials, they formed bags from used truck tarpaulins, using second-hand car seat belts as straps and used bicycle inner tubes for edging. Recycling materials positioned them to take direct advantage of the emerging environmental trend, and guaranteed that every Freitag bag is as original, customized, and personal as the truck that hauled its skin in the first place.

Explained:

Locus of control

Locus of control is a term in psychology considered to be an important aspect of personality. Developed by Julian B. Rotter in 1954, it refers to whether a person believes that the main underlying causes of events in his/her life are internal or external. People with an internal locus of control believe that they control their lives. People with an external locus of control believe that some other external power—fate, luck, other people—controls their lives.

Attribution theory

Attribution theory is concerned with how individuals interpret the behavior of others or themselves. It assumes that people try to determine why people do what they do. In their quest to explain "why," they may attribute one or more causes to a particular behavior. According to Heider, who first developed the theory in 1958, there are two types of attribution: 1) external or situational attribution, which infers that a person is behaving in a certain way because of an outside factor, such as the weather; 2) internal or dispositional attribution, which infers that a person is behaving in a certain way because of something about the person, such as intelligence level, attitude, character, or personality. The theory, which was further developed in the 1970s and 1980s by various scholars including Harold Kelley (1967: 192–238), explores the connection between individuals' attribution of causes to events and their usefulness in an organization.

The environmental trend Sigg helped in a small way to create multiplied Sigg sales, and as the company grew Sigg took advantage of the trend in personalizaton. Success has brought the humble Sigg bottle to more than 40 countries, and today there is a Sigg in the collection of the Museum of Modern Art in New York. Designing an opportunity around an existing trend, Freitag bags have also achieved success. They currently sell about 200,000 bags per year online, in five Freitag shops across Germany and Switzerland and in 300 stores around the world. Freitag has done so well that they have created their own genre around using recycled materials that other designers have started following.

The stories together show that trends can form a basis for opportunities and opportunities can form a basis for trends. But the insight is that it is always entrepreneurs who create opportunities. Whether taking advantage of trends or initiating them, entrepreneurs use what is available to them to create new products and markets. To illustrate the authorship of the entrepreneur, consider the environment without the Freitag brothers or Sigg. Would there be a market for customized, colorful aluminum drinking bottles? Would consumers pay high-fashion prices for bags made of commercial waste—or would such bags even exist? Likely not. Entrepreneurs do more than just meet existing market needs and discover business opportunities: they narrate novelty in the market.

TRUTH: ENTREPRENEURS DON'T PREDICT, THEY CONTROL

Niels Bohr, one of the most influential scientists of the the twentieth century, once said: "Prediction is very difficult. Especially when it's about the future." If by now you still want to use prediction in uncertain environments, we suggest you call a blue chip company and get a corporate job. Do not mistake us: We are not saying prediction is useless. It has its time and function. But more important is that control works in both certain and uncertain environments. So using control is independent of your environment. And there are many ways in which you can exercise control:

- Form partnerships because they give you a greater reach.
- Use your means—and other people's slack.
- Limit what you put at risk, what you might lose.
- Begin viewing surprises as something positive to work with.

TAKEAWAY: YOU CAN SHAPE THE FUTURE

Consciously or not, entrepreneurs act as if the future is not "out there" to be discovered, but an artifact created through the actions and interactions of the players. Yet they do more than

Explained:

Bounded cognition

I can't process everything—so I select the first workable solution.

Explained:

Isotropy

There is so much information out there. What is important?

toss a coin or shoot from the hip while hoping for the best. Their decisions have a logic of their own and there is method in their madness even when they appear to be acting on their gut feeling.

In fact, we can identify a consistent and coherent pattern of behaviour that we call effectuation. Combined with the philosophy that control can be achieved even in a totally unpredictable or unknowable situation, the logic of effectuation will allow you to construct elements of the environment in which you will build your venture and help you to shape the future in ways that matter to you and your stakeholders—even if you cannot imagine exactly what that will or should look like.

Before we turn to explicating that logic in a systematic way, we need to examine a couple more myths and a few more reasons why people hesitate to take the plunge into entrepreneurship.

Roadmap

Think about the following:

- [ ] Think about five things you can control as you launch into a new venture.

- [ ] Think about five things you cannot control as you launch into a new venture.

- [ ] Look at what you can use to help you control: What you have, who you know, what you know. Imagine ways that you might be able to influence and control those items you identified as beyond your control.

- [ ] What are your own biases around what you can control, based on your education and background? Are you holding yourself back?

So what?

Prediction works best in mature, stable environments, but, for the lack of other tools, it often gets called into duty in the wrong settings. Expert entrepreneurs work hard to directly control and influence uncertain environments and these same efforts may also apply in relatively mature and stable environments.

Bigger questions

- [ ] What industries benefit from prediction?

- [ ] In predictable situations, how should control be used?

- [ ] How do you behave in a culture that does not believe in control?

CHAPTER 6

Taking the plunge into a new venture is a deeply personal decision with motivations that range from aspiration to necessity.

The important thing is this: To be able at any moment to sacrifice what we are for what we could become.

Charles Dubois

I don't know how to take the plunge

∎ ∎ ∎

WE ALL HAVE friends, colleagues, and acquaintances who jumped ship and started their own businesses. Ask any class of students, whether they are undergraduates or mid-career executives, and two-thirds will respond that they want to start their own business. Most people we know, though, never go all the way.

The reasons we don't do it are varied and sometimes culturally bound, and sometimes highly idiosyncratic to the individual.

Instinctively, we compare what we know and have with an opportunity that we cannot quantify. We look at our current job, salary, location, and comfort and map out our future. And then we look into the uncertainty of the entrepreneurial idea we are considering and see a path we cannot chart. We balk at the unknowable and our egos fear the stigma of failure.

Even in a world where job security is a thing of the past, this thinking persists. We feel we can predict a safe, comfortable future for ourselves, and it makes us uncomfortable to plunge into the unknown.

Beyond the entertaining stories of entrepreneurs who quit school at 16, started something in Mom and Dad's garage, and were billionaires by the tender age of 23, how does one take the plunge?

One of the most important research questions in trying to understand the plunge decision is the following: What kind of decision process leads potential entrepreneurs to comfortably take the plunge? There are practical reasons why this question is important because governments and economic development organizations spend large amounts of money trying to "seed" entrepreneurship. There is also a thriving industry of entrepreneurial educators who, either directly or indirectly, teach potential entrepreneurs how to best make the plunge decision. At the same time, the statistics offered by the press on new venture success and failure are used to bias decision-makers against plunging. Only overconfident, risk-seeking, or mildly crazy people would tend to become entrepreneurs.

Practically speaking

The making of Sears

America, in the late 1880s, had 38 states, a total population of 58 million with 65 percent of folks living in rural areas. Only a dozen or so cities had 200,000 or more residents. The whole country's income was only US$10 billion. In 1886, when a Chicago jewelry company shipped some gold-filled watches to an unsuspecting jeweler in the Minnesota hamlet of Redwood Falls, it started a chain of events that led to the founding of Sears.

Richard Sears was an agent of the Minneapolis and St. Louis railway station in the neighboring hamlet of North Redwood. On the side, he sold lumber and coal to local residents for extra money. When the shipment of watches arrived, unwanted, at the Redwood Falls jeweler, Sears went into action. He purchased them himself and sold the watches at a nice profit to other station agents up and down the line. It went so well that he ordered more. The following year Sears moved his business to Chicago and placed an ad in the *Daily News*.

> **WANTED: Watchmaker with reference who can furnish tools. State age, experience and salary required.**
> **ADDRESS T39, *Daily News*.**

Alvah C. Roebuck answered the ad, telling Sears he knew watches and showed a sample of his work to prove it. This began the association of two young men, both still in their twenties. In 1893 Sears, Roebuck & Co. was formally named and they were off.

Farmers in rural America were selling their crops for cash and buying what they needed from rural general stores. But when they laid their money on the line for goods, they were in the red. In 1891 the wholesale price of a barrel of flour was reported to be US$3.47, while the price at retail was at least US$7, a 100 percent increase. Farmers formed protest movements, such as the Grange, to do battle against high prices and the "middleman."

Sears, Roebuck and Co. and other mail-order companies provided the answer. Through a combination of volume buying and making use of the railroads, the post office, and, later, rural free delivery and parcel post, they offered a happy alternative to the high-priced rural stores. Sears prospered in the 1890s, and over the next 100 years they built a huge product line, created countless successful brands, rolled out retail locations around the world, and added insurance and investment services, ultimately making a tremendous impact on the world of retail.

Was it market research? Deliberation? Luck? Opportunism? Richard Sears took advantage of a chance occurrence, and rather than focus on learning before doing, he focused on learning while doing. Sometimes the best way to figure out whether an idea is really a good idea for a business, or the "right" opportunity for you, is to buy the box of watches and try to sell them. Richard couldn't envision what Sears would become, but the initial opportunity was one that he was able to take on, and he made good things happen from there.

Over the next few pages we will dissect the decision-making process behind the plunge decision, starting with a real-life example, the creation of Sears. As you read, decide for yourself whether a plunge is really a plunge.

TELL ME WHO YOU ARE AND I WILL TELL YOU HOW YOU PLUNGE

Why plunge? Or, why not plunge? The answer varies greatly depending on where you are in your life and on your entrepreneurial motivation. To help see the range of different views on plunging, we offer three stories that illustrate some of the different stages in life. Clearly, there are more stages in life and more motivations for entrepreneurship than those we mention. The point is to see how the rationales change with context. In the following pages we also look at three common life cycle phases. Where would you situate yourself?

PRACTICALLY SPEAKING: YOUNG AND CAREFREE (SERENDIPITY)

As a sophomore at Harvard in 1984, Evan Marwell watched with interest as the doctoral students at the university struggled with the very last stage of their program, the seemingly trivial step of printing their theses. Laser printers were brand new, and small self-service print shops like Kinko's had not yet emerged in the market. As a result, doctoral students had to wait for days to gain access to the university's only public laser printer, and

had to pay several dollars a page to print their lengthy documents.

Marwell realized that just a small number of theses would completely offset the cost of buying a laser printer. So he bought a laser printer and posted flyers around campus announcing that he could print theses with no wait and at a lower cost than the university printer. And so a business was launched right from his dormitory.

Marwell did not end up as the head of Kinko's, but the experience started an entrepreneurial career. Since then, he has been in the call center business and the customer relations business, and he has also launched a new kind of hedge fund.

PRACTICALLY SPEAKING: MIDDLE-AGED AND ENCUMBERED (NECESSITY)

Patti Peery worked at Whirlpool's Maytag plant in Newton, Iowa. When Whirlpool closed the plant in 2006 the working mother of three faced the need to take control of her financial situation. So she entered the local community college, completed the management program, and started Fireside Camper Rental, LLC. Fireside provides full-service camper rentals to people interested in exploring Iowa's state parks. Working with her son and her husband, Peery delivers a camper to the customer's campsite, prepares it, fills it with water, sets it up, and then retrieves it and cleans it when the

customer's vacation is over. Her business has been so successful that she has expanded to four campers.

The interesting element to this story is that Peery was not alone in her entrepreneurial pursuit. Newton had been a Whirlpool town, and when the announcement of the plant closure was released, the future of the community was in question. Remarkably, however, Newton is today economically vibrant. Why? Iowa Telecom acquired Maytag's former corporate headquarters in Newton and went on to create 140 jobs. As a consequence, another Iowa company, Caleris, moved into town to set up helpdesk operations. And Central Iowa Energy took advantage of a trained and available workforce to staff a new biodiesel plant in the town. Using entrepreneurship as an economic solution for a middle-aged and encumbered town was just as effective for these companies as it was for Patti Peery.

PRACTICALLY SPEAKING: OLD AND WEALTHY (ASPIRATION)

Larry Hench spent 40 years developing and commercializing a breakthrough in life sciences technology called Bioglass®—a successful innovation that has helped millions of people who suffer bone damage. Bioglass has also been the basis of numerous books and patents, and it has resulted in Hench being well recognized in the field.

Nearly a septuagenarian, Hench wanted to extend his creativity into new areas, so he took stock of his means—the interests, knowledge, assets, and relationships he had accumulated over his full life. One area was his understanding of core scientific research, particularly in the repair of human bone through his work with Bioglass®. Another was his interest in his grandchildren having accessible information about science. But Hench was disappointed with what was available. And with more than 500 research papers and 22 books to his credit, he had a strong ability as a writer.

So what did Hench do with this seemingly unrelated set of means? He created Boing-Boing, the bionic cat. Or, more specifically, he wrote fictional children's books about the adventures of Boing-Boing—tales that combine Hench's penchant for storytelling with his understanding of and passion for technology, and his interest in offering education to children.

It is easy to imagine dozens of other aspirations Hench might have had given the means he had available to him: A life sciences start-up special-

izing in solutions for children with bone damage, a summer program for children wanting to get into medicine or clinical research, children's games built around science, etc. Seeing all these different business options offers two insights into entrepreneurship. The first is that there is no one right choice—no best opportunity. It is impossible to compare what he did with what might he might have done. The second is that by starting down the entrepreneurial path with his personal means, Hench gained perspective into a broad range of possibilities where he had a unique insight, a differentiated approach, and a competitive advantage. By starting with his means, Hench was able to determine that Boing-Boing was the best opportunity

for him. It's about doing what you can with what you know—who you are and who you know.

Research roots

The key to happiness

In a series of papers entitled "Being Independent Is a Great Thing," Benz and Frey (2008) have explored the role of happiness (subjective well-being) in the decision to become an entrepreneur. Their work has really highlighted how "being your own boss" enables people to feel more in control of their lives and therefore have more of what they really value, such as self-determination, flexibility, and the ability to use their skills in the best ways they think possible.

TAKING THE PLUNGE: MOTIVATION AND SITUATION

	Young and carefree	Middle-aged and encumbered	Old and wealthy
Necessity	What are you going to do with your life?	Here's your chance to take control of your life—now.	This will keep you alive (or at least from being bored to death).
Serendipity	What do you have to gain?	Don't miss the boat.	Why the heck not?
Aspiration	Here's your chance to change the world.	If you're going to make a difference, why not now?	Now is your chance to give something back.

Boing-Boing started life as a robotic "cat substitute" for a boy with allergies, and it has already gone on to wrangle with lion's claws and chase jewel thieves in subsequent adventures. Hench has also extended the product line to include Boing-Boing branded educational materials such as workbooks, experiment books, and hands-on kits for schoolchildren.

The fun question now is: What's next? Having added children's book publisher, "brand owner," and children's science educator to his set of means, Hench has expanded his range of opportunities to create in the future. Imagine the possibilities ahead of Hench, who is in his eighties. More important, imagine the possibilities for you to combine your means into something novel. It could even be more interesting than the golf course.

ANATOMY OF THE PLUNGE DECISION

There are at least four ways in which we can think about the plunge decision. They are closely related to the affordable loss principle—how an individual decides what he or she is willing to lose in order to make the plunge into entrepreneurship.

What you can lose

This is a twist on the textbook approach. Instead of calculating the opportunity cost of starting a business in terms of your current salary and its future earnings potential, you calcu-late two relatively simple values. First, estimate the absolute maximum amount you are willing to lose. Second, decide on the absolute minimum you want to earn. Now evaluate only those opportunities you can afford with your maximum investment that will pay you at least the minimum earnings you need. Typically, the approach—called the min max or max–min approach—provides a useful filter that reduces the number of possible ventures you can seriously consider and then leads you to a go/no-go decision on each of them.

Staged efforts

This is a "real options" approach to new venture creation. Instead of all or nothing, it involves potentially starting multiple ventures while still working in an existing job. It involves taking smaller steps in more directions until you learn which one is the best and then focusing on growing that one. Essentially, it means keeping more options open by delaying investments.

Toes first

This is about choosing the least risky of the various options that exist when looking at what business to launch—a min–max approach. As we saw with the "Curry in a Hurry" example in Chapter 1, there is a portfolio of ways to pursue a particularly entrepreneurial idea. One way to go about taking the plunge is to always choose the option that involves the least risk—for example, running a catering service on the side while continuing to work at one's job, rather than launching a restaurant with all the associated costs right at the start. This is what Pierre Omydar, the founder of eBay, did.

Opportunity cost

What if you never do it? Just like there are opportunity costs associated with starting a new business, there are opportunity costs associated with *not* starting one. People often overlook these costs. There are costs to staying

Why NOT plunge? (Skip the delayed life plan)

Many people do things they don't like in the short term in the hope that one day they will be able to live their true life plan. There are two major flaws with the delayed life plan. The first is that nobody is going to sit down and tell you when its okay to stop doing what you don't want to do and switch to your true life plan. The second is that we have limited time. If you plan to live forever, you can have as many life plans as you want. But given you only have one life, why not use it to do the things you want to do, make the impact you want to make, and not wait another minute to do it?

Practically speaking

The hobby that became a venture: The case of eBay

Back when I launched eBay on Labor Day 1995, eBay wasn't my business—it was my hobby. I had to build a system that was self-sustaining . . . because I had a real job to go to every morning. I was working as a software engineer from 10 to 7, and I wanted to have a life on the weekends. So I built a system that could keep working—catching complaints and capturing feedback—even when Pam and I were out mountain biking, and the only one home was our cat. If I had had a blank check from a big VC (venture capitalist), and a big staff running around—things might have gone much worse. I would have probably put together a very complex, elaborate system—something that justified all the investment. But because I had to operate on a tight budget—tight in terms of money and tight in terms of time—necessity focused me on simplicity: So I built a system simple enough to sustain itself. By building a simple system, with just a few guiding principles, eBay was open to organic growth—it could achieve a certain degree of self-organization. So I guess what I'm trying to tell you is: Whatever future you're building . . . don't try to program everything. Five year plans never worked for the Soviet Union—in fact, if anything, central planning contributed to its fall. Chances are, central planning won't work any better for any of us.

Pierre Omydar, eBay founder

It is not the critic who counts, not the man who points out how the strong man stumbles, or where the doer of deeds could have done them better. The credit belongs to the man who is actually in the arena, whose face is marred by dust and sweat and blood, who strives valiantly; who errs and comes short again and again; because there is not effort without error and shortcomings; but who does actually strive to do the deed; who knows the great enthusiasm, the great devotion, who spends himself in a worthy cause, who at the best knows in the end the triumph of high achievement and who at the worst, if he fails, at least he fails while daring greatly. So that his place shall never be with those cold and timid souls who know neither victory nor defeat.

Theodore Roosevelt

in the current job and forgoing both the potential financial upside and the psychological returns of starting the new business venture. These are often difficult to really quantify, and they can be quite emotional. In a plunge decision, where this approach domin- ates, the entrepreneur believes the costs of not becoming an entrepre- neur outweigh the calculable costs of taking the plunge. Understanding that you can start small and proceed step by step in the direction you have chosen is critical—not starting at all guarantees you will never build a successful venture.

Finally, it is important to realize that failing can have very positive side effects. For one, it will help you build relationships with people who are willing to walk through failure with you. If you don't try, you won't know who these people might be. And there are larger implications. Many would-be entrepreneurs say they cannot fail because they live in a cultural setting that does not look kindly on failure. But research shows that in every country there are pockets of entrepreneurship and support groups. By refusing to make the plunge, would-be entrepreneurs turn their fears into a self-fulfilling prophecy, encouraging the further stigmatization of fear.

WALK BEFORE YOU JUMP

Every company that we know today was started by an entrepreneur. So, clearly, others have successfully created their own maps for this difficult journey.

The examples in this chapter demonstrate that the plunge decision is not about a sudden dive into unfathomable depths. It is a process that happens step by step, depending on your means and what you are willing to lose. It is just another way in which you achieve your objectives.

TAKEAWAY: ACTION TRUMPS ANALYSIS

In general, expert entrepreneurs emphasize action rather than analysis. If we look at the history of entrepreneurship, it includes several examples of entrepreneurs whose ideas were not considered blockbuster opportunities, but who went ahead with mundane ideas and built successful businesses simply by doing the next thing and the next thing and the next.

Expert entrepreneurs are means-driven and not goal-driven in formulating their venture models. The more experienced they are, the better they become at using readily available bits and pieces of ideas—the bird in hand—to create amazing new possibilities they themselves had not dreamed about, including new strategies, new business models, rapid responses to changes in the environment, valuable new applications for mundane technologies, and even new markets no one quite knew existed or could exist.

■ ■ ■

Bigger questions

- What really makes it a bad time to plunge?

- What is the downside to you of not plunging, of not doing the things you want to do?

- If starting a business were your *only* option, how would you manage the plunge?

Roadmap

Think about the following:

- What's holding you back?

- What are you willing to lose?

- What can you do *today* to get started? It could be something as simple as coming up with a name for your venture and getting a business card printed.

So what?

Looking at the plunge decision as a series of small steps driven by your means and what you are willing to lose, rather than hope to gain, makes "starting" much less daunting.

The plunge is not really a plunge.

WELL, AFTER FORTY DAYS AND FORTY NIGHTS, IT APPEARS I'M READY TO GO INTO THE FERTILIZER BUSINESS...

Expert entrepreneurs have learned to control or shape the future using these basic principles:

1. **Start with means.**
2. **Don't risk what you can't afford to lose.**
3. **Be open to surprise.**
4. **Build the future together with partners.**

These enable control, so the entrepreneur need not rely on prediction.

Myth: Entrepreneurs are not like the rest of us

Most of what you hear about entrepreneurship is all wrong. It's not magic; it's not mysterious; and it has nothing to do with genes. It's a discipline and, like any discipline, it can be learned.
Peter F. Drucker (1985)

IN PREVIOUS chapters we explored some common myths that surround entrepreneurs—namely that they see opportunities others can't, seize them faster, make better predictions than others, and are brash risk takers.

What our research revealed is that somehow expert entrepreneurs excel in making decisions in the face of uncertainty, even though they cannot predict better than others, or are braver or brasher than others. This makes sense when you consider that their success depends on their ability to operate in truly unknowable environments where prediction is of little use, visions can be illusions without other people's buy-in, and the whole point is *not* to place big bets at all.

Why study expert entrepreneurs?

Experts develop unique heuristics for pattern matching and problem solving within their domains. Chess masters are no smarter than the guy on the street—they have just developed expertise in chess. It is the same with expert entrepreneurs who have developed expertise in making opportunities in uncertain environments.

How do expert entrepreneurs accomplish this? Our research revealed a difference in an expert entrepreneur's fundamental assumptions about the future compared with those of a novice:

- Novice (causal): To the extent that we can predict the future, we can control it.
- Expert (effectual): To the extent that we can control the future, we do not need to predict it.

While causal reasoning may or may not involve creative thinking, effectual reasoning is inherently creative. Both can be learned and taught—they need not (or perhaps cannot) be born to an individual. In other words, everybody can learn to think and act like an entrepreneur. Of course, there are some people born with extraordinary talent, just like prodigies in music, athletics, or any other domain. So our claim is not that we can produce entrepreneurial genius on cue, just that each and every one of us can learn to become better entrepreneurs if we want to.

In Chapter 3 we briefly introduced the idea that, stemming from the desire to control their environment, expert entrepreneurs apply a set of common principles. In this chapter we will look more closely at each principle, giving you a flavor for the logic of effectuation.

FIRST PRINCIPLE: START WITH YOUR MEANS

When expert entrepreneurs seek to build a new venture, they start with their means. These means can be grouped into three categories:

- who I am—my traits, tastes, and abilities
- what I know—my education, training, expertise, and experience
- who I know—my social and professional networks.

Using a combination of these means, the entrepreneur begins to imagine possibilities and take action. Most often, s/he starts very small with the closest means, and moves almost directly into implementation without elaborate planning (fire, aim versus aim, fire). With each action, the possible outcomes are reconfigured. Eventually, certain emerging effects coalesce into clearly achievable and desirable goals—landmarks begin to appear on the blank map. The end goals are the combined result of the imagination and aspirations of the entrepreneur and the people s/he has interacted with during the process.

PRACTICALLY SPEAKING: GOODKAARMA

What do you do when you wake up one day in San Francisco and realize you actually want to be living on a sparsely populated Estonian Island in the middle of the Baltic Sea? You make sure you will be able to support yourself by starting a company there, of course. That is what Stephen and Ea (pronounced e-ah) Greenwood did when they moved to the island of Saaremaa in 2004. But then come the details—what kind of company, where

to start, and how to make it work?

The answer to some of those questions lies in starting with what you have. The Greenwoods took stock of their assets:

- a derelict farmhouse on 4 hectares of Estonian island real estate
- the island of Saaremaa with its numerous beaches and spas, and more specifically, their town of Kaarma
- access to €10,000 in seed investment, through a friend managing an EU entrepreneur incubator fund, if they could come up with a convincing idea
- an appreciation of a sustainable, organic lifestyle.

While it may have been difficult to conceive new venture directions after the first paragraph at the start of this story, after we look at their means it actually becomes easier to imagine the Greenwoods in the organic farming industry, in the eco-tourism business, or in the promotion of Estonia to potential US visitors, for example.

The Greenwoods knew that start-up costs for their business could not exceed the €10,000 funding they might receive from the EU (as they had no more cash to put into the venture), and they decided their business had to have year-round revenue potential.

After taking the complete set of inputs into consideration, the Greenwoods decided to launch a business making organic soap. Potential customers needed to wash all year long, the business required no expensive equipment, and the product would meet

their personal desires for a pure and healthy offering.

With the basic idea clear, the Greenwoods were able to put together a plan that enabled them to secure EU funding. And with the money, they started renovation of the farmhouse (their production facility and first retail location). They also started experimenting with soap manufacture (using less expensive non-organic ingredients for practice). Stephen learned computer programming so he could set up an internet site for the company, and the Greenwoods, continuing to use what they had, named the firm GoodKaarma after their town of Kaarma. Next, the couple began putting together partnerships. They approached local spas, to see whether GoodKaarma could work with them to develop customized soap products that would enhance the spagoers' experience. And they worked with local designers and printers to create packaging using organic local materials.

Today, all of GoodKaarma's soap production happens in the farmhouse kitchen using simple household equipment and wooden molds they made. The soaps are created by hand (using certified organic ingredients) in small batches of about seven kilograms. Production is year-round with all 13 varieties available on the internet, as well as exported to retail outlets in Ireland, UK, Sweden, Finland, Denmark, and Germany. The soaps are also available throughout Estonia and under private label at many of Saaremaa's best spas. Over 5,000 people visited the GoodKaarma Talu (farm) in the summer of 2008 to buy soap, many of them also participating in the Greenwoods' second business, hands-on soapmaking classes. And GoodKaarma was recently recognized by Estonian President Toomas Hendrik Ilves and his family as a model of sustainable entrepreneurship. Perhaps most important, the Greenwoods are now permanent residents of Kaarma.

SECOND PRINCIPLE: SET AFFORDABLE LOSS

In a predictive world, the manager in charge of launching a new product analyzes the market and chooses segments with the highest expected value. It is a natural reflex that is the result of years of training around a single mantra: Maximize returns by selecting the optimal strategy for your target.

Yet entrepreneurs turn this logic on its head—they think in terms of affordable loss rather than expected returns. They decide what they are willing to lose rather than what they expect to make. Instead of calculating upfront how much money they will need to launch their project and investing time, effort, and energy in raising that money, the effectual entrepreneur tries to estimate the down-side and examines what s/he is willing to lose. The entrepreneur then uses the process of building the project to bring other stakeholders on board and leverage what they can afford to lose together.

An estimate of affordable loss does not depend on the venture but varies from person to person and even across his or her life stages and circumstances. In the Pet Rock example (Chapter 1), Dahl had time on his hands and enough cash to prototype his idea.

By allowing estimates of affordable loss drive their decisions about which venture to start, entrepreneurs stop depending on prediction. Instead, they focus on cultivating opportunties that have a low cost of failure, and that generate more options for the future. The combination enables cheap failure and learning that can be applied to the next iteration of the opportunity.

This does not mean that entrepreneurs choose projects that won't cost a lot if they fail—or that they do not expect to make a lot of money. It simply acknowledges that uncertain new venture opportunities are difficult to value upfront, while investment of time, money, and other resources is quantifiable, manageable, and controllable.

PRACTICALLY SPEAKING: COMING TO TERMS WITH AFFORDABLE LOSS

Tom Fatjo was an accountant in Houston in 1967 when a meeting in his community challenged him to take up the garbage collection problem the neighborhood was facing. Having borrowed US$7,000 for his first truck, he would wake up at 4 a.m. each day and collect rubbish for two hours before changing into a suit to go to work in his accountancy office. This went on for over a year before he sat down to make the hard decision of whether to go it on his own.

"The pressure just kept building," wrote Fatjo in his 1981 book, entitled *With No Fear of Failure: Recapturing Your Dreams through Creative Enterprise*:

Even though it was cold, my body was damp from continuous perspiration. Since so much of what I was doing in the accounting firm had to be done by the end of the tax year and involved important decisions with key clients, I needed to spend time thinking through their problems and consulting with them as they made decisions. I was caught in a triangle of pressing demands, and I felt my throat constricting as if there were wires around my neck.

Fatjo recalled lying in bed one night, exhausted but unable to sleep. As he stared at the ceiling, he imagined all his refuse trucks breaking down at the same time:

I was trying to push each of them myself in order to get them going. My heart began beating faster in the darkness and my body was chilled. The horrible thought that we might fail almost paralysed me. I wanted to quit and run away. I was scared to death, very lonely, sick of the whole deal. As hard as I tried to think about my life and what was important to me, my mind was just a confused mass of muddled images. . . . I remembered committing myself to make it in the garbage business "whatever it takes!" I lay back on my pillow and felt a deep sigh within myself "Good lord, so this is what it takes,"

I thought, then rolled over and got some restless sleep.

When Fatjo let go of the security blanket of a white-collar profession to found the waste management company Browning-Ferris Industries (originally American Refuse systems), he had no way of knowing he would end up building a billion-dollar enterprise that shaped an entire industry. But what he did know was his worst-case scenario. For him, making the commitment meant understanding what he could afford to lose. Instead of considering the potential upside opportunity in waste management, the important information in Fatjo's decision was what the possible downside looked like and whether he could tolerate it should the worst happen. By focusing on the prospect of the negative, entrepreneurs effectively manage the risk inherent in a new venture down to only what they find personally acceptable.

THIRD PRINCIPLE: LEVERAGE CONTINGENCIES

If you come across lemons, make lemonade! The third principle of

effectual reasoning is at the heart of entrepreneurial expertise—the ability to turn the unexpected into the profitable.

Expert entrepreneurs learn to not only work with the surprise factor, but also how to take advantage of it. In most contingency plans, surprises are bad—the "what if?" scenarios are usually worst-case scenarios. Entrepreneurs do not tie their idea to any theorized or preconceived "market" or strategic universe. Instead, they are open to surprises when it comes to the market or markets in which they will eventually end up building their business, possibly even creating new markets. James T. Russell had no idea what it would take to make a market for the CD or how the CD might be used when he invented the technology in 1970.

PRACTICALLY SPEAKING: SURPRISE IN A GLASS

Aging in the New

Think innovation, and whisky isn't the first market that comes to mind. Yet in the moist cellars where distillers are patiently waiting for their current batch to reach a delicious age in exotic oak barrels, they are also dreaming up new combinations. For William Grant and Sons, that dream is the perfect beer-finished blended whisky. Which is why the firm engaged Dougal Sharp, head brewer at Scotland's largest craft brewery, to create a special brew that would infuse the oak barrels with a malty, hoppy flavour that could become part of a whisky during the aging process.

Success and the Drain

William Grant and Sons were pleased with the results. The Grant's Ale Cask Reserve whisky that had rested in the barrels after the beer had been discarded had an exciting and distinctive taste. But as the ever diligent distillery staff discovered during the process of emptying the barrels, so did the beer itself. So Sharp arranged a partnership with William Grant and Sons that enabled him to take the waste beer from the whisky manufacture and bring it to market under a new label bearing the middle names of Sharp and his brother, Innis & Gunn.

Success from the Drain

From there, things have gone well for Innis & Gunn. Starting with an advance commitment from Safeway and Sainsbury's in 2002, before the brand had even been introduced, the firm shipped nearly half a million cases of beer in 2009 that would otherwise have gone to waste. The product has also been a hit internationally and is now the leading British bottled brew

in beer-loving Canada and number two bottled import ale in Sweden.

Business Surprise

The story of Innis & Gunn offers two insights into innovation. The first is that many innovations are not true inventions—created from scratch—but rather new combinations of things

we already have. The second is the role of surprise. Had not the employees of William Grant and Sons sampled from the waste, the world would have one fewer premium micro-brew. What is also surprising is how many of the products we know and love today came from accidents and unintended results of completely different ideas. Consider these three beer-compatible products:

Crisp Surprise

At the pub, you might enjoy a crisp with your beer. Legend describes these popular snacks as born of customer complaint. In 1853, tired of having fried potatoes sent back to the kitchen of Moon's Lake House near Saratoga Springs, New York, because they were soggy, a frustrated George Crum sliced potatoes as thinly as he could, then fried and salted them. The popular result has gone on to please beer consumers around the world.

Transparent Surprise

Perhaps after a pint in the lab, French scientist Edouard Benedictus accidentally broke a glass container and observed that the shattered pieces remained bound as a result of a plastic liquid that had formed a thin film inside the container. The year was 1903, and safety glass was born.

Romantic Surprise

While we will leave the connection with beer to the reader, Viagra was also discovered completely by accident. The active ingredient never met its intended solution to heart disease, but in lab tests, new applications popped up. Viagra was created and became the first oral treatment for men with erectile dysfunction.

"Forget lemonade. The real money's in bottled water."

The Surprising Entrepreneur

In thinking about where new opportunities come from, these examples highlight the importance of doing, and the role of the entrepreneur. While we love to tell stories of divine inspiration, the actual events behind many of the products we know are unplanned surprises that an entrepreneur was able to transform into an opportunity. The implication is clear. Those waiting for the perfect idea will have to be patient, while those taking action will likely create something interesting and then need only figure out how to make a business of it. Maybe that will change the way you see your next surprise.

> One only gets to the top rung of the ladder by steadily climbing up one at a time, and suddenly all sorts of powers, all sorts of abilities which you thought never belonged to you—suddenly become within your own possibility and you think, "Well, I'll have a go, too".
> **Margaret Thatcher**

FOURTH PRINCIPLE: FORM PARTNERSHIPS

Another key principle of effectual reasoning, which we touched upon in Chapter 3, is the focus on building partnerships rather than on beating competitors. Since entrepreneurs tend to start the process without assuming the existence of a predetermined market for their idea, detailed competitive analyses have little value since it's not clear who the competition will be!

Instead, entrepreneurs will almost always take the product to the nearest potential customer. Some of the people the entrepreneur interacts with self-select into the process by making a commitment to the venture.

The strategic partnership principle dovetails well with the affordable loss principle to bring the entrepreneur's idea to market with very little cash expenditure. Obtaining pre-commitments from key stakeholders helps reduce uncertainty in the early stages of creating an enterprise. Finally, since the entrepreneur is not wedded to any particular market for his or her idea, the expanding network of strategic partnerships determines, to a great extent, which market or markets the company will eventually end up creating.

PRACTICALLY SPEAKING: NAVIGATING A SEA OF POTENTIAL PARTNERS

William Dick is a physicist and a sailor who spent most of his career in the Irish whiskey business. During the early 1990s he became interested in escalating environmental issues, and set up a consultancy focusing on environmental impact, biomass, and the future of energy. Combining this expertise and his physics background with a realisation that fossil fuels were becoming exhausted—plus tough experience in small yachts in the North Atlantic—it is little wonder that he latched on to the idea of capturing energy from ocean waves. In 1999 he founded Wavebob™, an alternative energy firm intent on capturing the "blue power" of the sea.

But turning the idea of harnessing the ocean's relentless energy into commercial power is a big, complicated, and resource-intensive job. The ocean is a hostile environment presenting a host of challenges in delivering a

reliable, scalable, and cost-effective alternative to burning fossil fuels. Together with CEO Andrew Parish, Dick had to find the money, people, companies, and technologies necessary to assemble a complete solution.

Parish explains:

> **A popular first stop for an entrepreneur with a big idea is the financier—a venture capitalist or a banker. We made up our minds early on that we would take a different tack. In order to maintain control over our own destiny for as long as possible, we proactively sought funding partners who share a business interest in what we are doing. Not only would our incentives be aligned with these partners, but they would also understand our technology, our timelines, our financial requirements and, probably most important, the challenges we face.**

For Wavebob™, this meant building relationships with core technology researchers such as universities and commercial labs, as well as firms in the oil and gas industry, firms with expertise in electrical utilities and renewable energy, and even marine defence specialists who might help Wavebob™ with the durability of marine energy devices. The strategy appeared appealing, as it promised to bring together the expertise of larger diverse organizations to inexpensively accelerate development at the nascent Wavebob™, but where to start?

Perhaps with the luck of the Irish, Wavebob™ won an award in 2006 for their novel technology. At the Art of Innovation, an Engineers Ireland seminar where the awards were presented, they got talking with people from Intel, who had received similar recognition. It turned out both teams were working on long distance wireless networking, with Wavebob™ focused on communication over water. Both teams realized that Intel's Wifi and WiMax project was exactly what Wavebob™ needed to control arrays of energy generating buoys, and a collaborative relationship was formed.

Building on the Intel partnership, Wavebob™ has since announced strategic relationships with Chevron in oil and gas, and with Vattenfall in electric utilities and renewables, which have brought technology, expertise, and funding to the venture. "It's easy to be intimidated as a start-up working with such impressive players," reflects Parish. "But I quickly came to the conclusion that in a new market, companies of any size can come to the table and interact as peers, because both have something to offer and something to gain." And with the momentum Wavebob™ is gaining, they might just be the next wave in alternative energy.

PRINCIPLES ROOTED IN REALITY

Using effectuation, entrepreneurs begin with who they are, what they know, and who they know. From there, they set in motion a network of stakeholders, each of whom makes commitments that, on the one hand, increase the resources available to the network, but on the other hand, add constraints to their budding businesses. Effectual commitment has several characteristics:

- It focuses on what is controllable about the future and the external environment.
- The entrepreneur commits only what s/he can afford to lose.
- The goals of the venture are determined by who makes commitments and what they negotiate.
- The key to the process is not the selection between alternatives but the transformation of existing realities into new alternatives.

Going back to our example in Chapter 3, the entrepreneur using effectual logic says:

Whatever the initial distribution of balls in the jar, I will continue to acquire red balls and put them in the jar. I will look for other people who own red balls and induce them to become partners and add to the red balls in the jar. As time goes by, there will be so many red balls in the jar that almost every draw will obtain one. On the other hand, if I and my acquaintances have only green balls, we will put them in the jar, and when there are enough, we will create a new game where green balls win.

Research roots

Entrepreneurs made

Vivek Wadhwa (2009) looked at 549 successful entrepreneurs and did not find a connection with even the few things prior research had suggested might be associated with successful entrepreneurs—entrepreneurial parentage and early entrepreneurial activity. In his study he found 52 percent of successful entrepreneurs were the first in their immediate families to start a business. Furthermore, only a quarter were interested in entrepreneurship in college. Half didn't think about it, and had little interest in it when in school. Their main finding was that education was the biggest predictor of success. Education enabled a huge advantage. Interestingly, the source of that education was not important. Firms founded by Ivy League graduates and the graduates of other universities experienced reasonably similar success.

Of course, such a view may express hopes rather than realities, and many entrepreneurs in the real world do fail. In fact, being in an unpredictable market is often perceived as an advantage by entrepreneurs because they feel they can shape it through their own decisions and actions, working together with pre-committed stakeholders and customer-partners. Together they use contingencies along the way as part of the raw materials that constitute the very urn they are constructing.

Unlike causal reasoning that comes to life through careful planning and subsequent execution, effectual reasoning lives and breathes action. Plans are made and unmade and revised and recast through action and interaction with others on a daily basis. Yet at any given moment, there is always a meaningful picture that keeps the team together, a compelling story that brings in more stakeholders, and a continuing journey that maps out uncharted territories. By consciously

disregarding the history of the past, the entrepreneur effectually creates the future of his dreams.

PRACTICALLY SPEAKING: PERSIST EASY; SWERVE HARD

Snarly problem

The city of Bangalore, India, has over 200,000 three-wheel auto rickshaws— short distance, open taxis that provide critical transportation in a metropolis of more than six million inhabitants with no metro or underground rail system. Efficiently ferrying both people and goods, these simple machines challenge the urban environment. Their entrepreneurial drivers cruise the edges of the streets eagerly soliciting passengers, choking traffic and adding smog to an already congested city. Meanwhile, frustrated businesspeople, merchants, and families await rides in other locations without a free auto rickshaw in sight.

Smooth solution

So when the commissioner of traffic police approached Padmasree Harish, an entrepreneur and self-taught web designer, to build a software system that would connect available auto rickshaws with waiting passengers, Harish saw both a natural answer to her city's problem as well as a good business opportunity. The system would receive SMS messages from drivers indicating location and availability, and calls from passengers with location and interest. The system would match passengers with the closest auto rickshaw and dispatch the vehicle to the passenger. Harish could charge a setup fee for each driver, and a small fee for each fare her system was able to connect. All she had to do was let the software do the work while the rupees rolled in. And so, in 2007, Easy Auto kicked into gear. In theory, that is.

Hard stop

In practice, after the announcement of the initiative, the system never got beyond the rave press write-ups of its potential. This left Harish with a software system she and her team had spent six months developing, a call center filled with people hired to take calls from passengers, a tech team ready to roll out the system, extra uniforms for the drivers of the spruced-up rickshaws and even 50,000 rupees worth of coolers and inventory from Pepsi for in-transit sales and additional revenue. The bumps in the road seemed never-ending. Drivers were reluctant to pay a setup fee and were unwilling to send SMS messages with their current location. But the unseen pothole that derailed Harish was the regulatory environment. It turned out that the traffic commis-

sioner who initiated the project did not have permission from the branch of the bureaucracy that oversaw auto rickshaws. So the entire project was brought to a screeching halt.

U-turn?

Harish's inclination was to return to her profitable web hosting and design business, leaving physical traffic to someone else. But her personal cell phone was one of the three numbers provided in the Easy Auto announcement for passengers to call an auto rickshaw on demand. And whenever it rained, as it often does in Bangalore, Harish would get 200–250 calls. The market had her number, and it simply would not hang up. But when does tenacity become foolishness? And how does an entrepreneur know when to quit?

A new route

Harish started looking for workarounds. She took courses in entrepreneurship so she could get others chewing on her problems. She actively observed every auto rickshaw she rode in and then some. In one, she saw an advertisement. She saw taxis with GPS

units. Nearly every website she saw offered services for free to end users, but made money from someone else. So when the head of transportation came back to her in 2009 and asked her about getting Easy Auto going again, she had learned what to negotiate for and was ready to say, "Yes, and . . .":

- The approvals had to be complete before she would spend a rupee.
- The auto rickshaws would have to be equipped with units containing LCD screens showing promotional videos and GPS units for precise location information.
- The video would be funded by a company that builds the auto rickshaws.
- The drivers would receive compensation for signing up with Easy Auto.
- The GPS and LCD hardware would be provided by the manufacturers in advance with payment once the system started generating income.
- The call center would be outsourced to a firm willing to set it up at no charge.

Absolutely everything would be upside down from her first try. Harish had left behind the choice between the straight road of persistence and the sad U-turn. She had learned to swerve hard.

Enduring logic

Conventional wisdom describes the doggedly determined entrepreneur enduring in the face of adversity. But a closer look reveals an unexpected combination of persistence and flexibility. Persisting hard for a particular solution can be counterproductive and even end in despair. But hardheaded flexibility may transform the problem into an opportunity that attracts unexpected shareholders. Especially when problems persist, entrepreneurs need to be able to swerve hard to co-create new answers that can form the basis of new firms, new products, new markets, or even that unlikeliest of novelties—smoother traffic flow in Bangalore.

TAKEAWAY: A DIFFERENT WAY OF LOOKING AT THE WORLD

Beyond mapping the future, effectuation carries certain assumptions about the world. Effectual thinkers:

- See the world as open, still in the making. They see human action as having a genuine role. They see firms and markets as human artifacts.
- Do not see opportunities as given or as being outside of their control. On the contrary, they believe in creating, as well as recognizing and discovering opportunities.
- Do not have an instrumental view of the world. On the contrary, they see companies as a tool that allows them to create novelty for themselves and the world, they see markets as being made rather than found, and stakeholders co-create with them rather than being used.
- Work on making success happen rather than trying to avoid failure. They see failing as a normal part of venturing. Because they are willing to fail, they often create portfolios of ventures, knowing and learning to kill those that will lead nowhere and nurture those with potential.

Now you have a complete overview of effectuation. The rest of this book will dot the 'i's and cross the 't's of the principles outlined here and explicitly relate them to the nitty-gritty details of actually starting a new venture.

However, before we dive into the real tasks of new venture creation, we need to tackle one last and very important reason that most people do not become entrepreneurs—the biggest monster under the bed: *fear of failure*.

Roadmap

Think about the following:

- ☐ Think about the companies you admire. To what extent did the principles in this chapter contribute to their creation/success?

- ☐ In what ways do these principles work together, reinforce each other?

- ☐ For each principle, what is it that makes it work in uncertain environments?

- ☐ Identify five companies around you where you can see these principles in action.

Bigger questions

Potential answers?

- ☐ Is this the only thing I can do when faced with uncertainty? No, it's an alternative.

- ☐ Does it mean prediction doesn't matter? No, use it if you can; if not, use effectuation.

- ☐ Is it just for small firms? No! Big firms strive for innovation too.

- ☐ Is this just about making decisions? Yes, and it helps to take control and think about where to start.

So what?

Sometimes the principles and tools learned in school don't work. Expert entrepreneurs regularly turn our MBA lessons upside down.

Fewer than 2 percent of new ventures reach an IPO.

92 percent of ventures exit without outstanding debt.

If success is an initial public offering, then 98 percent of ventures fail.

If failure is bankruptcy, then 8 percent of ventures fail.

I'm human: I'm afraid of failing

■ ■ ■

NOBODY SETS OUT to fail. But the statistics above demonstrate that failure is something which means very different things to different people.

The matter is further complicated by the cultural aspects of success and failure. In Silicon Valley an entrepreneur is regarded with suspicion if s/he has never failed, whereas, in Europe failure is perceived to be a death knell, financially and socially. In some cultures failure in business can impact personal aspects of an individual's life such as the ability to marry.

Finally, we all have different subjective personal definitions of success and failure. For some, quitting is the only form of failure. For others, earning less than they could working for someone else is equivalent to failing.

Similarly, for some, only an initial public offering (IPO) can be considered a true success, while for others, just being able to make a decent living without answering to a boss is success enough. So how should you look at failure if you are starting a new venture? What does success really mean to an entrepreneur?

In this chapter we will look at four elements of what we call the failure equation, namely that:

- success ≠ success
- success ≠ money
- failure of the firm ≠ failure of the individual
- failure = learning

And finally, we will think about the following: Is failure terminal?

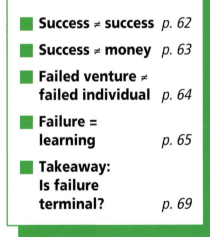

In Europe, a serious social stigma is attached to bankruptcy. In the USA, bankruptcy laws allow entrepreneurs who fail to start again relatively quickly and failure is considered to be part of the learning process. In Europe, those who go bankrupt tend to be considered as "losers." They face great difficulty getting financing for a new venture.
Communication by the European Commission, 1998

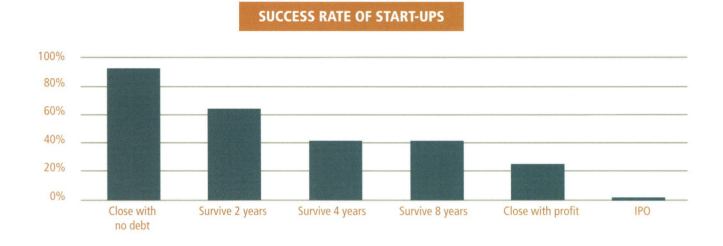

SUCCESS RATE OF START-UPS

SUCCESS ≠ SUCCESS

What does failure really mean? The "Success rate of start-ups" chart and the statistics at the start of the chapter (Headd, 2004:51–61; US SBA, 2009; Kirchhoff, 1997; Knaup, 2005) show us that the breadth of success and failure is in how you define both. If your definition is running a business that closes with no debt, then you have a 92 percent chance of succeeding. If your aim is an IPO, your chance is less than 2 percent. Obviously, those differences have implications for how you see your business and, ultimately, your success. The chart tells us that one in every four companies that closes down closes with a profit—clearly financial "failure" is not the only reason why people close down a business; a company may close down because the owner retired, moved to another country, accepted a job offer, or simply got bored with the business. Regardless of the circumstances, a Barclay's local business poll (McDougall, 2008) showed that 87 percent of the business owners polled would start their own business again if the current one failed.

With this spectrum of "failure" and "success" in mind, refer to the following short stories. For each story, think about whether you would label them as successes or failures, and tick the appropriate box.

Lucy launched four ventures that failed before she moved onto her fifth one. This one and the one that followed were enormously successful, financially. Unfortunately, the fifth venture was wiped out by a natural disaster in which the entrepreneur lost everything.

❑ Success   ❑ Failure

Mark meets a San Francisco venture capitalist (VC) to pitch his next idea. He is feeling confident. His previous venture sold after only 18 months, making over four times its original investment for its founders and stakeholders. The VC looks at the venture as a failure. Her argument: They sold too soon and could have made more money.

❑ Success   ❑ Failure

Jack, a serial entrepreneur, looks at the company he founded 15 years ago. It makes an 8 percent return for its shareholders, pays the bills, and is highly respected in its industry. Jack quit the company seven years ago, selling his shares to his managers because he knew he could never take it public.

❑ Success   ❑ Failure

Clearly, how you look at failure (and success) depends on your environment as well as on the expectations of those with whom you interact. What you view as success or failure also depends on your role in the process: If you are a VC, you want at least ten times the money you invested. If you are a supplier, you only worry about whether the start-up will be able to pay your bills. The fact that success and failure can mean different things to different people de-dramatizes the statistics, because whether you succeed or fail really depends on what your objectives are and what your committed stakeholders want. This takes us to our next point in our failure equation: Success and the reasons why entrepreneurs start businesses have to do with more than just the financial return.

SUCCESS ≠ MONEY

Before you launch your venture, hoping to become the next Bill Gates, consider the following:

- On average, the self-employed earn about the same as the employed.
- Having said that, the distribution of earnings is skewed by a few superstar entrepreneurs who make incredible amounts of money (i.e. Bill Gates) while most earn below average.
- For those who do earn below average, it's about one-third less than a comparable employed person.

So if typical entrepreneurs make less money than if they were employed, why do they choose to invest their net worth in (presumably) high-risk ventures when they do not stand to gain a substantial premium over less risky investments in public equity markets?

The most likely answer to this puzzle is that there are other things than money that matter (being your own boss, doing something that matters to you, or even just trying to solve a problem that irks you). Consider the story of the MGA Entertainment.

PRACTICALLY SPEAKING: FAIL TO SUCCEED

Isaac Larian is a busy man. Since his immigration from Iran to the United States 38 years ago, he has washed dishes, studied engineering, imported brass goods from Korea, and sold refrigerators and microwave ovens. Building on his Asian connections, he was the first to bring Nintendo handheld LCD games to the US, and from there he expanded into the toy

business by licensing popular brands like Mighty Morphin Power Rangers, Hello Kitty, and The Hulk.

All that got Larian started, but the reason you likely already know him is because of Bratz. In 2001, tired of making profits for his licensors, Larian decided to create his own toy brand and launched a line of fashion dolls. A runaway success, Bratz dolls successfully challenged Barbie's supremacy on toy store shelves and created more than US$2 billion a year in revenue for Larian's firm—MGA Entertainment —within just three years.

(Bratz) are everything Barbie is not. Who in Britain can identify with a six-foot-two blonde? The Bratz exist in a changing world—children today are exposed to change at a very fast pace, so the Bratz change too . . . In ten years, they will be something completely different.

Isaac Larian

In 2007 Larian was Ernst & Young's Entrepreneur Of The Year® overall national winner. But with the award

On the origins of failure

Scott Sandage (2006) studied the historical origins of failure in his book, *Born Losers*. What he discovered was interesting: Before the late 1800s the idea of failed individuals didn't really exist. This led Sandage to the thesis that failure is a social construct that was literally invented during the nineteenth century. Of course, people have stigmatized others for one reason or another throughout written history. The Greeks and Romans stigmatized slaves, criminals, and traitors. And because failure is still a reasonably new idea from a social perspective, people are still figuring out both how to define it and how to deal with it.

came disappointment. The year proved a bittersweet one for Bratz. Panned by the critics, the *Bratz Fashion Pixiez* movie that Larian released with LionsGate Entertainment generated less than US$3 million in revenue. And adding insult to injury, 4Kids.TV canceled the Bratz animated television series. A closer look at these disappointments offers the real insight into Larian's entrepreneurial expertise. In neither case did he put MGA Entertainment at grave risk. His investment in the experiments was sufficiently low that failure of the project did not translate into catastrophe for the firm. Instead, and in both cases, he shared both the risk and the potential rewards with partners. As Larian says, "You should not be afraid of failure. In order to succeed, you need to fail."

Looking back at Larian's career offers another insight. Entrepreneurship is less about vision and more about the journey of creation. From his start, it would have been impossible to predict that he would become the head of the third largest toy company in the world, yet in retrospect the pieces come together and make sense. And by failing gracefully when failure came, Larian was always ready to learn from the experience and do something better in the next round.

Quick fact:

Only 6 of 1,000 business plans get venture funding, and 60 percent of those go bankrupt.

Explained:

Right and wrong

"Sir, what is the secret of your success?" a reporter asked a successful businessman.

"Two words."

"And what are they, sir?"

"Right decisions."

"And how do you make right decisions?"

"One word."

"And what is that, sir?"

"Experience."

"And how do you get experience?"

"Two words."

"And what are they, sir?"

"Wrong decisions."

FAILED VENTURE ≠ FAILED INDIVIDUAL

Entrepreneurial performance is almost always confused with firm performance—the success or failure of the company is the success or failure of the individual. This is a mistake for several reasons.

First, as we have seen, although entry is common, survival is less so. Second, many companies enter a market in its infancy. As this market matures, only the fittest survive.

A lot of work has been done on the corporation, looking, for example, for a correlation between the age of the firm and survival rates (do firms die young or degenerate with age?). But little is known of the success or failure rates of entrepreneurs.

The primary reason for this lack of evidence about the success and failure of entrepreneurs (as distinct from their companies) is that whereas evidence on failed firms is hard to obtain (the data usually disappear along with the firm), evidence on failed entrepreneurs is well nigh impossible to come by. People just simply do not walk around with business cards that say "failed entrepreneur." Most founders of failed firms either dust themselves off and go on to start other firms, or they are serial entrepreneurs who have previously been successful. Both groups tend not to mention their failed firms, except long after the fact and as part of uplifting anecdotes in public speeches. The few truly "failed entrepreneurs" seemingly disappear off the face of the economy forever, leaving few traces for researchers to follow.

The corporation was invented to separate the individual from the business—separating the success or failure of the firm from that of the individual. If the individual closes the business to pursue a new opportunity, does that constitute individual failure? Too often, we think that if the business fails then the individual has failed. Remember that this is not the case, as the Hershey story illustrates (see the nearby box)!

FAILURE = LEARNING

PRACTICALLY SPEAKING: PRODUCT LAUNCHES AT APPLE COMPUTER

Apple is well known for its innovativeness and its incredible product successes—creating a mass market where there was none. Yet did you know that it has had to survive a failed product launch almost every year since 1983? And many argue it was those failures that set the ground for later successes. For a company known to focus all its resources behind each new product, each one of these product failures could have spelled the end of innovation at Apple. But each time the company learned from its failures and applied the learning to the next product generation.

> Success is a lousy teacher. It seduces smart people into thinking they can't lose.
>
> Bill Gates

Persistence pays, or who decides it's a bad idea?

Within a month of submitting the first manuscript to publishing houses, the creative team behind the multimillion-dollar book series *Chicken Soup for the Soul* (Canfield and Hansen, 1993) got turned down 33 consecutive times. Publishers claimed that "anthologies don't sell" and the book was "too positive." Total number of rejections—140. Then, in 1993, the president of Health Communications took a chance on the collection of poems, stories, and tidbits of encouragement. Today, the 65-title series has sold more than 80 million copies in 37 languages.

Practically speaking

Milton Hershey

Born September 13, 1857, on a farm near Derry Church, a small Pennsylvania community, Milton Hershey was the only surviving child of Fannie and Henry Hershey. His mother raised him in the strict discipline of the Mennonite faith. Frequent family moves interrupted his schooling and left him with a limited education. He only completed the fourth grade.

Following a four-year apprenticeship with a Lancaster candy-maker, he established his first candy making business in Philadelphia. That initial effort failed as did his next two attempts in Chicago and New York. Returning to Lancaster, Pennsylvania, in 1883, Hershey established the Lancaster Caramel Company, which quickly became an outstanding success. It was this business that established him as a candy maker and set the stage for future accomplishments.

Hershey became fascinated with German chocolate-making machinery exhibited at the 1893 World's Columbian Exhibition. He bought the equipment for his Lancaster plant and soon began producing a variety of chocolate creations. Hershey sold the Lancaster Caramel Co. for US$1 million in 1900 in order to concentrate exclusively on his chocolate business. Three years later, he returned to Derry Church to build a new factory. There he could obtain the large supplies of fresh milk needed to perfect and produce fine milk chocolate.

Excited by the potential of milk chocolate, which at that time was a Swiss luxury product, Milton Hershey determined to develop a formula for milk chocolate and market and sell it to the American public. Through trial and error he created his own formula for milk chocolate. In 1903 he began construction on what was to become the world's largest chocolate manufacturing plant.

All in all, Hershey failed six businesses before setting up the plant that turned HERSHEY® into a world renowned brand.

FAMOUS FAILURES FROM APPLE COMPUTER

Product	Launch	Apple's product failures: Lessons learned
Lisa	1983	The Lisa was the first computer to boast a graphical interface and a mouse. Aimed at the business community, it was priced at today's equivalent of US$20,800. Unsurprisingly, the business community voted for the cheaper IBMs. Lesson learned: Price does matter.
Apple IIc	1984	The Apple IIc was hailed as the first portable computer. It did have a carrying case, external power supply, built in floppy drive, and peripheral expansion ports. But it lacked upgradeability, and it had an extremely short-lived LCD display. The lessons learned from Apple IIcs shortcomings would drive the design of the next generation of Macintosh.
Mac TV	1993	A combination of a Sony Trinitron and an Apple Performa 520, the product barely lasted 12 months before it was discontinued. Its major problem? It was incapable of showing TV feeds in a desktop window. Although only 10,000 units were produced, it was in its way the precursor to the successful AppleTV.
Newton	1993	The best-known of Apple flops is probably the Newton. Released in 1993 as a revolutionary personal digital assistant (PDA) (but not as revolutionary as its first prototypes) it was available for four years with nearly no sales. When Steve Jobs returned to Apple in 1997, he axed the product he had tried so hard to launch. The Newton was bulky and it relied on handwriting recognition software, which wasn't yet very good. The lesson: The Newton is a good example of a product ahead of its time.
PIPPIN	1996	With the Pippin, Apple tried (once again) to enter the video game market with a product that was co-marketed with toymaker Bandai. The Pippin was sold as a cheap machine on which one could play games but which also served as a network computer—one of the first multimedia platforms. It failed for several reasons, including a lack of software and competition in a market dominated by players such as Sega, Sony Playstation, and Nintendo. Rumor has it Apple has just filed a patent for a new 3D gaming device. Time will tell whether they learned from the Pippin flop.
Hockey Puck Mouse	1998	The mouse that was shipped with the first iMacs was small, un-ergonomic, and awkward to control. It was almost immediately phased out and replaced by the Mighty Mouse. Lesson learned: Sometimes a classical shape is good.
G4 Cube	2000	While the Cube was meant to fill the gap between the iMac G3 and the PowerMac G4, it was killed by the critics before it got anywhere. Its major problems: It lacked a monitor and it had a high price tag. However, its designer, Jonathan Ive, won several international awards for its design, and he remains as head designer for Apple. Apart from its design, it also set the stage for fanless cooling in PCs. The G4 was also an improvement on the NeXT computer that Jobs had designed during his time there, based on a major learning: Don't build in proprietary software.

There are smart ways to fail and not so smart ways. Take, for example, the joke about a barber who routinely called his errand boy the village idiot. To prove his case to skeptical customers, the barber would invite the boy to choose between a rusty dime and a shiny quarter. The boy invariably chose the dime. Finally, it occurred to a customer to ask the boy when he was alone running an errand why he chose the dime over the quarter. And the boy replied, "Choosing the quarter would end the game." Not all failures are the same. Some are smart and they lead you to play the game better and win more over time.

Failure is simply the opportunity to begin again, this time more intelligently.

Henry Ford

Twain on learning

We should be careful to get out of an experience only the wisdom that is in it—and stop there; lest we be like the cat that sits down on a hot stove lid. She will never sit down on a hot stove lid again—and that is well; but also she will never sit down on a cold one.

Mark Twain (1897)

In fact, the essence of the scientific method is comprised in the design of well-thought-out failures—experiments that seek to falsify hypotheses. And slowly, as some hypotheses are shown to be false and others continue unscathed, we begin to get closer to workable truths that can be cumulated into valuable technologies and cures for diseases.

The same is true of good engineering as well. In a book entitled *Success Through Failure: The Paradox of Design*, Henry Petroski (2006) shows how success often masks potential modes of failure and how failures have again and again through history led to technological progress and better design.

Words of wisdom: A culture of learning

. . . part of creating an entrepreneurial culture is to celebrate failure. It's very hard to be an entrepreneur inside a company if you feel you're going to get crucified for failing because there's risk in being an entrepreneur. If you've tried ten things, five will fail. Besides, if you wait too long so that you can do enough research to be sure an idea will work, you're probably going to be too late. So you've got to create an environment where people know it's okay to fail and, that way, they'll try a lot more. They'll think outside the box. They're willing to think differently because they know that if it doesn't work, they won't be scorched and they'll still have a career.

At times, like when we've closed out a business, we've had something like a celebration of what we've learned. We celebrate what we now know that we did not know before because it will help us make much better decisions in the future. We celebrate those people who fail and everyone around them knows that they produced value. It wasn't the value we intended, but it's okay as long as we learn from it.

In one of the businesses we launched last December, the marketing person was someone who had failed on her prior assignment. She had worked on a project where we were trying to set up a business for lending to small businesses on a very low-tech basis. We developed, launched, and got ten financial institutions to back it, but we couldn't get the volume to make the business fly. But then last December, working out of our Boston office, which is one of our most entrepreneurial operations, the same person and her team succeeded at launching a whole new business called QuickBase. It's a revolutionary product and is off to a huge start.

Scott Cook, founder of Intuit

Passion?

If you're about to start your own business, you've got to have a passion for whatever it is that you want to do. We can't teach passion; we can teach everything else. If you have passion and you do your homework, don't let fear of failure stop you from going into a new business. Fear of failure is the number one reason people don't go ahead in starting a business. They're just afraid to pull the trigger. They start analyzing what the fear means. There is the fear that the business won't succeed and the fear that their ego will be damaged. At least in your head, you've got to separate the two fears. Many people won't do things, like a sales call, because they're afraid they'll be turned down. Ego shouldn't be a concern. Every rejection is a learning experience. You deal with the fear of a business failing by doing all those things. There is risk in everything in life. Don't let fear of failure keep you from moving ahead.

Robert Reiss,
founder of R&R

Resilience at work

When greeted by a heckler's boos—generally acknowledged to belong to Reginald Golding Bright—during the curtain call on the opening night of his play *Arms and the Man*, George Bernard Shaw responded with his now famous remark: "I assure the gentleman in the gallery that he and I are of exactly the same opinion, but what can we do against a whole house who are of the contrary opinion?"

William Butler Yeats, who witnessed the event, wrote of the sensation that ensued: "From that moment Bernard Shaw became the most formidable man in modern letters, and even the most drunken medical student knew it."

The key to learning from failures, of course, is to keep them small and kill them young. The affordable loss principle is very useful here. Limiting one's investments only to what one has consciously chosen as an acceptable level of loss has the double benefit of reducing the magnitude of failure as well as the psychological hit that is likely to come with unanticipated failures.

Passion serves an important role as well because passion breeds resilience. As the comedian Seinfeld quipped: "It is not that bad things do not happen when you love what you do. It is just that passion makes it easier to live with and deal with and overcome those difficulties."

All the same, failure is not easy. It can be painful and even result in real grief and serious loss of morale. It is possible, however, to deal with failure and come through it stronger, wiser, and more likely to succeed.

Shepherd (2003) suggests that the emotions associated with having to close down a business are somewhat similar to those felt when we lose someone dear to us (albeit not as dramatic). Business owners see the closure of their business as a personal loss, and are bereft with feelings of grief. Shepherd uses the psychology literature on grief and emotions to understand how entrepreneurs can overcome their feeling of loss and learn from their failures.

Learning from the loss of a business depends on grief recovery processes. Shepherd suggests that accepting that feeling grief is normal and working through a dual path of loss orientation (confronting the reality) and restoration orientation (suppressing and moving on) may help the entrepreneur pick him- or herself up and not see failure as terminal.

Perhaps the first and most important rule of failure is: *don't fail alone.* Success is sweeter and failure is more palatable when we have supportive people around us and people who share our ups and downs with us.

And interestingly, people who have gone through adversity together tend to strengthen their bonds of trust, friendship, and mutual self-beliefs. As the founder of Teledyne remarked, "My co-founders and I are blood brothers. We have been through failed ventures in the past."

And David Shrank, the founder of Pupcups, a promising start-up that he was forced to close down due to a cash crunch, mentioned this about his entire team, "The Pupcups alumni meet regularly and exchange memories and hopes. The question is not whether I would start another venture with them. I don't think I would start another venture without them."

© Copyright Michiel Jonker 2006

TAKEAWAY: IS FAILURE TERMINAL?

The failure equations show us that some of the most common myths about failure are actually just that—myths.

In Chapter 13, we will look at ICEHOTEL. The beautiful and popular winter destination created by Yngve Bergqvist was not the result of a flash of vision or insight, but rather an act of desperation from a man who had invited artists, press, and tourists to an ice-sculpting event which was washed out by rain. The rain could have put an end to Bergqvist's career

Research roots

Adversity motivates successful UK entrepreneurs

Personal adversity is a driving factor motivating successful UK entrepreneurs according to a survey by the Aldridge Foundation (2009).

The "Origins of an Entrepreneur" survey asked 370 of the country's successful entrepreneurs about their backgrounds, education, motivations, and personal characteristics.

Seven out of ten (69 percent) said they had been motivated by adversity including parental divorce, a car crash, cancer, and under-achieving at school. And the majority (56 percent) said determination is the most important characteristic for a successful entrepreneur, followed by passion (22 percent).

"Adversity forged my independence and was a major influence over my drive for success in my career," said Glen Manchester, CEO of Thunderhead (CBI/Real Business Entrepreneur of the Year).

Laura Tenison said under-achieving at school made her want to prove her teachers wrong and she set up her acclaimed baby wear brand, JoJoMaman Bébé, after suffering a severe car crash in France. Bar Hewlett said beating cancer gave her the determination to set up weight loss business, LighterLife. TenUK founder, Alex Cheatle, cited the breakdown of his parents' marriage when he was three: "A government minister once asked me how we can boost entrepreneurship in this country," he said. "My flippant response was, 'More misfortune.'"

as an entrepreneur and sent him back to the mines (literally). Instead, the fact that the ice could not be preserved led to the creation of the ICEHOTEL —something that had to be built anew every year.

Milton Hershey's numerous failures did not stop him from building the Hershey empire; and the rejections of the *Chicken Soup* team did not stop them from trying again and again. Apple's product failures did not stop it from being hailed by *Fortune*, in its March 2008 issue, as the most admired company in the world.

Success is not the same for everyone; entrepreneurs don't start companies for financial reasons alone, failing a business does not mark you for life as a failed individual, and if you can overcome the grief of a failed business and learn from it, then you have a fair chance of doing better (and smarter) the next time around. In addition, failing can also tell you who you can trust and who will go along with you— those that stay with you when you fail will be valuable partners for your next venture.

Remember that the only real measure of failure is those companies that close down owing money to debtors, which represent only 8 percent of all the companies that close their doors. In fact, some may argue that you are a successful entrepreneur only if you have failed once and continue to want to be an entrepreneur.

Roadmap

Think about the following:

- [ ] Think of failure as an option. Paint the picture of everything consistently going wrong. How bad is bad?

- [ ] Detail what you might lose if you fail versus what you will lose if you don't try. List five points for each option.

- [ ] What are your options after each situation? After which experience are you in a stronger position?

- [ ] At what point would you stop trying/move on?

- [ ] How are you going to survive failure?

- [ ] What could be the next thing to try?

So what?

By creating more companies, trying more often, your probability of success will increase—each experience will add to your learning. Along the way, your definition of success will change as a function of your changing means, what you learn, and your aspirations. Think of yourself as an emerging chess master, learning new moves with each game and using them in the next.

Bigger questions

- [ ] How much does our ego get in the way of accepting failure?

- [ ] How different is the failure of a managed business to the failure of an owned business?

- [ ] How do we deal with the cultural aspect of failure? Does it mean that it's easier to be an entrepreneur in some countries than others?

The nuts and bolts of venturing: Effectuation in action

But when I said that nothing had been done I erred in one important matter. We had definitely committed ourselves and were halfway out of our ruts. We had put down our passage money—booked a sailing to Bombay. This may sound too simple, but is great in consequence. Until one is committed, there is hesitancy, the chance to draw back, always ineffectiveness. Concerning all acts of initiative (and creation), there is one elementary truth the ignorance of which kills countless ideas and splendid plans: that the moment one definitely commits oneself, the providence moves too. A whole stream of events issues from the decision, raising in one's favor all manner of unforeseen incidents, meetings and material assistance, which no man could have dreamt would have come his way.

William H. Murray (1951)

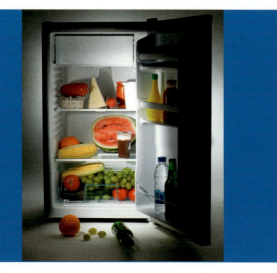

CHAPTER 9

The journey begins:

Start with your means.

The bird-in-hand principle: Start with what you have

■ ■ ■

AFTER YEARS OF thinking about it, huge investments, and months of preparation, the ancient mariners had to face the day of reckoning: the day they cast free of the dock, where their vessel was safely tied, and ventured forth into the uncertain sea.

Likewise, when facing the prospect of entering the entrepreneurial world, you may feel the same sense of leaving a safe harbor. But it need not be so.

In Chapters 5 and 6 we looked at the very start of the plunge decision: How the criteria change based on different times and situations in life, and also different ways of approaching the decision. In Chapter 2 we looked at where good ideas come from, building on our argument from Chapter 1 that opportunities are not found, but rather created by the entrepreneur and his or her partners. The implication is that it is not critical or even necessary to have the perfect idea when you leave the dock. The idea will more likely be created as a result of you starting; it simply does not exist until you create it. Finally, in Chapter 8 we looked at how success and failure are a matter of perspective, and how they depend on what you and your partners decide to do.

In the end, we found that "the plunge" does not have to be as dramatic as it sounds. It is possible to venture gradually into uncertainty, constructing the business in components while preserving your ability to return to the dock.

Research roots

The Corridor Principle

The "Corridor Principle" describes how new and unintended opportunities often arise for entrepreneurs when they are launching a new venture. This can be compared to standing at the entrance of a corridor. Until you proceed down the corridor, it is impossible to see what it holds. The Corridor Principle explains how entrepreneurs are able to "proceed down the corridor," and apply knowledge and insight from earlier ventures to the current situation.

Research further indicates that when entrepreneurship is a multi-venture process, and entrepreneurs go from one venture to the next, they can build corridors of opportunity that appear as they learn, thereby building new opportunities.

Robert Ronstadt (1988: 31–40)

In this chapter we develop the first principle of effectuation—working with your means. People focus so much on whether they will be successful or not, whether their idea is a good one or not, that they forget about all the other things they could be doing with what they already have. We start by looking at how effectual entrepreneurs use means, while causal entrepreneurs work with goals, and the difference between the two approaches. We then look at means in greater detail, helping you work with what you already have (and may not even know you have).

WHAT DO WE MEAN BY "START WITH YOUR MEANS?"

There are three categories of means available to all human beings: who I am, what I know, and who I know. Who I am consists of the stable of traits, abilities, and attributes of the entrepreneur. What I know includes your education, experience, and expertise. Who I know refers to your social networks. Your pool of resources (i.e. what I have) is the sum of the above three categories of means. The fundamental agenda then becomes: What effects can I create, given who I am, what I know, and whom I know? The effectual entrepreneur begins by imagining several possible courses of action, the consequences of which are, for the most part, uncertain. Therefore, these courses of action are evaluated in terms of their potential downside (affordable loss) rather than their benefits and the effectuator prioritizes them according to downside risk.

At the same time these courses of action (what you choose to do) are co-determined by stakeholders who are willing to commit resources. In general, stakeholders not only provide resources, but also set immediate agendas and generate new sub-goals for the venture. Since these stakeholders have to make commitments in the face of uncertain consequences, they in turn have to act based on what they can afford to lose. The entire decision-making process for each individual involved is focused on what can be done, given who s/he is, what s/he knows, and who s/he knows.

This is in stark contrast with the causal approach (search and select), described in Chapter 1. As the diagram illustrates, with the causal approach, you view your goals as given. These goals may be externally imposed (e.g. maximization of shareholder value in a public corporation), or they may be self-imposed (e.g. I want to make US$10 million before I am 40 years old). In both cases, the goals are taken as given before the decision is made. And the only real decision becomes: What resources or means do I need to accumulate to achieve my goal? Often, this question leads to the formation of a vision that will induce the necessary stakeholders to come on board so the required resources can be gathered. The accumulation of resources becomes the predominant goal for the venture, and stakeholders are primarily seen as resource providers.

Why be "means-driven" versus "goals-driven?" After all, there is a common (mis)conception that entrepreneurs are highly goal-driven individuals.

CAUSAL VERSUS EFFECTUAL REASONING

Managerial thinking (causal)

Distinguishing characteristic
Selecting between given means to achieve a pre-determined goal

Entrepreneurial thinking (effectual)

Distinguishing characteristic
Imagining a possible new end using a given set of means

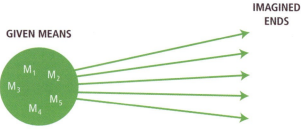

The key thing to realize is that goals exist in hierarchies. It is not that effectual entrepreneurs have *no* goals, it is just that when push comes to shove and the choice is between being tethered to means versus tethered to specific lower level goals, they are more likely to change their goals rather than go chasing means they have no control over. Understanding that goals exist in hierarchies entails realizing at least two things: (a) that higher level goals, such as wanting to be a millionaire by age 40, do not tell you what you should do on the first day of your new venture; and (b) tying yourself down to specific goals, such as starting an upscale restaurant in a high-income neighborhood, constrains your entrepreneurial actions to the pursuit of resources you currently do not possess. Instead, starting with what you can do with your readily available means is a practical approach, helping you take action now toward building your new enterprise without giving up your higher level, longer-term goals such as becoming financially successful or being your own boss.

What are some of the advantages of being means-driven rather than goal-driven?

- You are not chasing investors.
- You are not waiting for the perfect opportunity or the perfect set of resources.
- You are working with your strengths without having to overcome your weaknesses first.
- Good stakeholders want to shape goals, not just provide means.
- You are increasing the possible slate of stakeholders who can self-select into your venture.
- You are increasing the probability of innovative surprises.
- You are increasing the likelihood of finding or creating opportunities that are a better fit for you.
- You are increasing the likelihood of even failures being learning experiences that you can recover from faster and build on when you are ready to try again.

- You are forcing yourself to get creative with meager resources including slack resources and even waste.

WHO I AM: THE UNBEATABLE COMPETITIVE ADVANTAGE

We do not usually think of ourselves as the primary source of valuable new opportunities or the basis for unique competitive advantages that no one else can beat. Yet a little reflection will show that this can indeed be true and often is.

One of the most beautiful things about entrepreneurship is that there are probably as many high potential opportunities as there are individuals. Unlike other professions, such as medicine, accounting, dance, or sports, there is no one particular set of skills, abilities, or personality types necessary and sufficient for entrepreneurial success. An accountancy-based enterprise, such as H&R Block, can co-exist with an athletics-based firm, such as Nike, on the list of the most successful companies ever built. Similarly, a flamboyant risk taker, such as Mark Cuban, and a prudent calculator, such as Daniel Snyder, can both build thriving entrepreneurial careers resulting in eventual ownership of sports teams (the Dallas Mavericks in the case of Cuban and the Washington Redskins in the case of Snyder).

If we begin with the premise that who we are and what makes us unique could be not only the starting point, but also the basic ingredient of the venture and market opportunity we set out to create, we throw open the door to courses of action we would otherwise be blind to, especially if we seek to figure out first *the* set of necessary and sufficient conditions common to all successful enterprises. Curiously enough, the key member of that set appears to consist in the fact that successful firms and the entrepreneurs who found them leverage the idiosyncratic circumstances and eccentric quirks of personality that uniquely characterizes their inimitable life experiences.

PRACTICALLY SPEAKING: HOW ESTÉE LAUDER GOT INTO SAKS 5TH AVENUE AND NIEMAN MARCUS

Estée Lauder is a case in point. Born Josephine Esther Mentzer, daughter of Jewish immigrants, and married to Joe Lauter, the entrepreneur who created the cosmetic giant in the first half of the twentieth century, she unabashedly leveraged both what she loved and hated about her heritage to reinvent herself, including changing her nickname Esty to Estée with the acute accent on the first "e." And she helped all the women she reached out to "see" that they had the potential to grow into who they could be.

Even in her early days in business, instead of greeting potential customers with the usual, "May I help you?" the self-created Estée Lauder would approach women in beauty parlors with, "I have something that would look perfect on you, madam. May I show you how to apply it?" Later, in places like Saks Fifth Avenue and Nieman Marcus, she would say, "Try this. I am Estée Lauder, and these are the most wonderful beauty products in the world."

Because Lauder did not have the kind of money her competitors, such as Revlon, were spending on ad campaigns, she gave out free samples—a practice unheard of in the industry at the time and jeered at by professionals as a recipe for disaster because she was "giving away her whole business." However, Lauder averred this was "the most honest way to do business," and it turned out that people who trooped into the store to get free samples ended up not only buying products but also acting as word-of-mouth evangelists —something no ad budget could easily buy.

Her approach to her retailer customers was equally based on the means of her own personality. Stanley Marcus, head of the Texas-based department store, described her as ". . . a very determined salesperson; she pushed her way into acceptance. She was determined—and gracious and lovely through it all. It was easier to say yes to Estée than to say no."

The intersection of ask and slack

Novice entrepreneurs often think that crafting a perfect sales pitch or offering something they would value personally are the only two ways to get something they need from a potential stakeholder. This often leads them to either come up with overly "salesy" pitches that are hard to swallow and/or give up the very idea of asking others for anything.

Experienced entrepreneurs know that there is a simpler way—and that is to *ask* the potential stakeholder what would convince them to come on board. Try this and, chances are, you will be pleasantly shocked. Most people will actually tell you what they want in order to work with you or provide you with a needed resource and, more often than not, what they want is probably something you would not have anticipated and probably something that is actually a slack resource you have that you do not even know you have.

At the very least, people will give honest and useful advice, a variety of valuable leads, and/or bring to light your own hidden resources. Take the matter of titles on business cards, for example. Some people would take a cut in pay in return for a title or invest sweat equity in return for advice and leads from you—advice and leads you might not know would be of any use to them unless you open up and let them tell you exactly what they want. One example of such advice involved a good local lawyer willing to provide free intellectual property (IP) services in return for the entrepreneur working with his son on his application to business school—not something this particular entrepreneur had included in her original pitch to the lawyer!

PRACTICALLY SPEAKING: MEANS IN A TANK AT AQUASTASIS

If you have ever owned an aquarium, you probably know the state-of-the-art way to measure water quality in the tank: When the fish float, the water is no good. But as an avid keeper of tropical fish with a Ph.D. in chemistry (his means), Roni Kopelman knew there could be a better way. Scientific test kits existed, but they were expensive, complicated to use, and did not provide continuous monitoring of water quality.

During his doctoral studies, Roni created a test strip that continuously changes color as the pH levels in water change. His patented invention turns yellow when the pH level gets too low for aquarium fish, and turns blue when it gets too high. This could be a better way for people to keep their fish alive, but could it be a business? To help answer that question, Roni enrolled in an entrepreneurship class with Stuart Jamieson, with a background in physics and software development (his means), and the pair wrote a business plan for the venture.

The potential for a simple and cheap water quality tester looked promising. Pet retailers in the US alone sold millions of new fish tanks each year, and casualty rates for fish continued to be high. So Roni and Stuart formed AquaStasis, and went to work with Slipstream Design turning Roni's invention into a product. They faced the usual challenges of making it function correctly, making it easy to use, and making it inexpensive to produce. But the biggest difficulty lay beneath the surface.

PETCO and PetSmart provide the primary channel to market for most of the pet goods sold in the US. Naturally, Stuart and Roni's first step with a prototype of their new LivepH product was to visit these huge retailers. Both loved LivepH. But neither was willing to work with a start-up: too much uncertainty of supply and too expensive to do business with a company offering only one product. Disappointed, Stuart and Roni sat down with their new head of business development, John Thuma, to make a new plan.

The team decided to demonstrate their innovation at a pet product trade show where they met a number of large pet product companies, including Virbac. Virbac already had relationships with PETCO, PetSmart, and a host of smaller independent pet product retailers. They too loved LivepH and wanted to sell it. But the offer came with a catch. Virbac wanted exclusive rights to Roni's invention for the pet product market.

The AquaStasis team decided to work with Virbac. They reasoned that the

speed to market, the legitimacy of working with a large firm, and the potential future opportunities it might create outweighed the loss of control.

What happened with AquaStasis illustrates not only how starting with your means enables you to get going right away and positions you with an idea where you have a competitive advantage (nobody else has your exact set of means). It also illustrates how means change with partners. Bring on a new partner, and the range of things you can do immediately expands because you can also use their means.

WHAT I KNOW: BRINGING LEARNING TO THE VENTURE

What I know is unique to each individual person. Because information is generated through idiosyncratic life experiences, the stock of prior knowledge held by individuals differs considerably, making this one of the elements that generates significantly different ventures from two different people at the same starting point in the same environment.

Because of the knowledge corridor, particular entrepreneurs may be better off working to develop opportunities where they have the advantage of information others don't have. This doesn't mean just scientific or technical information—it could just as easily be an understanding of customer needs, product bundling, or distribution.

A good example of this can be found in a study of eight entrepreneurs who sought to commercialize a new technology called 3DP (three dimensional printing) that was developed at MIT. All eight entrepreneurs heard about 3DP technology from someone directly involved in its development. None of the entrepreneurs had contacted MIT's Technology Licensing Office about the technology. In each case, friends or acquaintances introduced them to 3DP technology. However, they already knew about a possible use for the technology. The result of this matching process was the discovery of a possible opportunity.

PRACTICALLY SPEAKING: THE BIG IMPACT OF SMALL ENVELOPES

Very often, the way ventures develop is by entrepreneurs accumulating knowledge as they go—i.e. starting with one idea, finding out the idea doesn't work or isn't favored by customers, and then moving on to the next thing. Thus, entrepreneurs build knowledge corridors by learning what works and what doesn't work as they try to gain commitments from different stakeholders. The following re-usable envelope story is a good example of exactly this. Ann DeLaVergne started with a very small idea—one the size of an envelope. Looking at the stack of used envelopes in her recycling, and thinking of a paper processing plant, it occurred to her that a lot of small envelopes could make a big impact.

Further investigation told Ann that indeed there are a lot of small envelopes. At least 81 billion return envelopes are produced and sent through the US mail each year. Tough on the environment, using 1.8 billion tons of wood, generating 1 billion pounds of greenhouse gases and requiring more than 71 trillion BTUs of energy to process and transport. Tough on the bottom line too, as return envelopes represent between 15 percent and 45 percent of a business's direct mailing costs.

As an organic farmer with a philosophy of reuse, Ann already saved large envelopes to send out again herself. But what if she could apply that thinking to 81 billion return envelopes? With that idea, Ann founded EcoEnvelopes, a firm built on the simple goal of using one envelope instead of two for round trip business mail transactions.

Figuring out how to transform her small idea into a big impact, however, was not obvious. So Ann, who had also worked as a graphic designer, sat down at her kitchen table with some office supplies and a sewing machine (to make perforations in paper) and prototyped her reusable envelope idea. Her first effort yielded ten

envelopes, which she mailed off to friends around the country. When all ten came back, she knew she was on to something.

Partnerships and communities can provide the critical mass for an entre-

Working with what you have

Barbara Corcoran runs a real estate empire worth US$US4 billion. This success comes after failing at over 20 jobs. Her secret: listening to her mom's advice. In her book, *Use What You've Got* (Corcoran & Littlefield, 2003: 6), Corcoran lists her first bit of advice as follows: *If you don't have big breasts, put ribbons in your pigtails.* She learned this during her job as a waitress when she felt her life was going nowhere fast. One day she came home complaining to her mother that the other waitresses were getting all the attention because they had big breasts and she did not. And her mother replied, "You're going to have to learn to use what you've got. Since you don't have big breasts, why don't you tie some ribbons on your pigtails and just be as sweet as you are." Which is exactly what she did . . .

Lesson: Get away from what you don't have and focus on what you have.

preneurial idea. Ann began extending her community beyond her friends to include businesses that both use the mail and have an environmental mission. The first were the Land Stewardship Project and the Minnesota Landscape Arboretum. In addition to feeling better about their direct mail efforts and saving money too, these organizations have increased response rates using EcoEnvelopes to as high as 8 percent, roughly ten times the average for mail campaigns.

Today, EcoEnvelopes produces and markets a range of patented zip-close reusable envelopes, manufactured with paper from managed forests and containing up to 100 percent post-consumer waste content. In January of 2008 EcoEnvelopes received a US$570,000 investment from TC Angels, the largest single investment the group has made to date, to help Ann hire employees, secure patents, and take her invention to companies around the globe. Just a month later, the US Postal Service granted Ann a National Consumer Ruling, making EcoEnvelopes the first reusable envelope certified for standard mail.

WHO I KNOW: SIX DEGREES OF SEPARATION

One of the greatest assets of an entrepreneur is the people s/he knows. Expert entrepreneurs build firms by building stakeholder networks— adding others' means to their own means. There are people that are directly accessible to you, and that you

can pull in almost immediately— friends, family and acquaintances.

There are two other aspects of human interaction that help you add to your means. The first is that you often meet people through interactions that are contingencies/accidents/serendipitous —as did Burt Rutan and Paul Allen in the creation of SpaceShipOne (see the following section). The other is what is known as the six degrees of separation principle. This is about the fact that you are linked to people you don't know by people you do know. The people you know, know people, who know people who could become helpful partners. Described as "the strength of weak ties," you learn more from people you know less well. The combination of the two can connect you with anyone on the planet to give you the means to create something truly novel.

What we see is that entrepreneurs build stable stakeholder networks out of people they already know, out of people that they are connected to through others, and out of contingent interactions—three different sources of who you (eventually) know. The story of SpaceShipOne is an illustration of how who you know and what they have/know can lead to a successful venture coming to life. The entire story is almost too paradigmatic of the entrepreneurial spirit, in part because of the larger than life personas involved: Burt Rutan, the brilliant designer of the craft; Michael Melvill and Brian Binnie, the daredevil pilots; Paul Allen, billionaire sponsor of the enterprise; and, of course, the swashbuckling Sir Richard Branson.

PRACTICALLY SPEAKING: SPACESHIPONE

The story of SpaceShipOne is tied up with the story of its designer, Burt Rutan. Rutan built his first flying model at age 10. His father was a dentist who teamed up with four other pilots to buy his own plane; his brother, Dick Rutan, was a decorated Air Force pilot who served in Vietnam. Rutan earned a degree in aeronautics from California Polytechnic University in 1965, joined the Air Force testing new airplanes, and in 1972 became director of Bede Aircraft's test center in Kansas. In 1974 he moved his family into the Mojave Desert and went into business for himself. His first venture, Rutan Aircraft Factory, developed light aircraft and served the home-built plane market by developing and selling plans.

In August 2002 the White Knight, a spaceship carrier plane designed by Burt Rutan, took to the air. After that a series of 56 step-by-step flights were undertaken, culminating in the historic moment on June 21, 2004, when SpaceShipOne became the first private rocket ship to break the space barrier. And in October 2004 SpaceShipOne won the Ansari X-prize. The terms of the international competition for the X-prize included launching three passengers into sub-orbital space in a reusable aircraft twice within a 14-day period.

Rutan's comrade in arms on this venture was Paul Allen, co-founder of Microsoft, who came on board the enterprise as early as March 2001. After he left Microsoft in 1983, Allen became both an investor and a

Research roots

The six degrees of separation

The study of social networks dates back to the 1960s. The initial finding, in a US-sized population without social structure was: "It is practically certain that any two individuals can contact one another by means of at least two intermediaries. In a [socially] structured population, it is less likely but still seems probable. And perhaps for the whole world's population, probably only one more bridging individual should be needed." Simmulations of these early models were run in the 1970s showing that a more realistic three degrees of separation existed across the US population, a value that set the stage for Stanley Milgram (1967: 61–67).

Countless studies have since been conducted to measure connectedness. While the exact number of links between people differs depending on the population and the types of links, it is generally found to be relatively small. Hence, the phrase "six degrees of separation" is often used as a synonym for the idea of the "small world" phenomenon.

philanthropist in a variety of science and space related projects—a strong proponent of private non-governmental funding for space programs.

Three months after the historic flight on June 21, Sir Richard Branson, founder of the Virgin Group, announced an agreement with Mojave Aerospace Ventures (MAV) to develop the world's first privately funded spaceships that will carry commercial passengers on space flights. MAV is Paul Allen's company, and it owns the technology embodied in SpaceShipOne, which in turn was designed by Burt Rutan and built by his company, Scaled Composites. Branson formed a new company called Virgin Galactic with a view to kick-starting the space tourism industry. Virgin Galactic's business plan calls for 3,000 astronauts and a ticket price of US$200,000 (including three training days) per passenger (Virgin Galactic Online, 2009).

Commenting on the announcement, Virgin Galactic founder Sir Richard Branson (2004) said: "We've always had a dream of developing a space tourism business and Paul Allen's vision, combined with Burt Rutan's technological brilliance, have brought that dream a step closer to reality."

The market opportunity for space tourism (and any profits it may or may not entail) has ensued from what Rutan and his stakeholders did. Their actions in turn grew from the inter-subjective interactions between Rutan (with his love of and skill for designing aircraft), Allen (with his passion for the exploration of space), and a variety of stakeholders, each of whom self-selected into the venture by committing what s/he could afford to lose without worrying about positive cash flows down the road.

INVENTORY YOUR MEANS

Who you know	Who you know	What you know	What you know	Who you are	Who you are
Your rolodex (Linkedin, Plaxo, Facebook)		Your prior knowledge and education		Tastes, values, and preferences	
Classmates, alumni		Knowledge from your job		Passions	
Serendipitous encounters		Knowledge from your life		Hobbies	
The strangers in your life		Informal learning, hobbies		Interests	

HOW IT WORKS

To see how this means-driven process works, consider examples from the history of entrepreneurship. Be it Sears, Staples, Starbucks, or CNN, the entrepreneurs who founded them worked closely with their means to shape, step by step, the opportunities they ended up with. The beginnings of those opportunities, however, were usually rooted in the way entrepreneurs wove together the mundane realities of who they were, what they knew, and whom they knew into projects that they personally believed were worth doing. Those enduring ventures tended to start small, without elaborate market analyses. The entrepreneurs then continually added on to their original projects, pushing them outward, reshaping them to work with new stakeholders, stretching themselves— just a bit at a time, to reach higher and thrust farther—until eventually they transformed both their means and ends into unimagined new possibilities.

MAP YOUR MEANS

Start by printing off a one-page version of your resume. Be creative about what you consider; it needn't be things that you would normally include in a resume. To get started, look back at your life. What means did you acquire or build:

- as a teenager
- at school
- at university
- in your first, second . . . job
- in your private life
- with your hobbies, activities
- from your parents?

How would your friends, colleagues, family, or acquaintances describe your means?

Be as broad as you can. You will certainly need more room than in the "Inventory Your Means" table once you get going, but we hope this gives you a place to start.

SLACK AND OTHER RESOURCES YOU DON'T EVEN KNOW YOU HAVE

Sometimes unusual opportunities and the successful ventures built on them are forged from resources you don't even recognize as resources in the first place. Truth is, the world is full of "slack"—resources that are left over from other uses or simply lying around because nobody has paid any attention to them.

Slack can include anything from waste and empty space to loopholes in the law and buffers created for emergencies. Today, an entire world of new economic opportunities is being fabricated from waste recycling due to concerns about climate change and the fear of exhaustion of fossil fuels. But waste that could be recycled into products of value has always been a resource to entrepreneurs. Billionaire J.R. Simplot, founder of potato processing plants and the first frozen french fries, began his career by collecting and feeding hogs set for slaughter by farmers who feared a pork surplus. By simply waiting out the period until hogs went into short supply, he made enough money to buy an electric potato sorter. Throughout his career, Simplot was quick at picking up slack resources that he transformed into valuable products, often appearing to snatch opportunities right from under the noses of his competition.

We also saw the use of slack resources in the U-Haul case (see Chapter 3) where Leonard Shoen made a deal with a national gas station chain for the stations to become locations for U-Haul dealerships. The gas stations had unused space that Shoen could leverage and make valuable not only for himself but also for the owners of that slack resource.

Estée Lauder also used a slack resource in the early stages of building her business (see page 75). She had noticed that women sitting under hair dryers in beauty parlors had nothing to do with their time. So she offered them a free makeover using Estée Lauder creams and lotions. Most would accept and having actually experienced the benefits of the products would often buy at least some of them for home use.

Sometimes the slack resource comes in the guise of misfortune. As in the case of the Fad Doctor (see box below), who found himself in the woebegone state of a jobless Harvard graduate. If he had found a plush job like his classmates, chances are, he would be working for a living like the rest of us!

Practically speaking

Working with slack

Dr. Fad is Ken Hakuta, an identity he gave himself in 1983. Ken graduated from Harvard medical school but was soon disgruntled by the fact that his colleagues all seemed to have better offers than he did. As he mulled over this piece of information, he nonchalantly threw around a slimy, sticky, octopus-shaped rubber toy that his mother had sent from Japan for his children. In 1982 they were the only toys that could climb down walls. Ken bought US$100,000 worth of the toys, thinking that if his venture failed he could go back to Japan. He started selling them to small gift shops and toy stores in Washington DC, where he lived. And then one day CBS evening news did a feature on them, turning the Wacky WallWalkers into an overnight hit. Over 240 million Wacky WallWalkers were sold, making it one of the biggest selling fads ever. Dr. Fad ran his own shows about fads and published a bestseller called: *How to Create Your Own Fad and Make a Million Dollars* (1989).

TAKEAWAY: YOU CAN GET STARTED NOW!

Effectuation shifts the focus from "How to build a successful firm?" or "How to become a successful entrepreneur?" to "What types of ideas and opportunities should *you* pursue?" and "Given who you are, what you know, and who you know, what types of economic and/or social artifacts can you, would you want to, and should you create?"

Sticking very closely to who you are, what you know, and who you know not only tells you what to do, it is also very useful in telling you what not to do. The problem with most novice entrepreneurs is not that they do not have great new ideas for ventures, it is that they have too many. They see opportunities everywhere and feel tempted to expand product lines too soon or jump into too many new market segments all at once.

The bird-in-hand principle (starting with your means) tells you four things:

- You need not wait for the blockbuster idea or the multibillion-dollar opportunity to come your way. You can begin with a simple problem for which you see an implementable solution—or even something you simply believe would be fun to attempt—and go for it.
- Don't run after imagined "fantastic" opportunities that require you to chase money you do not have, work with people you are not sure you like, or deal with technologies and markets about which you know little.

- Means are about more than just money (and they often cost nothing).
- Means include not only your means but also those of your partners, and together the novel combination they create gives you a competitive advantage.

When you use the bird-in-hand principle, starting a new venture is no longer an incredibly risky act of heroism. It is something you can do within the constraints and possibilities of your normal life. You can start a new venture anytime you want. You can get started now.

So what?

Starting with means rather than goals helps you begin right away, with the bird you have in your hand: Who you are, what you know, and who you know. It reduces the feeling of risk and gives good ideas about where you can start. Means are not static—they change with time and as you bring in new people with means of their own.

Roadmap

- [ ] If you are having trouble deciding on an idea, how about starting with more than one idea at once and let the dominant path self-select in the process?

- [ ] On your way to school or to work today, look for slack resources that you could put to valuable use.

- [ ] Create an elevator pitch for yourself—if you had to sell stock in yourself, what would your prospectus look like, and who would want to buy the shares?

Bigger questions

- [ ] In goal oriented societies, how do we change mindsets to start with means?

- [ ] When are goals useful?

- [ ] If I do not have a goal, how do I know when I am successful?

- [ ] What are the pros and cons of goals (on one hand they give direction, energize, motivate to take the first step—on the other they might block the view towards upcoming opportunities)? How can you resolve this?

An entrepreneur is a person who is willing and able to convert a new idea or invention into a successful innovation, simultaneously creating new products and business models largely responsible for the dynamism of industries and long-run economic growth.
Joseph A. Schumpeter
(1942)

Innovation and the creation of new ideas is not a mysterious process.

There are simple approaches that can be easily learned and readily applied.

Worldmaking: Understand transformation

■ ■ ■

Y OU'VE TAKEN stock of your means—you know what you have, who you know, and what you know. But how do you turn that into something actionable and valuable—into a new product, a new venture, or even a new market? Clearly, there is some form of transformation involved—turning something into something useful.

But how does this actually work? To answer this question, we needed something that would help us visualize how entrepreneurs generate variety—how they turn something into many other somethings. So, we created an experiment—Venturing—that you will find detailed in the next section. Based on an imaginary company selling a game, the Venturing experiment allowed us to watch entrepreneurs transform ideas and opportunities.

The experiment and the transformation types we observed preclude any judgment as to whether the ideas are "good" ideas—i.e. valuable new combinations. We only intend to show how transformations occur and to take away some of the mystery around the process. As you already know from the first section of the book, idea + action = opportunity. This chapter is devoted to the foundation of the idea.

Following the description of the Venturing experiment is a typification of the four most common transformation types we found employed by expert entrepreneurs. For each, we describe how they were used to transform the product, firm, and market situation presented in Venturing into a novel outcome not offered in the scenario and give a sample quote from

Research roots

Effectuation improves research and development project performance

Kuepper *et al.* (2009) transfer the principles of effectuation in research and development management and show, using a survey of 400 research and development projects, that research and development managers tend to use effectuation in more uncertain projects and that using effectuation improves the performance of these projects.

The Venturing scenario
(exactly as it was presented to all participants)

Introduction

In the following experiment, you will solve two decision problems. These problems arise in the context of building a new company for an imaginary product. A detailed description of the product follows this introduction.

Although the product is imaginary, it is technically feasible and financially viable. The data for the problems have been obtained through realistic market research—the kind of market research used in developing a real-world business plan. So far, the entrepreneurs who have participated in this study found the project both interesting and feasible.

Before you start on the product description and the problems, I do need one act of creative imagination on your part. I request you to put yourself in the role of the lead entrepreneur in building this company—i.e. you have very little money of your own to start this company, and the experience you have.

Description of the product

You have created a computer game of entrepreneurship. You believe you can combine this game with some educational material and profiles of successful entrepreneurs to make an excellent teaching tool for entrepreneurship. Your inspiration for the product came from several reports in the newspapers and magazines about increasing demand for entrepreneurship education; and the fact that a curriculum involving entrepreneurship even at the junior high or high school level induces students to learn not only business-related topics but math and science and communication skills as well.

The game part of the product consists of a simulated environment for starting and running a company. There are separate sub-simulations of markets, competitors, regulators, macroeconomic factors, and a random factor for "luck." The game has a sophisticated multi-media interface—for example, a 3D office where phones ring with messages from the market, a TV that will provide macroeconomic information when switched on, and simulated managerial staff whom the player (CEO) can consult in making decisions. At the beginning of the game the player can choose from a variety of businesses and the type of business s/he wants to start (For example: manufacturing, personal services, software etc.) and has to make decisions such as which market segment to sell to, how many people to hire, what type of financing to go for, etc. During the game the player has to make production decisions such as how much to produce, whether to build new warehouses or negotiate with trucking companies, etc.; marketing decisions such as which channels of distribution to use, which media to advertise in, and so on; management decisions involving hiring, training, promoting and firing of employees, and so on. There is an accounting subroutine that tracks and computes the implications of the various decisions for the bottom line. The simulation's responses to the player's decisions permit a range of possible final outcomes—from bankruptcy to a "hockey stick."

You have taken all possible precautions regarding intellectual property. The name of your company is Entrepreneurship, Inc. The name of the product is Venturing.

an entrepreneur in the process of transformation. Each transformation type is also presented with a "Practically speaking" example of a real-world situation. Finally, we will look at how you can create your own transformations. As you work your way through the chapter, stop at each transformation type and look at the things around you—everything from the features of the chair you are sitting in to the caffeinated soda you are drinking. Imagine the transformations that are at the heart of these things you use every day. What pieces came together to join hydraulics with office furniture so it's easy to scoot your chair up and down? What combination of people and means provided the insight which transformed those two seemingly unrelated elements into something which is standard equipment for every business—even for a new venture (though perhaps second-hand)? Once you start looking, you will see transformation everywhere, because, of course, everything was created from something.

A WORD ON THE VENTURING EXPERIMENT

We wanted to create a situation that would let us observe and better understand how entrepreneurs transform ideas. The experiment had to have several characteristics. First, it had to present those participating with an uncertain business situation. Second, it could not be a real situation—otherwise participants could be influenced by the actual outcome. Third, it had to allow for any range of possible strategies so participants would be free to propose any transformed solution

they felt might be appropriate for managing the situation.

With these design goals in mind, we created a description of an imaginary company called Venturing that was preparing to offer an imaginary software game of entrepreneurship. Based on the description of this business idea, participants were asked to answer a set of questions pertaining to the development of an initial market for the product and think aloud continuously during the task. Their protocols were collected on tape and transcribed for coding and analysis.

In order to see what strategies were unique to expert entrepreneurs, we carefully identified three different groups of participants. We defined expert entrepreneurs as persons who had, either as individuals or as part of a team, founded one or more companies, remained with at least one company that they founded for more than ten years, and taken it public.

We compared the expert entrepreneurs with a novice sample of MBA students at a small university in the western United States and expert corporate managers who had spent a minimum of ten years operating in a multinational organization consisting of more than 500 individuals.

TRANSFORMATION TYPES

The results of the Venturing experiment clearly showed that expert entrepreneurs had adopted a unique set of decision-making strategies learned through their experience. These strategies form the basis of the

effectual logic described in this book. In addition to the strategies (of means, affordable loss, partnerships, and contingency), the experts were very creative in the way they transformed situations into opportunities. We have tried to categorize the four most common transformation types we observed in the experiment in this chapter and offer a more complete list later in the chapter.

Deleting/supplementing

We describe any form of (re)combination—adding to and subtracting from something existing—as transformation by deleting or supplementing. Supplementing can include elements related to the original product or service, or surprising combinations from unrelated domains.

In the context of a new venture, deleting/supplementing means looking at your product/service and thinking about which features you may want to add or remove to increase its attractiveness. There is really no limit to the possibilities for adding and removing product or service features in order to transform an offering.

In Chapter 11 we have a good example of deleting and supplementing. Ruth Owades' company, Calyx and Corolla, weeded out florists from the fresh flower delivery process by using a different channel from that of the traditional companies. She did this by mailing flowers direct from the growers to the customers via Federal Express, in the process recombining flower delivery and express postal services. By doing so she not only

Deleting/supplementing in Venturing

We witness the process in action in the Venturing scenario, as an expert entrepreneur talks about adding functional business areas, such as a simulation game for operations management in addition to the marketing oriented application of Venturing as it was presented (other participants added or deleted product features as well as service elements): "... rather than just developing the entrepreneurial spirit side, there may be some real opportunities of doing game development to enhance the skills of ... someone in the sales and marketing area ... or in the manufacturing area."

eliminated the intermediary, but also provided her customers with fresher, longer-lasting flowers. Here we provide a taste of the process with a venture in Belgium.

PRACTICALLY SPEAKING: CHOCOLATE MAGIC

Tucked in a quiet Brussels suburb behind an unassuming garage door is the factory of Manon Chocolatier. As easy as it is to miss the small sign, once inside the garage it expands into Christian (known as Mr. Manon) Vanderkerken's sanctuary of chocolate. The operation, founded in 1935 by Manon's grandfather, handcrafts 80 different types of bonbons using all natural ingredients, some of which even come from Manon's own garden. The treasured confections are offered at an equally unassuming retail location in downtown Brussels and those chocolates that are not too delicate to travel are exported to international destinations that include Europe, Japan, and the US.

Around 12 years ago Manon received a call. The caller was not someone asking to have a shipment of Manon's creations express delivered for a special occasion, as was usually the case; instead, he was looking to gain admittance to Manon's refuge–he wanted a private tour of the factory. Interested in sharing his expertise in how pralines are made and intrigued by the possibilities it offered, Manon agreed.

Combining his knowledge of chocolate and the history left to him by his grandfather with a bit of magic learned from an old Chinese man, Manon put together a tour that involved hands-on education, tasting, vintage chocolate-making equipment, and a surprise ingredient thrown in for good measure. The result was such a success that word got out, and Manon began offering regular tours of the operation, except during peak production times before Christmas and Easter.

Mr Manon says:

> When I did my first tour, it was for fun. Twelve years later, I still do the tours for fun. I never really imagined it as a business, but a chance to get paid for something I like doing anyway. In addition to eating 250 grams of dark chocolate per day (for health), I think that everyone should know about how chocolate is made, and that is my real goal.

Roughly, 3,000 people visit the enclave each year. At €12 per person (€10 for groups of 15 or more during the week), Manon is not in much danger of getting wealthy and retiring using tour proceeds. However, in creating a complementary business with little incremental cost (making the tour income highly profitable) he has also managed to get paid to do his own marketing. Most visitors purchase his handiwork at the tiny factory shop near the garage door following the tour, and word-of-mouth has placed him among the top 40 attractions in Brussels on TripAdvisor.com.

Is Manon in the business of selling chocolate? Certainly. Is he also in the business of education and entertainment around chocolate? Without a doubt. And by supplementing education he expands the scope of what constitutes a chocolate business, and effectively differentiates himself from the numerous other excellent (many larger and better funded) truffle traders in Brussels. He also teaches us where to look for these unique insights. They come from the things we already have, and support the things we already do. Manon has 100-year-old chocolate recipes and Chinese card tricks. Manon's story prompts us to ask what business you could be in. Chances are excellent that you have something equally magical to offer.

Composing/decomposing

Reorganizing material that is already there—decomposing and recomposing it (in contrast with the first approach, which takes away or adds material to or from the existing set) is what we mean by composing and decomposing.

In the context of a new venture, this means taking stock of what you have to offer—a product, a service, the way you work—and pulling it apart to recombine it in a new way. It's a

Composing/decomposing in Venturing

Taking apart the components of the offering and thinking about how to reconfigure them is something we saw often in participants using the Venturing scenario. In most cases, participants were doing this to redefine the market for Venturing, as we see an expert entrepreneur doing several times in the following quote:

The basic concept is a business simulator . . . start-up simulator . . . so you can hop into a business situation and practice and get a lot of reflexes and thought processes built up up front. A successful launch of the first product with a big marketing sales push to penetrate as many different markets as we could might have a successful second product.

. . . for example, you could have a product . . . how to succeed, prosper, grow, and get promoted within a large company . . .

. . . it could be a follow-on product. The research would be similar, the product development would be similar, and so the production part would be equivalent and some of the same marketing channels would also work.

. . . you could make another product . . . for students . . . simulate the learning process in the classroom and research traits that tend to make you successful or not . . . study habits that tend to make you successful or not . . .

. . . next, there is negotiation . . . you could practice being a good negotiator . . . I gave four or five endeavors. You can expand . . . so, maybe I'm gonna change my opinion about the growth potential for the company . . .

process similar to pulling apart and recomposing Lego blocks.

Consider, for example, the composing and decomposing that has emerged in the food industry as a result of the popular Atkins Diet. Initiated in the late 1970s by Dr. Robert Atkins' (1973) diet book, the attraction of a low-carbohydrate lifestyle has grown. Today, you can find compositions and decompositions of recipes in virtually every food category to make existing materials and ideas compatible with a low-carbohydrate diet. Remarkably, you can even find low-carb pet food.

Next, we look in more detail at an entrepreneur composing and recomposing using a more readily available ingredient: waste.

PRACTICALLY SPEAKING: DRAGON LADY

What would you guess happens to this page after you have read it? If you are a social person, you might share it with a friend. Or a resourceful person might use it to build a paper airplane. Perhaps, but chances are good it will end up with Yan Cheung of Nine Dragons Paper Holdings Limited in China. And it won't take long either. "The newspaper that you put in your newspaper bin—three weeks later, it's in the hands of someone in China," explains Bill Moore of Moore & Associates in Atlanta, a consultant on recovered paper. Amazing—but how does this happen?

Rewind to 1990. In that year Cheung created America Chung Nam (ACN) with just US$3,800. Her plan was to

buy recycled paper in the United States and export it to China. She observed that Americans love to consume paper, using more than 700 pounds per person each year. And the Chinese desperately need to produce paper-based cardboard boxes in which to export domestically manufactured goods throughout the world. Driving around the US from dump to recycling facility in a Dodge minivan, Cheung and her husband filled containers that had just arrived from China carrying clothing or electronics with waste paper, and sent them back. It wasn't long before they were filling a lot of containers.

Five years later, and armed with new means of a strong cash flow from ACN, a reliable source of high quality recycled paper through ACN, and a clear understanding of the appetite for packaging materials in China, Cheung returned to Hong Kong. There she launched Nine Dragons to take that stream of waste paper and process it into Kraftlinerboard, Testlinerboard, or corrugating medium—the basic

papers used to make a cardboard box. Over the next 15 years Cheung's operation may as well have been printing cash directly. Nine Dragons built capacity to produce more than 8.8 million tons of paperboard a year and today is the largest producer in China and among the largest globally. And the self-crowned "Queen of Waste Paper" rivals Oprah Winfrey and J.K. Rowling as one of the richest women in the world.

There are two useful insights from Nine Dragons that can be boxed up and shipped to entrepreneurs everywhere. The first is that new ventures can easily be created with things that already exist. It is easy to believe that in order to start a company, you need a technological innovation or a huge investment to build something else. But Cheung started with nothing more than trash—available to everyone—and free. Second, ideas don't become opportunities until somebody acts. The fact that Americans were gener-

ating paper waste and that China needed massive amounts of cardboard was no secret to anyone, even in 1990. Yet someone, an entrepreneur, had to get into her Dodge minivan and make the opportunity happen.

Also contained in this story is a bigger idea. It's about where solutions to big problems come from. The problem of paper waste is huge. For years people have known that every 120 pounds of recycled paper saves a tree, and that recycled paper requires 64 percent less energy than making paper from raw materials. Governments have tried endless and costly schemes to convince people to recycle. But Cheung's products use an average of 85 percent to 90 percent recovered paper in the manufacturing process. That's a lot of trees and a lot of watts. She and entrepreneurs like her that build sustainable businesses using problems create solutions packaged for success.

Exaptation

Exaptation is actually a term from biology, meaning to use something for a purpose for which it was not originally designed or intended.

In the new venture setting, exaptation involves employing existing technologies, products, services, or elements thereof for a use they were not intended to serve.

In 1897 researchers at Bayer, a drug company, found acetylsalicylic acid to be an excellent painkiller and fever reducer. They decided to call it aspirin,

---

Exaptation in Venturing

Exaptation can be a rich source of transformations. In the venturing scenario, we see some of the thought process as one expert entrepreneur "exapts" the game for use as an evaluation tool:

> . . . people who want to be entrepreneurs and want to evaluate their own ability and tune up their ability to do that. Uh. . . particularly people who are planning to leave a big company or who have been [laid off] by a big company . . .

Or as a tool for large organizations wanting to give employees a simulator for new ideas:

> [This product would enable] the entrepreneurs to suspend reality, if you will, and say, and make themselves believe in "wow this product I've got here this entrepreneurial program is gonna be a real hit, I believe in it and I'm gonna go out and make it happen" . . . They'd basically only understand the things that already exist. The entrepreneur identifies with and sees the imaginary as real. Things that don't yet exist . . .

---

and by 1899 a brand was born. The product was immensely successful, particularly with its effectiveness demonstrated during the Spanish flu pandemic of 1918. When the patent expired in 1917, copies populated the market. But the product's popularity only really fell with the launch of paracetamol (1956) and ibuprofen (1969). It seemed as though aspirin was doomed.

But in the 1970s, clinical trials showed the product's efficacy as an anti-clotting agent—it reduced the risk of clotting diseases. Aspirin sales grew once more, spurred by its use as a preventive treatment for heart attacks and strokes—far from its original use!

In more detail in the next section, we find an entrepreneur exapting furniture to become high-tech charging stations for mobile devices.

PRACTICALLY SPEAKING: CHARGING AHEAD

Today, there are about 3.3 billion cell phones in the world, a number roughly equivalent to half the population of the planet. Every one of these has to be charged at least every few days in order to keep its faithful user connected. That means a lot of little chargers to get lost, forgotten, or broken. But what if you could charge these devices wirelessly? Sounds like *Star Trek*? Surprisingly, the core technology (magnetic resonance) has existed since before the first *Star Trek* episode was aired. All that needs to be done is to bring the technology to the altar of the user.

But technology can sometime prove the reluctant groom. Wireless charging of mobile devices requires equipment to send the power and equipment to receive the power. It requires integration so the system functions as intuitively as a wedding ring. It requires consumer awareness and adoption. From a business perspective, that means bringing power adapter suppliers, telephone and laptop manufacturers, standards and certification bodies, and countless other industry players on board. Not easy for a single entrepreneur to accomplish.

Undaunted, Maija Itkonen set out to make this opportunity her own. But, as an industrial designer from the University of Art and Design, Helsinki, her first instinct was not to look for a technical answer, but to redesign the user experience in a way that intuitively integrates the technology into their daily lives. When she thinks about user experience, she starts with frustration: like that moment when you still have two hours in the terminal to wait for your flight, and realize you forgot to charge your cell phone. Itkonen is right there with you in your moment of pain when you sit down in weary resignation, and so is her product. When you put your dead phone down on the table next to you so you can collect your thoughts about how to spend the next two hours, without any action other than pleasant surprise, the phone on the table magically comes alive. And you sit up to notice: It's getting charged!

Approaching the problem from the perspective of design led Itkonen to partner with Martela and Isku, two of Finland's largest and most established furniture manufacturers. To her delight, she found these traditional,

typically stolid firms quicken with the excitement at the prospect of transforming their age-old product lines into active elements powering today's mobile lifestyle. A table, literally, was no longer a table. And so the romance was on. Together, with her first partners, Itkonen built a prototype as well as more relationships with local cafes so that she could pilot test the technology. Users in downtown Helsinki sipped coffee, talked with friends, and chewed on pastries while their cell phones, lying naturally on the table, were equally recharged. A perfect union, by design.

The initial introduction generated much attention for Itkonen and her 12-person start-up Powerkiss. She soon found herself CEO as well as chief matchmaker. Her ability to create the relationships that create a compelling user experience is what makes Powerkiss more than a simple technical company. These relationships define the product, inform Itkonen's venture-building activities,

and shape the new market as it emerges into the world. It also broadcasts the fact that this is simply not yet another technology company. The pink on her website makes it hers, while the "kiss" in Powerkiss keeps users happy, mobile, connected, and productive at all times.

Happily ever after? Not quite that simple, as spouses in long, stable marriages know. It is going to take ongoing effort and real work at balancing business and romance to keep the energy up in this as in all ventures. As she moves to scale deployment, the number of possible partnerships Itkonen could arrange is limitless. And each will involve more design and redesign of the product as well as the venture. And, given she pulls it all off in the long term, it will also end up transforming our world. This possibility was recognized by EUWIIN (European Union Women Inventors and Innovators Network) when they selected Itkonen as the 2009 Woman Innovator of the Year.

Itkonen teaches us that opportunities are generated not by a jolt of electricity, but rather crafted from a unique combination of the different elements partners bring together and realized through action and interaction with the environment. What kind of planned coincidences or purposeful leveraging of the unexpected is it going to take to recharge the venture that is our lives today?

Re-weighting

Re-weighting involves increasing and decreasing the relative emphasis of features or attributes of a product or market.

For entrepreneurs, re-weighting means changing the emphasis of a feature so that it bears a greater or lesser emphasis in a new and differentiated offering.

BMW has gradually increased its emphasis on "driver appeal" as it launches new product designs, emphasizing "The Ultimate Driving Machine." Volvo, in contrast, emphasizes the safety features of its cars. Next, we look at a much more sophisticated re-weighting task—the task of not only re-weighting the activities in the market, but also re-weighting the responsibilities of the organization to match.

PRACTICALLY SPEAKING: BIO GENERATION

Google offers a tool called "Trends" that lets you graph the number of searches on a keyword over time. For the word "biofuel," searches peak on April 30, 2008, which, coincidentally, was the date an article entitled "Scientists want to stop using food to make biofuel" was in the news. And if Google Trends arc any indicator of general sentiment, interest in biofuel has been cut by well more than half since spring 2008, dropping precipitously even prior to the global financial crisis. Whatever politics, preferences, or conspiracy theories might underlie, the fact remains that despite any historical correlation between biofuel production and food prices, first generation biofuels based on corn, soy, and rapeseed have lost public appeal and will likely not expand beyond today's production levels to provide the cure to our energy woes.

End of the story? Not for Per Falholt, chief scientific officer at Novozymes. Today, biofuel is made by physically grinding corn, breaking down the starch into sugar with enzymes, converting the sugar into ethanol with microorganisms, and distilling the

Re-weighting in Venturing

At one point in our study an expert entrepreneur said: "We're really talking about any learning in an interactive situation where simulation is a benefit." This involves a re-weighting of the relevant features of the possible market for Venturing. This re-weighting changes the relative emphasis the expert entrepreneur puts on aspects of Venturing from gaming to learning, thus transforming the potential market opportunities considered for Venturing. Weightings can be dichotomous or on scales, etc. Changes in the ways products are marketed commonly involve changes in the relative weighting of elements.

require more effort and consequently more cost to convert, around US$2.35 per gallon. With fossil-based fuel priced at less than US$120/barrel, the economics don't work.[1]

Must Per and his team wait patiently until the price of oil goes up for the next chapter of the story? Not necessarily. While scientists invent, entrepreneurs innovate. Entrepreneurs shape, package, and deliver an invention to make it useful and valuable. For Per and his scientific team at Novozymes, this means changing

ethanol. Per's research team of 150 scientists, in seven different locations around the world, designed the enzymes at the center of the process. From their expertise, they know that other vegetation also offers the sugars necessary to make energy, and they have been working on a second generation of enzymes capable of converting waste corn stalks or wood chips into clean fuel. Technically, Novozymes is successful. Novozymes can produce "cellulosic" biofuel (based on refuse or crops such as switchgrass, grown on marginal land) today. But there is a cost. Corn, rich in sugar, converts easily into fuel, at around US$1.88 per gallon. Corn stalks

---

1   The US government, anxious to enjoy the 85 percent reduction in CO_2 emission from burning biofuel instead of gasoline and reduce foreign dependence on oil, subsidizes biofuel at US$0.50 per gallon, making second-generation US biofuel competitive with US$80/barrel oil.

from white lab coat to white dress shirt to transform second-generation biofuel technology into a business. Their new tasks:

Re-engineer partnerships

First generation biofuel production involves a long "value chain" of partners: farmers, grain processors, processing plants, financiers, and oil companies. But second-generation biofuel can start with waste. That long chain of partners might now include organizations ranging from paper companies and municipalities that would pay to dispose of corn stalks and wood chips, to owners of marginal land where the acreage is not profitably cultivated today. Any of these partners could benefit by working with Novozymes to design a new business model around second-generation biofuel.

Reconsider the customer

If you buy corn to make fuel, you build large factories to drive down processing costs with volume production. If you help cities or companies save money disposing of waste, smaller distributed facilities located near that waste might be desirable. And while input is a cost in the first generation, it is maybe free or even a source of income in the second. Partners may also buy the finished product, as activities like paper processing have significant energy demands.

Re-weight involvement

Today, Novozymes is a technology supplier to only a single step in the process. The firm counts on external entrepreneurs to turn its inventions into innovations. Though this limits risk, it also limits the company's ability to shape the market. In the second

Research roots

Creative templates

Jacob Goldenberg is a professor at the Jerusalem School of Business Administration, researching creativity and innovation. Goldenberg (Goldenberg *et al.*, 1999: 200) writes about creative templates, similar to the idea of transformation types in this chapter. He describes five templates which his research indicates are the basis of about 70 percent of all new product ideas:

- subtraction, multiplication, and division, each of which is a specific approach to deleting and supplementing we have described here

- task unification (making some aspect of an artifact do more than one task) and attribute dependency change (changing a linkage between the artifact and the environment), which are both specific approaches to exaptation in that they both involve changing what a product or component is capable of doing.

So regardless of what you call them, it is useful to know that scholars consistently observe the systematic nature of idea generation. It's not magic, it's *method.*

generation, Novozymes may go beyond existing partnerships with grain processors and oil companies to build business models for cities or even design processing plants for industry in order to ensure its invention becomes the catalyst of a genuine innovation.

Biofuel illustrates the power entrepreneurs can have over markets. The fate of the second generation, a big potential answer to the energy crisis and to greenhouse gas emissions, lies in the hands of the entrepreneur, not the technologist. As with everything technical from internet search engines to hybrid car engines, the real innovation lies in creating the opportunity.

One of the approaches observed in expert entrepreneurs is the ability to invert a problem and imagine how

even unpleasant surprises can provide the foundation for new opportunities. Crises ranging from energy to malnutrition present transformation opportunities to make both impact and money.

ONGOING TRANSFORMATION

The previous sections outline only some of the ways expert entrepreneurs work to transform their means into ideas. If you need inspiration on more, feel free to explore the table below where we list some additional transformation types we also observed expert entrepreneurs using in the Venturing scenario.

ADDITIONAL TRANSFORMATION TYPES

Transformation type	Description
Deleting/supplementing	Adding and subtracting to something existing
Composing/decomposing	Reorganizing material that is already there; decomposing and recomposing it
Exaptation	Transforming existing artifacts by converting them to new uses
Re-weighting	Increasing and decreasing or re-ordering relative emphasis of features of a product or market
Manipulation	Inverting, mirroring, twisting, turning an idea or artifact inside out
Deformation	Deliberately deforming the original idea or concept; analogous to melody deformation in jazz
Localization/regionalization/globalization	Changing the scope of the market by proposing smaller or larger markets
Ad hoc associating	Drawing on prior experience and memory, by associating the current venture with some previous problem or opportunity

TAKEAWAY: COMMITMENT TRANSFORMS AN IDEA INTO A GOOD IDEA

The notion of turning "something into something" can be found at the heart of Schumpeter's definition of entrepreneurship from his 1911 book *Theory of Economic Development*: "Our assumption is that he who makes new combinations is an entrepreneur."

But while making new combinations is easy because there are an infinite number of possible new combinations, it is immensely difficult to find valuable new combinations for exactly the same reason. Most scholars of entrepreneurship, including Knight (1921), Schumpeter (1911), and contemporary researchers conclude that the entrepreneur has some kind of intuition or judgment that enables them to instinctively pick good combinations from the infinite set of all possible combinations.

In this chapter we outline the clinical mechanisms behind this process, but we omit one element common to them all: the importance of interaction.

The interaction sequence is a relatively easy one: I have an idea—I talk to someone—together we transform it into something meaningful. So while the transformation types here may allow you to generate ideas on your own, they also allow you to transform ideas collaboratively with others. Also critical to interaction is the importance of commitment. While you may be able to generate many ideas with these transformation types, what separates ideas from good ideas is whether key stakeholders such as employees, partners, and customers are willing to make a commitment to

them. Expert entrepreneurs make transformations based on stakeholder commitments, not merely new combinations pulled out of a hat. Transformations, as mathematicians know, require interactions in space—in the case of expert entrepreneurs, this interaction happens in the stakeholder space. This is what we look at in the next chapter.

So what?

Entrepreneurs who use transformational processes produce more new market ideas than those who search and select for an existing opportunity. If you're struggling to make connections to others, or to find ways to put affordable loss, contingency, and pre-commitments to work, transforming what you've got into something new may be just what you need to do. You don't have to invent something from nothing. Instead, transform something or several somethings into something else.

Roadmap

Use the transformation concepts from expert entrepreneurs to imagine three new ways to create value with three completely new audiences.

- ☐ Decompose what you've got into its most basic elements, and imagine different audiences that could connect to those elements.

- ☐ Imagine that a component of your current opportunity, which you consider to be the most irrelevant, turned out to be the most valued element of your whole idea. Create three new ways to connect to three new audiences building on that possibility.

- ☐ Practice your pitch and "sell" some of these new ideas to someone who might actually value what you assumed to be irrelevant.

Bigger questions

- ☐ Is transforming existing ideas and material really capable of creating something genuinely new?

- ☐ To what extent are your efforts really transforming/remaking the world?

- ☐ In the venture you dream about, are you adapting to the world or reshaping it?

CHAPTER 11

Managing risk like a seasoned entrepreneur means making decisions based on acceptable downside rather than guesses about upside potential.

The affordable loss principle: Risk little, fail cheap

■ ■ ■

IN THIS CHAPTER:

I MAGINE YOU ARE an entrepreneur. During your 12-year tenure as an engineer at a major computer manufacturer, you work on your own time to invent a device that recognizes and responds to eye movements. You imagine it might make a great alternative to the computer mouse. You can make it rest on the user's head much like headphones and set it up so that point-and-click navigation is accomplished with even the most minor head and eye movements. You are convinced there is a huge potential for change in the way things are currently done. But when you attempt to interest your current company in licensing the idea from you, they are uninterested. There are no firms currently offering anything close to this and you possess all the technical skills needed to create the product effectively and efficiently. You quit your job to further develop this idea and win a business plan competition with the idea. As soon as you have a demonstrable prototype, you have to make a decision.

You have presented your prototype and some initial market research on selling this device through the retail channel as an upgrade to existing or new computers. A venture capitalist who was one of the judges in the business plan competition likes your idea and believes that with an initial investment of US$10 million you could realistically capture 1 percent of the personal computer market worldwide. She believes your product should sell for US$30 and generate a

20 percent net profit margin. For that investment, the venture capitalist would expect to own 40 percent of your company.

In the meantime, you have been speaking with a friend of your father's who runs a large manufacturing facility. He is willing to pay you US$1 million to adapt your technology to a hands-free system that enables blue-collar factory workers to control systems from their work areas. The adaptation of your product, integration with the factory systems, and commercialization will cost you about US$950,000. He is willing to pay you upfront.

CHOOSING THE BEST OPPORTUNITY

Because of the development bandwidth you cannot do both simultaneously. Given what you have seen thus far in the book, what are some ways you would think about making this decision?

- Which is the bigger opportunity?
- What is the net present value of each opportunity?
- What would you be personally investing into each alternative?
- What is the downside risk of each alternative?

As you look at these questions, you will probably recognize that the first two are the more predictive ways of thinking about the decision, and the second two are the more effectual ways of thinking about the decision. Let us look at each question in turn, so as to get a better grip on what might—and what might not—help us make a

---

What goes into making an NPV prediction?

Predicting NPV is packed with a lot of detail that is forward looking.

Let's unpack it. Most NPV calculations are anchored fundamentally with a demand forecast. This typically involves gathering information on a consensus for the high side and the low side of demand for the product at certain price assumptions. The price assumptions, similarly, rely on predictions about the product and features developed over the time period in question, and the competitor reactions to those improvements and price strategies. So with some ideas on price and quantity forecasts, the calculations turn to the costs and margins it takes to deliver on that demand.

From a cost standpoint, individual material and input cost matter a lot. Will the product cost US$1 or US$3 to make? How will it change over time? Additionally, you need to create expectations around the costs of the assets and infrastructure. These things change over time, and they rely on the product roadmaps involved in improving the product over time, and how competitors interact on that front. Finally, the question of risk and discounting the cost of capital used to pursue the entire endeavor involves predicting and assessing the variability inherent in all of this forecasting. Put this together, and you realize that NPV is actually a calculation of future expected value with numerous dimensions that introduce variance which can generate wide margins of error.

---

good choice between the "venture capitalist" and "father's friend."

Which is the bigger opportunity?

How would you know? Take the case of the absurdly unlikely venture 1–800-Autopsy from Chapter 4. Until 1988 the world got along without the services of a company providing autopsies on demand. However, with the growing success and increasing demand for private autopsy services over the last two decades, perhaps one could argue that there was latent demand that simply went unnoticed until Vidal Herrera recognized it. But if we wind back to 1988, what would his elevator pitch have been to investors? Or, for that matter, what would Starbucks' pitch have been in 1980, at a point in time when US coffee consumption had been declining for 20 years straight?

Common sense suggests that while you might be able to calculate what you may lose by investing in a venture (namely, everything that you put at risk), it is much harder to calculate the potential upside, i.e. the size of different opportunities.

What is the net present value of each opportunity?

You can take out a piece of paper, or create a spreadsheet to calculate the net present value (NPV) of these alternatives. What is your forecasted demand? What is your product cost? What are your overheads? How will these costs change over time?

Put this together, and you can see the interrelated system of prediction involved in trying to assess opportunity value.

What would you be personally investing into each alternative?

Both options require you to invest a variety of resources in order to make it successful. Spend a moment thinking about how these alternatives differ in terms of the following:

• your wealth commitment
• your time commitment
• your reputation commitment
• your emotional commitment.

How would you measure these? How would you decide what constitutes an appropriate level of investment? These are highly subjective and personal assessments that also change over time in an individual's life.

What is the downside risk of each alternative?

Let's assume you choose the venture capital option. These are some of the uncertainties:

• The market is not there, and the venture capitalist "pulls the plug" on the company (shuts you down).
• The market is there, but the venture capitalist takes control of the firm and fires you.
• You don't get along with the venture capitalist, but you can't buy her out.
• The market ends up being 25,000 units per year, just enough to break even, but leaving you managing a firm turned into the "living dead."

Now, assuming that you have decided to work with your father's friend, these are some things you may want to consider:

• You miss a critical deadline that costs your father's friend a week's manufacturing output. You father's friend is unhappy with your father.
• You deliver something defective, and employee harm results.
• It costs you twice as much to implement the solution as you estimated.

• While you are working with your father's friend, a new company releases the product you wanted to put into retail and it is a runaway success.

In each case, which of these is worse and why? Which of these is within your control? Does the worst case depend on things you do wrong versus things that happen outside the firm?

What do you do next in each of these cases? Are you really losing one segment while pursuing another?

Using affordable loss as a decision tool

While NPV is a useful decision-making tool in many situations, because of its sensitivity to uncertainty, you have to be careful how you use it in entrepreneurial situations. The research upon which this book is based suggests that expert entrepreneurs favor thinking through the plunge into a new venture using an affordable loss approach, rather than NPV. Fundamentally, affordable loss

ASSESSING AFFORDABLE LOSS

	Venture capitalist	My father's friend
Time		
Reputation		
Opportunity cost		
My intellectual horsepower and property		

is based on things they know and can control, whereas NPV is based on predictions they don't trust and can't control.

In Chapter 7 we looked at how expert entrepreneurs work from the basis of affordable loss rather than expected returns. They decide based on what downside risk they find acceptable rather than on what they guess the upsides might be. So instead of calculating upfront how much money they will need to launch their project and investing time, effort, and energy into raising that money, effectual entrepreneurs try to estimate the downside and examine what they are willing to lose. They then use the process of building the project to bring other stakeholders on board to reduce the resources they need to start their venture, and share what they and the stakeholders can afford to lose together.

As we walk through how to think in terms of affordable loss, the key "perspective" point to remember is that affordable loss puts the entrepreneur front and center rather than the venture. Traditional business planning puts the venture front and center, asking what financing the venture needs to get it off the ground, independent of the entrepreneur's available means. Affordable loss is different because it starts with the entrepreneur's concrete situation, not abstract estimates of venture financing needs. As such, the emphasis is on taking the entrepreneur's context into account. Big decisions like taking the plunge into entrepreneurship depend a lot on the specific situation you are in, such as your family situation, your stage of life, and the social norms

"We've considered every potential risk except the risks of avoiding all risks."

around—for example, attitudes towards failure in your particular social setting and industry.

> ## To ponder
>
> A loser doesn't know what he'll do if he loses, but talks about what he'll do if he wins,
>
> And a winner doesn't talk about what he'll do if he wins, but knows what he'll do if he loses.
>
> Eric Berne

So affordable loss is about reasoning from your life situation, your current commitments, your aspirations, and your risk propensity. It is helpful to think of affordable loss as a two-step process:

1. The first step is to ask how much do you really need to start your

business: getting creative about different ways of bringing your idea to market using all the means that are available to you and reducing the means you need to launch the venture. The vast majority of new businesses are started with small sums of money, not big ones, and rely heavily on other contributions, such as the entrepreneur's time and (often) family support.

2. The second step is to ask what are you really able and willing to lose to start your business? This means actually to think through your available resources and your risk preferences, and using these to guide your decisions when starting your venture.

We'll look at these two steps in turn, starting with case of Ruth Owaldes next, who is a good example to help think through how much you really need to start your business.

Determining an acceptable level of red ink in the newspaper industry

Consider the launch of the *USA Today* newspaper. The newspaper's owners did substantial financial analysis on the launch decision. But all the analysis did not change the fact that the paper's success was critically dependent on advertising revenues (70 percent of the revenue base) that were driven by the reactions of several key competitors to the new paper (i.e. the success or failure of the venture hinged in part on the interaction between the different actors in the marketplace). However good the analysis that went into making the launch decision, the paper's financial future couldn't be controlled by its owners—it was in the hands of its competitors.

USA Today was launched in 1982. It was estimated to have lost US$400 million in its first 5 years, and continued to lose money for its first decade. It reported its first year of profits (US$7.5 million) in 1993.

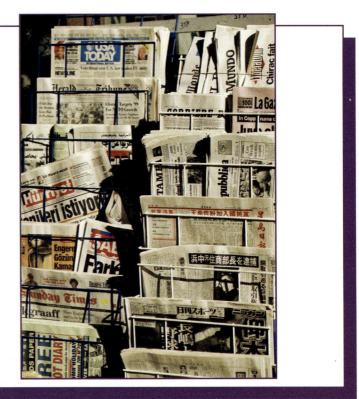

PRACTICALLY SPEAKING: IS A COST ALWAYS A COST?

As an executive at diversified mail order retailer Avion Group, Ruth Owades saw opportunity. Choosy gardeners did not have easy access to premium specialty gardening equipment. But these amateur horticulturalists could be profitable, easily reached, and extremely loyal if well served. She proposed the business to Avion, but they had no interest. Her next step was to ask them if she could take the idea and develop it on her own. Surprisingly, they agreed.

Ruth had not worked outside the comfortable confines of a corporate environment. A brief investigation

RUTH OWADES' CAPIAL EXPENDITURES

Cost of starting up	Cash "upfront" estimates	Same using affordable loss
Catalogue printing and mailing	US$100,000	Negotiated for two catalogues and 6-month payment terms
Mailing list rentals	US$30,800	US$30,800
Payment for merchandise	US$75,600	Negotiated long credit windows
Miscellaneous utility and other deposits	US$4,000	Negotiated no deposit
Other working capital: e.g. mailing supplies, employee, rent	US$15,000	US$15,000
TOTAL	**US$225,400**	**US$45,800**

into setting up her own operation revealed that investment money for an unproven entrepreneur with an unproven idea was not exactly forthcoming. Ruth's best offer for funding involved her providing 25 percent of the money for the venture from her own bank account, while giving up 49 percent of the company to a group of four private investors. Determined to make it work without the investors' money, she plunged into business, naming her venture Gardener's Eden.

Ruth's first stop was the printer. To a mail order company, the single largest expense is the printing and mailing of the catalog—a line item that can account for up to half the costs in the business. Ruth needed both a fantastic print job and good financial terms—two elements that are usually mutually exclusive. So she proposed a scheme where the printers would bid on her first two catalogs rather than just her first one. This showed the printers that she was willing to make a commitment to them, in exchange for favorable treatment on their part. Her suggestion was novel to the industry and was well received. So when she went in and said, "Gee, the other printers are offering me 90-day terms. Can't we do better than that?", the printer gave her six months to pay.

Gardener's Eden needed more than catalogs, however. And Ruth doggedly pursued each supplier necessary to make the venture happen. She negotiated with the utilities so that she did not have to tie up her cash with deposits for electricity and telephones. She arranged long credit windows with the suppliers that manufactured the exotic gardening items she intended to

sell. She drove hard bargains with both her landlord and with the credit card company for unusually low terms. She even pursued her local postmaster, visiting him again and again until he turned up a forgotten regulation that enabled her to collect her daily mail without any service charge.

Ruth's strategy was simple: figure out who would benefit from her success; tell them the story about what she was trying to accomplish; explain to them why they were critical to the venture and how they would be successful when she was; and push each entity to make an investment to help her be successful. She negotiated everything with everyone until she got what she wanted. Unknowingly, she was successfully applying affordable loss to her venture. Nearby is a comparison of what her costs should have been (using classical calculations) versus what they ended up being.

As the picture came together, Ruth had built an environment where everyone around her had a reason to do something special to make her successful—an environment where she had transformed suppliers to the venture into partners with the venture —an environment where she was able to succeed. Ruth's revenues well exceeded US$1 million when stylish

retailer Williams-Sonoma acquired Gardener's Eden less than four years after she launched the venture.

Think about who will benefit from getting their hands dirty with you, and how they can help you be successful too. It is easiest is to start from the estimated cost of the venture and work hard (and creatively) to make that number zero.

DECIDING ON YOUR AFFORDABLE LOSS: SOME GUIDELINES

Once you have gone through the process of creatively trying to find every way possible of lowering the amount of money that you need to get your venture off the ground, you are left with the question of what downside risk is acceptable to you in order to start the business. Here, the key thing is asking yourself the right questions. It's helpful to think through both what you can afford to lose and what you are willing to lose. We'll look at each of these in turn.

What can I afford to lose?

People "mentally account" for resources in different ways by putting them into different categories. For example, many individuals start new businesses based on contributing their time, but carefully limit how much of their cash they are willing to put into the business. Evidently, people account for their time differently from how they account for their cash. Similarly, some resources are mentally accounted for in ways that preclude them from being put at risk. A good example is savings that parents accumulate to fund education for their children. These monies are often considered as "out of bounds" for risking on a new business venture.

While everybody mentally accounts for their resources in this kind of way, what exactly they put into each mental account often differs. To understand what you can afford to lose you therefore have to know what your resources are, but you also have to make some decisions about what belongs in the category of "riskable" and what doesn't. As you are thinking about this, remember that some psychologists have argued that rational people never put at risk what is truly valuable to them.

Here are some of the big accounts that people view as being different. Use them to help think through what you can afford to lose, and what is "out of bounds" for you.

Your time

Contributing time to a new venture is often referred to as "sweat equity." A good proportion of entrepreneurs sweat it out over long periods of time. However, this may make sense to

them because time is a different "currency" from cash and therefore how an individual accounts for time they put into a venture is somewhat ambiguous. Also, because time is perishable, people feel differently about contributing it—after all, they might have wasted it anyway. Therefore, time may be a more affordable loss than losing money in a venture.

Windfalls

One of the interesting elements to the success story of Fedex is that Fred Smith's father passed away as he was creating the business plan for the venture. The initial funding for FedEx came from from Fred's inheritance of US$4 million and another US$4 million from his sister's share. In this case, because of the inheritance, Smith's level of affordable loss changed overnight, and by a very significant amount. This may be because inheritances are put in a different mental account than earned income, and therefore people feel differently about putting them at risk by using them to start a new venture. Other examples include lottery winnings and big upswings in asset prices such as shares and stock prices, both of which may significantly increase (or decrease) an individual's affordable loss.

In retrospect, Fred Smith's decision to invest his and his sister's inheritance into the fledgling FedEx looks prescient. But had he been a seasoned entrepreneur, he might have first tried to start the firm with US$0 of his own money.

Long-term savings

Some research suggests that most people apply rules of thumb to borrowing against or spending certain resources that are mentally accounted for as belonging to other parts of their life. Examples include funds set aside for their own retirement, and those set aside for the care of dependents, e.g. children and parents.

The family home/home equity

There are many instances in which people use home equity loans to fund a business start-up. However, other individuals appear unwilling to put their home at risk, indicating a difference in the way homes are mentally accounted for in different cultures around the world.

Credit card accounts

In entrepreneurship there are several well-known stories of entrepreneurs who started their businesses on their credit cards (e.g. EDS was started by Ross Perot on his credit card, as was

THE AFFORDABLE LOSS PRINCIPLE: RISK LITTLE, FAIL CHEAP

the founding of the US home improvement superstore Home Depot). There is some evidence that people mentally account for credit card expenses differently from other expenses because the link between spending and paying for items is weakened by using a credit card.

Loans from family and friends

Other examples of weak links between spending and paying may include loans from family members that have flexible or unspecified payback terms. Descriptions of family business, for example, refer to the relatives' money as "patient capital." Such funds may seem more affordable to use and lose than funds with heavy pressure to repay at specific deadlines.

What am I willing to lose?

Once you have decided what you might be able to afford to lose, you still need to decide what you are willing to lose on this particular venture. This issue largely comes down to a question of motivation. This will include factors such as the degree and intensity of your motivation to start this particular venture, since this will shape your willingness to lose any given sum. It will also depend on whether you have set certain mental thresholds as an entrepreneur, since if the downside case for your venture falls below or above a key threshold you have set, this will dictate your course of action. Ultimately, the question you have to ask yourself is,

> **You can't always control the wind, but you can control your sails.**
>
> **Anthony Robbins**

"Is the venture worth doing even if the invested amount is lost?"

Regardless of whether your motivation to become an entrepreneur is largely subject to pecuniary or non-pecuniary elements, there are several ways that reasoning through the plunge decision using affordable loss is likely to increase the chances that you'll decide to go ahead:

- It reduces the threshold of financial risk taking required. Going

Research roots

Affordable loss

The economist George Shackle refers to the term affordable loss in an early paper (Shackle, 1966: 765) where he postulated that the entrepreneur might characterize each venture opportunity according to the possible gains and possible losses and suggests affordable loss is used in the evaluation of which venture opportunity an entrepreneur might pursue:

It is practical and reasonable to regard the focus-loss, in absolute terms, as depending on the nature and scale of the enterprise concerned. Thus, by choice of an appropriate kind, or an appropriate size, of plant or enterprise, he can adjust the greatest amount he stands to lose, that is, his focus loss, to the amount which, given the size and character of his assets, he can afford to lose.

through the exercise of absolutely minimizing the start-up costs of the business lowers the bar for starting your venture.

- It allows you to focus on things within your control (the downside) and proceed in spite of things outside your control, which increases your confidence about starting a venture.
- It makes explicit that the upside potential for the venture is in large part contingent on your actions and the actions of your stakeholders, which again increases the perceived controllability of your venture, and therefore its attractiveness.
- It enables you to choose a venture to start that matters to you in ways beyond the economic upside. Bringing in factors that lay beyond financial calculation makes the decision more realistic, and in tune with how most people actually make major decisions.

In short, reasoning using the logic of affordable loss will provide you with more reasons for taking the plunge into entrepreneurship and fewer reasons for saying no.

TAKEAWAY: UN-RISKY BUSINESS

The statistics of new venture success and failure would seem to suggest budding entrepreneurs adopt a bias against starting new ventures, simply because a large number of new firms fail. However, affordable loss lessens the impact of possible failure because it makes failure clearly survivable by constraining the loss to something that

Research roots

Mental accounting

The notion of mental accounting was first developed in a paper by Thaler (1985: 199) and later summarized in another of his papers (Thaler, 1999). Mental accounting emerges fairly straightforwardly from bounded rationality: Creatures with limited cognitive processing capabilities require ways of keeping track of their money with limited memory space. Thaler theorized that people categorize resources in order to keep track of them, much like accountants do in firms. For example, they create separate mental compartments for long-term savings (such as that for retirement and children's education) and others for short-term expenses (such as entertainment and leisure activities). A key implication of mental accounting is the violation of the fungibility premise of economics, i.e. that resources are automatically arbitraged across different accounts (Thaler, 1999:183). A simple way to think about this is that for Homo economicus, "money by any other name is still money" but for most Homo sapiens, "money in one mental account is just simply not the same as money in another account." Because of this non-fungibility characteristic, mental accounting suggests that consumers may borrow at high interest rates in some accounts even while they save at much lower interest rates in others.

the entrepreneur regards as affordable and is willing to lose in order to pursue the venture. If the entrepreneur manages the downside risk to a low and acceptable level then, should failure occur, that entrepreneur is likely to lose less in terms of investment than an entrepreneur who invests on the basis of his or her guess about the upside potential of a venture. Also, should failure occur, the entrepreneur using affordable loss logic has kept his or her loss to a level s/he can live with, despite the failure of the venture.

Roadmap

Think about uncertain questions where affordable loss will help more than expected return.

- [ ] Do I hire at all? Whom specifically should I hire?

- [ ] How much, if any, do I invest in longer-term investments such as research and development?

- [ ] Do I stay with my plan, or follow this side opportunity?

- [ ] Can you specify what you are willing to lose at this point to find out if your opportunity "has legs?" Time, money, reputation, other?

- [ ] Who benefits from the efforts of your venture? Identify three things you can negotiate to your advantage with those people. Think big, be creative. How will you proceed?

Bigger questions

- [ ] What are some of the cultural aspects of affordable loss in different parts of the world?

- [ ] How does affordable loss encourage or discourage commitment?

So what?

Using affordable loss to reason through the plunge decision reduces the perceived barriers to starting your business, and helps you see how to get started right now, while still managing your risk. Starting a business doesn't have to be over whether the upside is big enough; instead, it can be about whether the downside is life threatening.

CHAPTER 12

Bootstrapping

There were others who had forced their way to the top from the lowest rung by the aid of their bootstraps.

James Joyce, *Ulysses*, 1922

Starting a business without any money is not only possible, it might actually give you an advantage.

Financing: Bootstrap the venture

■ ■ ■

AS WE SAW IN Chapter 4, one of the greatest perceived hurdles to new venture creation is, "I don't have enough money." Lulled by the stories of venture capitalists and angels that pour millions of dollars into small start-ups with barely a business plan to their name, the budding entrepreneur naturally assumes that the first step is to look for money, preferably a lot of it. But before you embark on that quest, think about the following:

- How much do you want?
- How much do you need?
- What do you need (investment) money for?
- What can you do without money?
- What does money cost?
- What are you willing to give up in return for the money?

This chapter and Chapters 14 and 16 will look to answer these questions and offer alternative views to the cash question.

In this chapter we will look at start-up financing—or how to bootstrap your venture without taking on external funding (or taking on as little as possible).

Chapter 14 will look at how you share ownership and control as other people invest with you.

Chapter 16 looks at the role of business plans in a more formal funding process —including venture capitalist funding and initial public offering/exit options.

To put bootstrapping into a very specific and detailed context, this chapter will take you through a real life case of a young couple who decided to launch their own business. At each breakpoint in the story, think back to the questions listed here, and think about how you would have approached the business, had you been the founder.

The base assumption throughout the case is, not surprisingly, that when you start your own business, cash in has to somehow be greater than or equal to cash out.

Bon voyage!

Tall boots may have a tab, loop or handle at the top known as a bootstrap, allowing one to use fingers or a tool to provide better leverage in pulling the boots on. The saying "to pull yourself up by your bootstraps" was already in use during the 1800s as an example of an impossible task. Bootstrap as a metaphor, meaning to better oneself by one's own unaided efforts, was in use in 1922. This metaphor spawned additional metaphors for a series of self-sustaining processes that proceed without external help.

Bootstrapping in business is to start a business without external help or capital.

(Wikipedia, 2010)

PRACTICALLY SPEAKING: BOOTSTRAPPING IN ACTION: STACY'S PITA CHIPS

Who I am, what I know, who I know (Chapter 9)

The year is 1996. Stacy and Mark are a couple, living in Boston. Mark is a psychologist and Stacy a social worker. They both have experience in the Californian food industry, having worked in restaurants. They know trends in the US often move from west to east. They believe Boston might soon acquire an appetite for Californian style food. They are strong believers in the healthy diets they experienced in the West. They know they want to be their own boss. Together they have debt of US$370,000.

Mark and Stacy are attracted to the food/restaurant business. Ideally, they would like to start a healthy bistro, but that dream is squelched by their debt and the lack of enthusiasm by their immediate family to support the venture. So they start selling sausages and hot dogs from a pushcart in the streets of Boston. It isn't exactly the healthy diet they had in mind, but it is a profitable and cash positive living.

What should they do next?

Keep selling sausages from the pushcart: it's making money?	Quit selling junk food and look for jobs?	Make healthier sandwiches Californian style?	Do something else (remember Curry in a Hurry, Chapter 1?)
Not consistent with values	Not consistent with goals	Interesting—what's the cost?	Possible—guided by partners

The opportunity cost of time

Spending money versus spending time are perceived differently. The value of time (or sweat equity, as it is sometimes called) is more ambiguous and perishable because time can't be saved for future use. Therefore, losses paid for in time may be experienced as more affordable than losses paid for in money because they can be accounted for more flexibly and are, therefore, seen as being more affordable than ventures paid for in money.

WHAT IS THE BALANCE SHEET FOR SELLING HEALTHIER SANDWICHES?

Income	Expenses	Money questions
From their first venture into hot dogs, they know there is demand.	Ingredients	Do you want fresh ingredients? Could you get yesterday's bread cheaper? Could you cut a deal with a pita manufacturer?
	Pushcart	You already have one, but are you willing to lose the revenue you might have generated selling sausages?
	Time	How do you account for your time?

The couple decides to make pita wrap sandwiches to sell on a pushcart in Boston's financial district. The date is 1997.

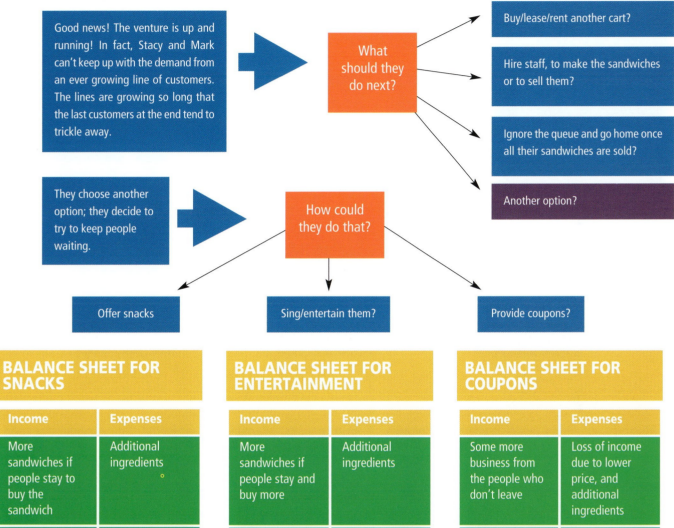

Good news! The venture is up and running! In fact, Stacy and Mark can't keep up with the demand from an ever growing line of customers. The lines are growing so long that the last customers at the end tend to trickle away.

What should they do next?

- Buy/lease/rent another cart?
- Hire staff, to make the sandwiches or to sell them?
- Ignore the queue and go home once all their sandwiches are sold?
- Another option?

They choose another option; they decide to try to keep people waiting.

How could they do that?

- Offer snacks
- Sing/entertain them?
- Provide coupons?

BALANCE SHEET FOR SNACKS

Income	Expenses
More sandwiches if people stay to buy the sandwich	Additional ingredients
If I sell the snacks, maybe some income	More time, and maybe loss of customers, cost of snacks

BALANCE SHEET FOR ENTERTAINMENT

Income	Expenses
More sandwiches if people stay and buy more	Additional ingredients
	The time it takes to learn and provide some form of entertainment

BALANCE SHEET FOR COUPONS

Income	Expenses
Some more business from the people who don't leave	Loss of income due to lower price, and additional ingredients
	Time to print the coupons

Mark and Stacy decide to offer snacks. But they cannot buy something off the shelf. Instead, each evening they take the left-over pita bread, dust it with spices—cinnamon, garlic, etc., and the next day they hand these "chips" out to the customers waiting in line.

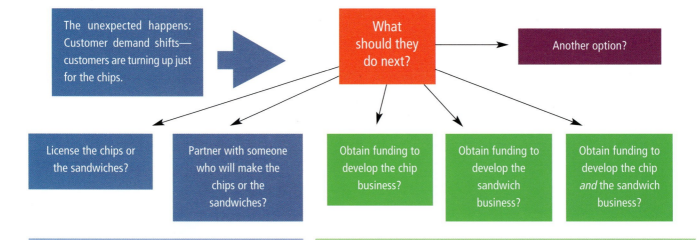

When it's partners you need

When confronted with choice, there is always another option. Sometimes, it's not money you need but a partner.

For Mark and Stacy, this is an easy time to bring on a partner. They have two opportunities, which have created demand, more demand than they have the resources to handle. A partner could add all sorts of resources to their set of means, ranging from broad distribution (a high-end grocery store interested in offering sandwiches), to factory capacity (a bread factory, idle during the day as most baking is done at night).

In addition, money is not always the only motivation for launching a partnership. As these two examples highlight, you may have investors interested for other reasons than money. And in turn, these partners can both offer resources that go beyond money and can also enable the pursuit of new opportunities that were not previously imagined (for example, flavored pita bread produced by the bakery partner to make the sandwiches more unique and exciting).

When it's money you need

It is important to remember that all money comes with strings attached. The relationships you create as you gather investments of all different sorts reasonably require your attention. People involved need to know how things are developing, they often have specific legal rights to be updated, and have a say in some of your major decisions. This relationship work takes real time and sincere attention, not unlike the attention and investment it takes to manage your relationship with a great customer. More money means more of this type of relationship management.

Like all relationships, it's a two-way street: People involved don't just listen to you, you also learn from them and include their resources in your portfolio. We made the case for the value of taking advantage of contingencies earlier in the book and we will look at it again in detail when we talk about contingency. The listening and cooperating involved in working with your investors/lenders/other sources of money can limit the degrees of freedom that you have in dealing with contingencies. Even with great sources of capital and shrewd big thinkers that trust you, the process can slow you down.

Finally, more money often leads to customer interactions that are relatively more directive than collaborative. Imagine you are in the business of selling garlic chips and you find an interested customer. He loves your garlic chips, but will only buy from you if you can modify them into cinnamon chips. If you are sitting on US$10 million in cash, you are imminently less inclined to say yes to that possibility than if you are sitting on US$1 in cash. As a result, you turn the customer away—your business is garlic!

Mark and Stacy are unsure what to do. They stop and think. They speak to other people in the industry, read trade journals, and talk to colleagues and competitors.

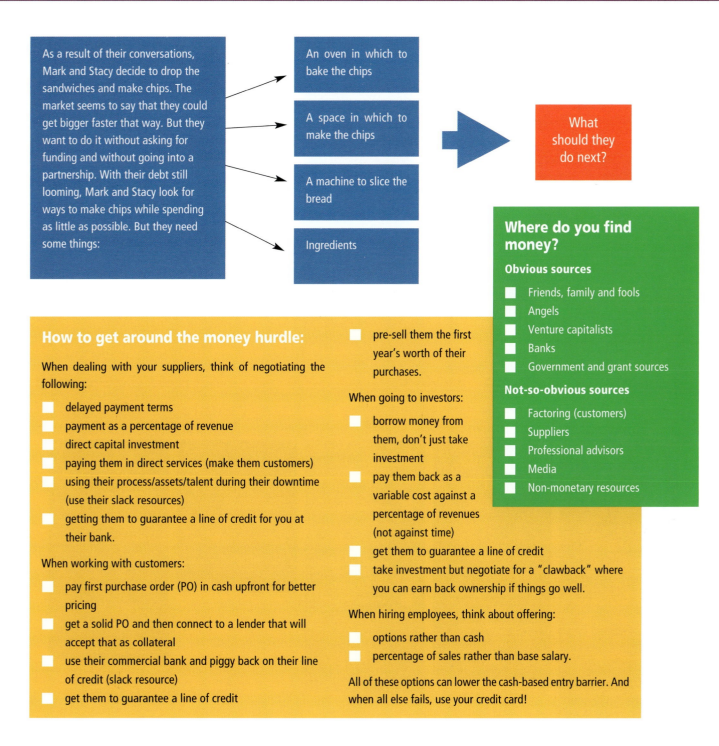

As a result of their conversations, Mark and Stacy decide to drop the sandwiches and make chips. The market seems to say that they could get bigger faster that way. But they want to do it without asking for funding and without going into a partnership. With their debt still looming, Mark and Stacy look for ways to make chips while spending as little as possible. But they need some things:

- An oven in which to bake the chips
- A space in which to make the chips
- A machine to slice the bread
- Ingredients

What should they do next?

Where do you find money?

Obvious sources
- Friends, family and fools
- Angels
- Venture capitalists
- Banks
- Government and grant sources

Not-so-obvious sources
- Factoring (customers)
- Suppliers
- Professional advisors
- Media
- Non-monetary resources

How to get around the money hurdle:

When dealing with your suppliers, think of negotiating the following:

- delayed payment terms
- payment as a percentage of revenue
- direct capital investment
- paying them in direct services (make them customers)
- using their process/assets/talent during their downtime (use their slack resources)
- getting them to guarantee a line of credit for you at their bank.

When working with customers:

- pay first purchase order (PO) in cash upfront for better pricing
- get a solid PO and then connect to a lender that will accept that as collateral
- use their commercial bank and piggy back on their line of credit (slack resource)
- get them to guarantee a line of credit
- pre-sell them the first year's worth of their purchases.

When going to investors:

- borrow money from them, don't just take investment
- pay them back as a variable cost against a percentage of revenues (not against time)
- get them to guarantee a line of credit
- take investment but negotiate for a "clawback" where you can earn back ownership if things go well.

When hiring employees, think about offering:

- options rather than cash
- percentage of sales rather than base salary.

All of these options can lower the cash-based entry barrier. And when all else fails, use your credit card!

They rent space from a bakery—using the bakery's down time to bake their chips in the bakery's oven. This solves the space, oven, and machine problem. But it does not allow for large-scale production.

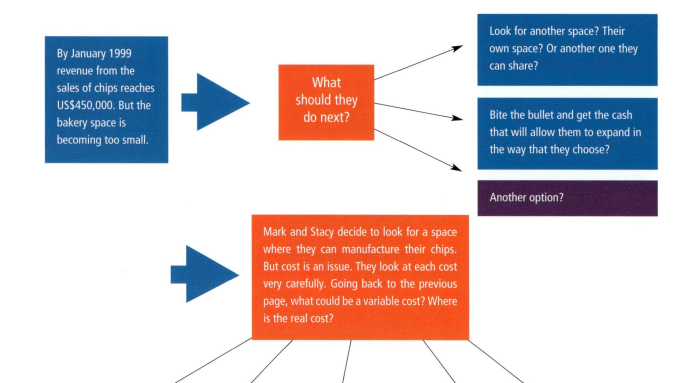

By January 1999 revenue from the sales of chips reaches US$450,000. But the bakery space is becoming too small.

What should they do next?

Look for another space? Their own space? Or another one they can share?

Bite the bullet and get the cash that will allow them to expand in the way that they choose?

Another option?

Mark and Stacy decide to look for a space where they can manufacture their chips. But cost is an issue. They look at each cost very carefully. Going back to the previous page, what could be a variable cost? Where is the real cost?

An oven
- Mark and Stacy can get a new one for US$160,000.
- They can also partner in developing one with an oven maker. If two ovens are made, each will only cost US$80,000.
- If they find a bakery selling a second-hand oven they could pay as little as US$13,000.

Ingredients
Stacy and Mark have always been keen on using the freshest ingredients. But if you are making chips, would yesterday's bread do just as well? Could they get leftovers from a pita manufacturer?

Slicing machines
- A bread-slicing machine costs US$100,000 and is available immediately.
- A second-hand carrot-slicing machine could be found for US$18,000.

Staff
At this point, they have 15 staff. Should they hire additional people to make more chips?

Packaging machines and supplies
With the business growing, they can no longer pack and send all the chips by hand. But this machinery seems impossible to buy second hand.

What should they do next?

Mark and Stacy expand the chip business

- They make Stacy the majority owner of the company so that she is eligible for funding from BankBoston, which has a loan program that assists women in business. They ask for a US$60,000 loan to buy automated packaging equipment and supplies. Six months later they apply for US$500,000. But in exchange for that amount, the bank wants equity, which the couple is not willing to give. They settle for US$300,000.

- They partner with an oven manufacturer to make the oven they cannot find, paying US$80,000—half the original price.

- When they realize they need a second oven, and that the banks will not lend them any more money, they buy a used oven from a bankrupt bakery. They pay for it with their credit card.

- Since they cannot find an automatic slicer at a price they can afford, they buy a 40-year-old carrot-cutting machine from Campbell Soup, which Mark modifies.

- They rent a suburban warehousing space from a contracting company. They spend nothing furnishing it, getting furniture for free from friends and family or making their own.

- They hire Stacy's brother into the company in exchange for a share of the profit.

- When they need more staff than the 15 they have, they hire temporary employees.

- They spend nothing on advertising—instead they give samples away in person at trade shows, cooking demonstrations, public appearances, and grocery stores everywhere across the US.

- They partner with Babson, a Boston area business school focused on entrepreneurship, to hire summer interns to design their website in exchange for them speaking at the school.

The story of Stacy and Mark illustrates the timeless rules of new venture bootstrapping:

- Never buy what you can rent.
- Never rent what you can barter for.
- Never barter for what you can borrow.
- Never borrow what you can get for free.

By 2000 Stacy's Pita Chips is a profitable business with US$1.3 million in revenues (double that of 1999).

Five years later Mark and Stacy sell their pita chips to PepsiCo's Frito-Lay. By then, they are the top-selling maker of pita chips in the US, with revenues of US$60 million and 100 employees.

SELECTING A FUNDING APPROACH

In an effectual approach investment is tightly coupled with what you can afford to lose. Clearly, there is a risk that you will under-invest in the opportunity. It could be that you will underestimate the upside potential of the market or that you choose to pursue only one aspect of it, leaving a chunk for someone else to pursue. On the other hand, it is the fear of missing out on something that often drives the entrepreneur to look for external funding.

That said, human entrepreneurial predictions tend to be optimistic, calling for rapid growth and the associated funding that may be required. The risk is that, should your predictions be optimistic, you will have built a larger business than you need (a rapid growth around more space, more people, more patents, more marketing, better sales channel investment), which will not be sustainable.

For most businesses, bootstrapping offers a better fit, because of the reduced risk, the obligation of proving the business before a large investment is made, and because of the simple odds against attracting large institutional investments.

Roadmap

Before you go for money, ask yourself the following:

- [ ] When do you need it, however much the amount? You don't need it all at once. Identify at least three clear points at which you would need different chunks of money. Can you prioritize them? Which can you hit first, for the least resources?

- [ ] When does cash flow into this business relative to when you need to pay your most significant bills? Create three ideas for how you can move that inflow forward in time. Create three ideas for how you can move that expense back in time. Even if you pay a little extra, or get a little less, matching ins and outs can be very worthwhile.

TAKEAWAY: MAINTAIN CONTROL BY DOING THE MOST WITH THE LEAST

The question among the top of budding entrepreneurs' concerns is, "How will I finance my venture?" What we need to remember is that there are countless ways, beyond money or in spite of money, in which you can grow your business.

In general, entrepreneurs either prefer the cheapest option or come up with creative ways of doing things at little cost and risk to themselves. But at some point in time, you may have to go for external funding. Think carefully about what you need and

So what?

Most start-ups could avoid venture funding, rather than pursue it!

whom you need. There is always a trade-off between investing too many resources and investing too few resources. Regardless, figuring out how to do the most with the least is rewarded by being able to maintain more control over the ownership of your venture.

Bigger questions

- [ ] What would have happened if Mark and Stacy had chosen different options at each decision point?

- [ ] What are the cultural aspects of financing that affect entrepreneurial start-ups in different communities?

- [ ] What is **not** a source of funding?

- [ ] Ask yourself, what is money—really?

CHAPTER 13

SOLUTION

The crazy quilt principle: Form partnerships

■ ■ ■

S O THIS IS IT. You have scribbled pages of notes; maybe you have even put something into PowerPoint. You are excited, and a bit anxious about the future. But a question nags you: What do you do first?

The first action is almost always something that involves a partner—a supplier who can provide something you need, a customer who may be interested in something you have to offer, an acquaintance that brings new means.

What distinguishes effectual partnerships from causal partnerships is the belief that those who choose to join the venture, those who self-select into it, ultimately make the venture

what it is. This is in sharp contrast to selecting partners to fit a given goal. It is effectual partnerships that create the venture and not the venture that dictates the partnerships. The partnerships may transform the venture into something very different from what it started out to be. In this logic, the end goal is not known, but the means grow and change with each new partner.

THE PATCHWORK QUILT AND THE PUZZLE

Following effectual logic involves negotiating with any and all stakeholders who are willing to make actual commitments to the project. Metaphorically, we contrast the two approaches using the image of a quilt versus a puzzle. Making a patchwork quilt differs from solving a jigsaw puzzle in at least three ways:

- The quilter has wider latitude than the puzzle solver in putting

together the pattern. Even when s/he begins with a basket of random patches, s/he can choose which patches to use and juxtapose them in a way that s/he

personally finds pleasing and meaningful. A puzzle has only a single solution.

- Large quilting projects are usually communal: A good quilter works with others who bring their own baskets of patches along with their tastes and talents. In the process, the quilter must decide who s/he will work with and why, manage various problems of coordination, and deal with unexpected contingencies.
- The quilt not only has to be pleasing and meaningful, but also has to be useful and valuable—ultimately, it has to keep human bodies warm or embody their aesthetics.

An effectual logic for building a new firm or a new organization or any type of collaborative institution incorporates similar subjective, intersubjective, and objective elements that make it more analogous to stitching together a patchwork quilt than solving a jigsaw puzzle.

WHY ARE PARTNERSHIPS IMPORTANT?

Entrepreneurs begin their venturing journeys with who they are, what they know, and whom they know, and they act on things they can do. For example, in Chapter 9 we looked at a pair of students who wanted to make a fish tank-monitoring product because of their interest in fish and the chemistry background of one of the team members. But a computer professional could also decide that she wanted to make an electronic fish tank-monitoring product with digital

"I'll agree to a fifty-fifty split, But I get the hyphen."

readout and synthesized voice. In either case, the final "product" monitors the water in the tank, but one entrepreneur began with his knowledge of chemistry while the other would have worked from the possibilities suggested by computer hardware and software technology. What they do next will depend on what they can create or transform through their unique abilities, prior knowledge, and social networks.

In the next step of the process, the entrepreneur will start to reach out to other people to obtain advice and other inputs on how to proceed with some of the things they could (possibly) do. The people s/he interacts with could be potential stakeholders, friends, and family or random people s/he meets in the routines of his or her life. As the entrepreneur finds people who want to participate in the effort to build something (at this point, the "something" may be vague or concrete, but it is always very much open to change), s/he moves toward obtaining actual commitments from them. In this step, what counts is the willingness of stakeholders to commit to the construction process—not their

fit with or alignment to some pre-conceived vision or opportunity. Each person who concretely stakes something to come on board contributes to shaping the vision and the opportunity, as well as enabling and executing particular strategies to achieve them. Whatever each stakeholder commits becomes a patch in a growing quilt whose pattern becomes meaningful only through the continual negotiation and re-negotiation of its appeal to new stakeholders coming on board. In other words, stakeholders commit resources in exchange for a chance to re-shape the goals of the project, to influence what future will ultimately result.

The process of negotiation and persuasion has two effects: On the one hand, with each new partner, the means of the venture increase (and once again, we are not talking only or even financial means here). On the other hand, with time, the goals of the venture crystallize and become increasingly hard to change.

At some point in the process, the converging cycle ends the stakeholder acquisition process; there is no more room for negotiating and maneuvering the shape of what will be created. As the structures of the market begin to take visible shape, it becomes important to re-evaluate the balance of prediction and control in the venture's strategies.

It is clear, therefore, that stakeholder commitments drive the dynamics of the effectual model. But how do the stakeholders decide whether to make that commitment or not? Later in this chapter we will look at elements such as persuasion and negotiation, but right now, let's look at those decision-making elements that are directly related to our effectual model:

- **Each stakeholder brings new means to the venture.** Each interaction combines means to create something novel and valuable, whether or not they are important to the new world they are transforming. In this way, the entrepreneur and the stakeholder select each other. Initially, every stakeholder interaction is as likely to change the shape of the new market being created, as it is to change the original set of means.

- **Each stakeholder strives to invest only what s/he can afford to lose.** Since it is not clear at the early stages of the effectual process what the pie will be, let alone how much each piece will be worth down the road, stakeholders cannot effectively use expected return as their immediate criterion for selecting resource investments. Instead, stakeholders have to reconcile within their own minds whether they can live with the loss of what they are investing in the enterprise. Here as well, the selection process goes both ways.

- **Any environment and epoch in human affairs contains unexpected contingencies.** If you don't allow contingencies to influence your venture, you end up with purely transactional relationships aimed at reaching a predetermined goal. Contingencies don't only undermine the value of current means in achieving given goals; they also provide opportunities to create new value through those means in pursuit of new goals. In the pre-commitment phase, surprises are an important shaping factor.

In the end, the new venture is the result of sufficient conditions as opposed to necessary conditions. As we illustrate in this chapter, Yngve Bergqvist created the ICEHOTEL by finding and working with enough interested stakeholders who were willing and able to invest enough to make the venture viable. If he had weighed all the evidence—both for and against the potential opportunity for an ice hotel—and waited to discover all the necessary conditions for the success of his venture, the venture would probably never have come to life.

OVERVIEW OF EFFECTUATION IN ACTION

The individual begins with an inventory of his or her means, deciding what s/he can do with the means at hand and enlisting others to join in co-creating the new venture.

The chain of commitments launched at the start of the venture has two impacts: It increases the resources available to the venture by increasing stakeholder ownership, while at the same time constraining the venture, crystallizing its goals, and helping it converge towards something specific, which may or may not be what the entrepreneur had in mind at the beginning.

As the effectual network grows to include more and more of the external world, it tends to become less effectual, slowly turning into a distinct new market.

The new market gets created, not through the designs of any one person, but as a result of the interaction between the current members of the network and those outside that network.

Any changes in the environment can provide the individual with new means, and kick start the cycle again. And any interactions that fail to gain the traction of commitment are considered dead ends, at least for the moment.

PRACTICALLY SPEAKING: ICEHOTEL

After five years working for a mining company in Kiruna, Sweden, Yngve Bergqvist realized what he did not want to do with his life—work for a big company. His colleagues' lack of enthusiasm for the job grated on him. And he found it impersonal and unpleasant having people refer to him by his employee number. But Yngve was an outdoorsman, and as an outlet from his job he took up river rafting. One day a tourist asked Yngve for a ride on the river. Suddenly, he was in business. He began going to the tourist office on weekend mornings, and nearly always found clients. Yngve

ultimately resigned from his mining job, and gradually expanded the rafting business to 40 summer employees and 30 boats.

But summer in Sweden is short, and rafting on the Torne River in winter is impossible. For starters, the river is frozen solid. Yngve needed to find a winter business to complement his summer earnings. He had heard about Japanese tourists visiting Alaska in winter to see the Northern Lights (Aurora Borealis), and wanted to learn more. In 1988 he traveled to Sapporo and Hokkaido, Japan, for the Snow Festivals, and there he met an ice sculptor from Asahikawa. Over beer, the two men planned a winter ice-sculpting workshop in Sweden. The

workshop received a lot of press, as numerous international artists, spectators, and local people flocked to Jukkasjärvi.

In recalling the event Yngve described the evening before as cold and clear. His family was there watching the beautiful ice sculptures take shape and they were so impressed. The local people in the village were taking photos.

But then, as Yngve recalled, "The next morning when I woke up at six, I heard something strange. I couldn't believe it . . . it was raining and it was plus seven degrees." The ice workshop was scheduled to start at 11 and the sculptors wanted to know what to do. Rather than trying to preserve something that belonged to nature, Yngve said, "Let it be destroyed and make something new when it is destroyed."

What they made new was the ICEHOTEL. It is a business that is the embodiment of Yngve. It is constructed each winter using ice from the Torne River, where he runs rafting trips, and employs skills learned during his ice-sculpting workshop. Yngve's friends at the Swedish tourist board then introduced him to Sakata, owner of a Japanese travel agency named Northern Express. A natural partnership ensued where Sakata generated interest in Japan for travel to Jukkasjärvi and Yngve provided Sakata's clients a wholly unique experience in Swedish Lapland including ice fishing, getting married in an ice chapel, or simply marveling at the art which is the ICEHOTEL itself.

WHAT MAKES PARTNERSHIPS WORK?

When it rained on Yngve Bergqvist's ice sculpture exhibit, there was more than one way to deal with the unpleasant surprise. Yngve could have gone back to the mines, or to the summer canoe job; his employees could have seen the madness in a project that was so weather dependent and cut their losses. Instead, some of them picked up their ice-sculpting tools and turned to the guests and press people who had come to see the sculptures. Some chose to learn the art of ice sculpting; others chose to make igloos. When night fell, the group that had been busy building igloos invited others to come and try to spend a night in their creations. Contrary to what they had imagined, it was not cold in the igloos. And it was not dark: in fact, the light coming through the ice made it shimmer in a translucent manner that was almost magical in its quality.

It is this partnership between ice sculptors and guests that truly launched the ICEHOTEL. There was no money involved, no big venture capitalist cash deal, nothing but a group of people who came back the following year to build another group of igloos.

Next, we map out the sequence of effectual partnerships that led to the creation of the ICEHOTEL.

Effectuation in Action

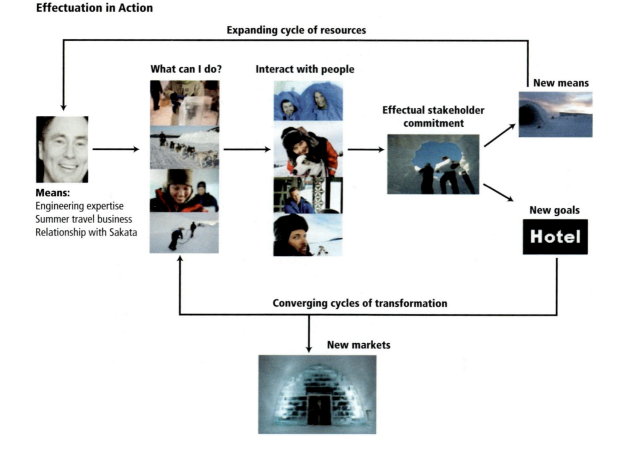

Vodka "in" the rocks

Yngve Bergqvist did not stop with the success of the ICEHOTEL. This "first round" provided him with new means. Even from the original ice sculpting exhibit, Yngve wanted his own Swedish icon to be associated with another Swedish icon, the premium vodka brand Absolut. In 1994 he wrote to Absolut, suggesting a partnership. Initially, Absolut was not interested in partnering with a tree-hugger building igloos in the far north of Sweden. Yngve persisted. And as often happens, he was helped by a little serendipity.

The ICEHOTEL featured a sculpture of a giant Absolut bottle as the centerpiece of its bar. As a result of an ICEHOTEL press release, a picture of the bottle made its way back to Absolut. At first incensed (the sculpture had not received their approval), the company started seeing the potential in a partnership. But their aspirations were much greater than ICEHOTEL.

Together, the tree hugger and the world's fourth largest spirit brand came up with the idea of launching ICEBARS around the world, using the ice from the Torne River—the very same ice that was used to build the ICEHOTEL.

The bars are kept at a constant temperature of –5°C. A selection of international artists and designers are invited to design the bars, which are transformed every six months. As with the ice hotel, everything is sculptured from ice—the bars, the stools, the glasses, the walls. While the original ice bar sits in the ICEHOTEL, today there are ICEBARs in Copenhagen, Tokyo, London, and Stockholm.

Ice in space?

Thanks to the partnership between ICEHOTEL and Absolut, ice is now the largest export product of that part of Sweden. The success of both ventures could have encouraged Yngve Bergqvist to stop there and focus on running the existing business. But the most unexpected partnership was yet to come. The ICEHOTEL has decided to link up with Virgin Galactic to sell space travel. Kiruna is the home of an ESA Space station and trips into space will start from this base, beginning in 2012. The trips will allow travelers to experience the Northern Lights in the winter or the midnight sun in the summer. Virgin had been looking for accredited space agents to take in bookings, and ICEHOTEL was looking to add new trips to the list of excursions available to their guests. And so a new partnership, and a new business venture, was born. Who knows what is next?

ON THE CONSEQUENCE OF COMMITMENT

The ICEHOTEL example helps us understand how stakeholder commitments shape ventures. The mutual commitments between the first stakeholders (Yngve and the tourist office, the sculptors, the press, the

travel agents . . .) forges an initial network that eventually transforms a budding reality into a new market. To the extent that neither party (Yngve nor his initial partners) had an idea of what the end product would look like, the market is not discovered but transformed, leading to the creation of something new. As such, the market truly is an outcome of the interaction between the partners. Initially, neither party knows what this new "thing" may or may not be worth down the road, or whether it will even end up looking like what they may be imagining. The entire process is driven by interaction—the stakeholders prospectively negotiate the very existence and shape of what will be.

Effectively, all the partners are negotiating for what the "thing" will be—not in a predictive sense (although prediction may be part of the reasons for negotiating), but merely in the sense

that all parties invest in and start making the "thing" happen. Even more importantly, their negotiations proceed as though everything and anything is possible until the last minute. There is always room for the actual transformation to surprise them with something neither knew existed. This cycle of effectuation in action is illustrated in the "Effectuation in action" diagram. As you appreciate the process behind ICEHOTEL, consider how Yngve used persuasion in order to bring partners together.

THE ART OF PERSUASION

In the first chapters we looked at the myth of the entrepreneur conquering the world through his or her unique vision of the future—nothing short of a genius able to convince others of the validity of his or her perspective. There is one point here that is important—if

you are going to work in an uncertain environment, with a product or service that is yet to be defined, you will need a strong ability in persuasion.

Back in the 1790s Adam Smith (1798:493–4) had already stated the following:

> Different genius is not the foundation of this disposition to barter which is the cause of the division of labor. The real foundation of it is that principle to persuade which so much prevails in human nature . . . We ought then to mainly cultivate the power of persuasion, and indeed, we do so without intending it. Since the whole life is spent in the exercise of it, a ready method of bargaining with each other must undoubtedly be attained.

Persuasion is critical. If you can't convince anyone to work and create with you—be it potential customers, suppliers, etc.—then you have no business. We are all persuadable to varying degrees. But what we tend to forget is that persuasion works both ways—the stakeholders, the partners who are co-opted into the venture by the entrepreneur, also persuade him/her.

Does this mean that to be a successful entrepreneur one needs to be an exceptional salesperson? The short answer is no.

Being persuadable and being able to persuade others of the validity of your proposition, however, is important. And, of course, there are many ways of doing this. For example, Robert Cialdini, a social psychologist and author of the bestseller *Influence: The Psychology of Persuasion* (2006), looks at what he calls "weapons of influence." We have listed them below. Think about how often you have been persuaded by one of these tools of influence:

- **Reciprocation**. If someone does you a favor, you tend to return it. Birthday presents and Christmas gifts are examples. Another example that Cialdini uses is that of Ethiopia donating humanitarian aid to Mexico after the 1985 earthquake, even as the country was going through famine and civil war. Ethiopia was reciprocating for the support received from Mexico when it was invaded by Italy in 1935.
- **Commitment and consistency**. Once a person has committed to do something, they will typically honor that commitment (with some variation depending on culture) even if the original incentive or motivation disappears. This speaks to basic principles of human psychology.
- **Social proof**. Human beings imitate each other.
- **Authority**. People tend to obey authority. This was strikingly demonstrated in a social sciences experiment run in the late 1960s in which people chosen randomly on the street were taken to a lab and asked to turn a dial on an electric chair. On the chair sat an actor posing as a criminal. When ordered to do so, the majority acted according to the instructions given to them, even though they knew very little about the facts.
- **Liking**. People are more likely to be persuaded if they like the person doing the persuading.
- **Scarcity**. Perceived scarcity creates demand, as everyone wants the product before it runs out. Apple did this well with the iPhone, as did Lipton with its green tea flavor—for a short period of time, the drink was available only at specific bars, which created demand for the drink.

In addition, Schotter's (2003) experiment (highlighted in the nearby box) points out that, in general, people prefer advice to information. This is contradictory to the commonly held wisdom that human beings are

Research roots

Advice

Recently, experimental economists have looked at the role of advice in decision-making. In a recent presentation of experimental results with naive advice, Schotter remarks: "Despite the prevalence of reliance on advice, economic theory has relatively little to say about it . . . [E]xperimental results . . . indicate that word-of-mouth advice is a very powerful force in shaping the decisions that people make."

Schotter's (2003) key findings:

- Subjects tend to follow the advice of naive advisors with hardly more expertise at the task than the subject.
- Advice changes behavior, with subject playing experimental games differently as a result of receiving advice.
- Given a choice between information and advice, subjects tend to opt for advice.
- Decision-making with naive advice tends to be closer to economic rationality than decisions made without advice.
- The process of giving and taking advice tends to foster learning.

Research roots

Persuasion

In his book *The Venturesome Economy*, Amar Bhidé (2008: 429) discusses the role of users in the innovation process, noting that entrepreneurs often start off with a component of a solution that customers then add to, and that the interaction is far more intense than the traditional model of focus groups for market research. He concludes that, "Buyers of new products face significant . . . uncertainty about the utility of their purchases, and in addition to good information, they need persuasion. In fact, persuasion is an essential ingredient of technological progress."

rational and make decisions divorced from emotions. If this were the case, we would prefer information over influence. In reality, it is influence and our willingness to be influenced that makes interactions possible. In turn, those interactions allow us to create something new.

PRACTICALLY SPEAKING: DRIVING THE FUTURE

Clean solution

Depending on whom you ask and where you look, automobiles account for at least one-fifth of the CO_2 we emit into our planet's atmosphere. Combine that with the fact that only 7 percent of the world's population owns a car today, and it is clear that to meet future transportation aspirations, and to aspirate ourselves, we need to rethink the fossil fuel car. This should pave an easy route for electric vehicles—except for a few small bumps in the road. Like the fact that the few electric cars on the market today have a short range. There are no charging stations. And even if

you do find a station, charging an electric car takes much more time than filling up a fuel tank.

Dirty job

So what is it going to take to drive electric vehicle adoption? Massive government legislation prohibiting automobiles with tailpipes? CO_2 levels so high there is a broad-based market for bottled oxygen? We suggest something even more extreme—the entrepreneur. By definition, the job of entrepreneurs is to create novelty from the things they have to work with and the people who join them on the journey. Enter Shai Agassi, founder of Better Place. In devoting his start-up to servicing electric vehicles, 42-year-old Agassi has positioned himself as the mechanic fixing the business problems associated with electric cars. And like any good entrepreneur, he already has his hands dirty.

Local limitation

Most electric automobiles today can travel a maximum of 150 miles on a

charge, or about a third as far as their fossil fuel peers. Without the immediate means to create an electric car with greater range, Agassi has focused on what he can control. As an Israeli, he chose his geographically constrained home country, where 150 miles is a long way, as the first place to roll out Better Place. And he is adding new geographies according to both the size and commitment of Better Place partners. Just about anywhere in Denmark is within about 200 miles of just about anywhere else in Denmark. And DONG, the local energy provider, invested US$140 million in Better Place. Denmark will host the second Better Place rollout.

Pricey placement

But whether it's in tiny Israel or sprawling India, a Better Place charging station for electric vehicles costs around US$500,000. Here again, Agassi has combined what he knows with who he knows to generate a solution. Prior to launching Better Place, Agassi founded TopTier Software, a provider of enterprise information portals, which was acquired by SAP in 2001. Using his knowledge and credibility in building cash flows around an emerging business, Agassi successfully attracted US$350 million in investment into Better Place in 2010. One of the major money sources was HSBC, which promised to partner with Better Place to expand into cities in China.

Slow current

Agassi has brought the power of partners to the problem of battery charging time as well. Together with electric vehicle manufacturer Nissan, he announced a plan to enable a battery exchange at Better Place vehicle charging stations. In less time than it takes to wrestle the hose to and from a fossil fuel pump, an automated process would remove an exhausted battery from the bottom of a car and install a fully charged one.

Spark of creation

Whether Better Place will turn out to be the future of driving or lose its charge remains to be seen. What is evident is what it takes to drive the future. In addition to being a transformation of the entrepreneur's resources together with his committed partners, Better Place is guided by something you might not expect: flexibility. Agassi's vision is simply to

Research roots

Markets are co-created

The explanations for how new markets come into existence cover the entire field of human studies, from psychology and sociology to institutional economics, strategy, and entrepreneurship. But none of these approaches agree or offer a comprehensive explanation for the generation of new markets.

Goodman (1983) was the first to move away from the search and select view of opportunity creation to look at markets from the perspective of transformation (something which he called the grue principle), and in particular transformation through co-creation. He theorized that when two stakeholders make a commitment, they transform what is there into something new—creation being an outcome of the interaction between the different stakeholders.

The field of marketing has also adopted a co-creational view through what is referred to as a service-dominant logic (Vargo and Lusch, 2004: 1–17).

make the world a better place by the year 2020. But whether that amounts to renting batteries, building service stations, renting electric cars, selling them, or installing home vehicle charging equipment seems secondary. By being open to a variety of possible goals, Agassi expands the ways he can steer his company. Is it time for you to move over to the driver's seat?

CREATING MARKETS THROUGH PARTNERSHIPS

Effectuation emphasizes pre-commitments from stakeholders as a way to reduce and/or eliminate uncertainty in the environment and as a way of expanding your means to generate something that may be very different

from the starting point. Effectual entrepreneurs do not choose stakeholders on the basis of preselected ventures or venture goals; instead, they allow stakeholders who make actual commitments to participate actively in shaping the enterprise.

Partners can come in very different shapes and forms—what matters is that they commit to a future in which they all find a stake, and influence/persuade each other as to what shape that future venture should take. In an effectual partnership, what matters is that both parties find something in it for them. The partnership between an environmental adventurer and a vodka manufacturer (see previous chapter) was an unlikely one. But the Absolut ICEBAR concept created something new for both parties, something beneficial to both, and something neither could have created on their own, irrespective of the size of their business or their values.

Getting started on building a stakeholder commitment could be the hardest part. Once the conversation has begun, the possibilities begin to unfold. So if you need a bit of inspiration to get yourself started, try the following exercise. Using a grid like this one, ideally on the back of a napkin (all good entrepreneurial ideas are first inked onto a napkin), sketch out that first interaction. Consider a specific individual you would like to approach to initiate a stakeholder commitment. On the left-hand side, inventory your own means and motives. On the right-hand side, do the same for your prospective partner. Then draw lines across the middle from your means to the partner's motivations and from his or her means to your motivations. Each line

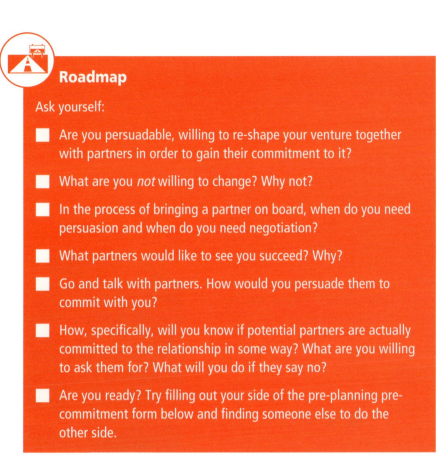

Roadmap

Ask yourself:

- Are you persuadable, willing to re-shape your venture together with partners in order to gain their commitment to it?
- What are you *not* willing to change? Why not?
- In the process of bringing a partner on board, when do you need persuasion and when do you need negotiation?
- What partners would like to see you succeed? Why?
- Go and talk with partners. How would you persuade them to commit with you?
- How, specifically, will you know if potential partners are actually committed to the relationship in some way? What are you willing to ask them for? What will you do if they say no?
- Are you ready? Try filling out your side of the pre-planning pre-commitment form below and finding someone else to do the other side.

PRE-PLANNING PRE-COMMITMENT

Me	Commitment	Other stakeholder
Means		Means
Motives		Motives

represents the basis of a possible commitment, and certainly gives you the foundation to start a conversation.

TAKEAWAY: BUY-IN IS BETTER THAN SELLIN'

We close this chapter with a practical answer to the philosophical question of how you balance persuasion with rationality. The answer is simply that *buy-in is better than sellin*. In other words, persuasiveness and rationality come together at commitment. So as nice as it is to have someone who is willing to make a transaction with you, what you really want is that concrete and rational commitment to co-creating an idea with you.

So what?

Partners self-select into new ventures, and commit different means to the effort. Without commitments, you don't have a partner; you have merely a potential partner. Committed stakeholders co-create ventures that don't always look like the original venture you had in mind. You influence them *and* they influence you.

??? Bigger questions

- How does focusing on how everyone is persuadable change how you view the world?

- When should you refuse to be persuaded?

Partnerships work through an effective sharing of risk, reward, and control.

CHAPTER 14

Ownership and control: Manage investors

■ ■ ■

AS YOU CONSIDER setting up your business, it is critical to understand the difference between ownership and control. Most people think they are the same. As a result, the natural reaction is to focus on how to retain equity in order to retain control. In this chapter we challenge you to think more deeply about what you really want from the venture. Do you want ownership? Do you want control? How are they different? Where does each come from? And how does the combination help you to design partnerships that work well for everyone involved?

THINKING BEYOND OWNERSHIP

The expected connection between ownership and control is clear. If you own more than half of the company, for instance, you control it—from the day-to-day operations to the overall shape and direction of the new venture—in theory at least. Venture capitalists know better. They understand that decision rights are a matter of the principle they establish with the entrepreneur and the terms they build into the contract. For example, they will negotiate specific rights on how the assets of the firm will be distributed in case of liquidity. They can specify when and where the venture can raise subsequent rounds of funding and even the conditions under which they can fire the founding CEO and members of the top management team. Additionally, they will have seats on the board with voting rights on a variety of issues. And they can do all this with only a minority ownership share in a venture. As you forge partnerships, whether it's with investors, customers, co-founders, or friends and family, this chapter will help you consider what you can offer each in terms of ownership versus control. If you can match the terms outlined above to the different kinds of relationships and objectives you envision in your own venture, you will be ready to build partnerships that are low on friction and high on productivity.

WHAT DOES OWNERSHIP BUY?

If ownership does not automatically give you control and decision rights, what does it buy you? The answer: residual claims.

Residual claims refer to anything of value that remains after all contractual rights and obligations have been fulfilled. In plain English, this means the owners of a new venture possess anything that remains after the firm's contracts are met and bills are paid. For example, if the firm is being liquidated, a variety of trade creditors, debt-holders, preferred shareholders, and others, who have specific rights written down in contracts, get paid before the common shareholders.

The intuition underlying the separation of ownership and control in a new venture is very similar. To the extent you can predict and plan for contingencies, you can write detailed contracts that specify who will do what, who has control over which decision, and how things will proceed. But ownership gives you control over all the things that cannot be predicted upfront and, therefore, cannot be contracted for in any reasonable detail. We know already from our understanding of entrepreneurial expertise and effectual logic that the key to building enduring ventures lies in the unpredictable. Hence, understanding and wisely allocating equity ownership—i.e. residual claims or control over the unpredictable—is an extremely important skill in the development of entrepreneurial expertise.

WHEN AND HOW TO USE EQUITY

Does this mean that you want to try to hold as much equity as possible at all cost and at all times? Not always. It means instead that you think through the subtleties of how to use equity—when to give it away and how much,

> **Trust**
>
> With self-selected stakeholders, you don't need to worry about trust and opportunism. Instead, you just focus on the commitments they make.

how to design contractual provisions, and so on. What is the mastery of colors and knives and brushes to the artist, so is the mastery of the role of equity for the expert entrepreneur.

First, through appropriate contractual provisions, you can share ownership of the financial returns of the venture without giving up decision rights. In other words, investors and other stakeholders can be entitled to receive a large percentage—say 70 percent of earnings—while having no rights whatsoever in making management decisions.

Second, you can provide equity on a temporary basis, with the right to buy it back based on meeting specific milestones. This is frequently a condition associated with short-term debt or loans.

And third, you can offer equity to bring high potential partners on board, using equity to align everyone's interests while keeping day-to-day management control through contractual provisions. It is up to you to decide, at any given point in time, exactly what you want and need in building your venture. Sometimes you might find the ability to make decisions in the face of unpredictable contingencies more valuable than the daily management of the venture. Depending on the direction of the venture, the right to a larger piece of the return may be more important than a hold on the day-to-day control of operations. And yet, at other times, you might want to give away equity to get great people on board and share larger pieces of the pie you co-create with these stakeholders.

Ultimately, it is up to you. You can make specific judgments as you build the venture and ensure technicalities are taken care of by good advisors. But it is crucial to understand the subtleties of ownership versus control before you take the plunge.

Food for thought

There are many alternatives to equity that will encourage people to join you in creating your venture, market, or product. You can offer investors a fraction of revenues, or even discounted products as opposed to equity. You can offer co-founders a sliding scale of salary versus stock. You can even offer new employees a better title or a nicer office instead of equity. If you are intent on holding onto equity you can, provided the alternative keeps the stakeholder engaged in the venture.

However paranoid you might feel about your venture, most outside stakeholders, even venture capitalists, do not want control over your venture. They want protection from downturns and optimal participation in upturns—the slice of the pie that matches their appetite to invest.

NOT ALL RECTANGLES ARE SQUARES: NOT ALL CONTROL IS COMPLETE CONTROL

We consider control to be the ability to direct the use of any particular resource. When can control be utilized? To what extent? To what end? By what processes? Control is never absolute. Different types of decisions involve different players, and when people are involved, it also involves persuasion, as everyone is self-directed. Sometimes you have a say in a matter, sometimes, you have *the* say in a matter. Control is rarely simple.

Ownership is connected to control, but it is not control. A clear example is ownership of public companies. There has been an entire body of academic research around agency theory. The fundamental observation is that owners explicitly *don't* control the operation of the firm, they sub contract the control to agents, i.e. the CEO, etc., who exercise that control. It is possible to control a large firm with relatively small amounts of ownership, if any at all. Then again, what does it mean to "control" a firm? Clearly if you own 100 percent of a firm you have significant control, but even then you do not have 100 percent control of

the entire venture, you simply have control of how you will lead the venture in reaction to the actions of the other stakeholders involved.

> Even Bill Gates, who clearly exercises a great deal of control over software giant Microsoft Corporation, only actually owns 9.4 percent of the outstanding shares of the firm (as of May, 2009).

Consider customers versus lenders versus investors versus co-founders and the ownership and control they enjoy in exchange for their commitment to the venture. Customers might have no ownership of your organization, yet they exert a lot of "control" in the form of influence and leverage, especially early on in the life of your organization.

Lenders might not have any ownership of the venture, but they exert significant control in how you use cash, while likely exerting little control on anything else. However, should financial problems arise, lenders can take complete control of the organization, without taking complete ownership. Investors have a range in the extent to which their ownership, purchased by providing cash to you, translates into control. In fact, venture investors are quite nuanced in the nature of their ownership, and the specific rights and situations over which they retain control. And that's the point—there is a suite of options and a mix of choices involved in the structure of ownership and the delineation of control.

The purpose of ownership

Ownership is primarily about two things: rewarding risk takers and providing incentives for success. A key difference between these two ideas is that the first is about the past, and the second is about the future. Ownership tends to spread to those people who assume risk when they commit resources to your venture. Obviously, it doesn't have to—people are often compensated directly for their commitments with salary, purchase orders, etc. But early in the life of a venture, sharing ownership is often involved in rewarding the risk takers.

Early investors will generally not buy out the entrepreneur of a venture entirely. While they may want to capture all of the "rewards" that have come from the success of the venture, they know that incenting the commitment of the entrepreneur going forward is even more important. As a venture grows up, there are a lot of "rules of thumb" about what the percentage of ownership ought to be. You can Google it for the latest variety of opinions. But we will offer one basic, not too unusual and reasonably fair, distribution here as food for thought: one-third to the founding team, one-third to venture investors, and one-third to the employees of the organization. It doesn't have to be that way—spending two-thirds of the equity of your venture to attract resources—but it's not outlandish.

Explained:

Agency theory

Dating back to the times of land barons and feudal farmers, the incentive difference between the owner and the worker has always been appreciated. It is the incentive of the worker to be paid as much as possible by the owner to do as little as possible. And it is the incentive of the owner to pay the worker as little as possible and get as much productivity as possible.

Management scholars refer to the owner as the "principal" and the worker as the "agent." The agent works on behalf of the principal. Land barons tried to resolve the agency problem by taking only a fraction of the crop the farmers produced. Thus, the farmer had some incentive to be productive, as the more they produced, the more they benefited. The same is true today for the sharing of equity. It is the goal of the owner of the venture, be it the founder or the investor, to provide incentives to the agents to be productive. Equity offers a strong incentive as the agent benefits directly from any value created. There are many other approaches to overcoming the agency problem, ranging from financial rewards, such as raises and bonuses, to less tangible rewards, such as promotions, more interesting work assignments, and public recognition of accomplishments.

BUILDING EQUITABLE PARTNERSHIPS

If everyone is equal, and receives an equal share of the pie, there is no issue. But what if some partners are senior and bring a lot of money, skills, credibility, or contacts? How do you divide the equity?

How does one share ownership wisely?

The secret: There is no right answer at the level of detail most entrepreneurs are seeking. What we know is that the split needs to sufficiently reward people for the risks they've taken, and sufficiently incent them to continue to risk their time, talent, and resources on the venture. Notions of fairness can get mixed into this discussion. Feelings can get hurt. Lawyers can even get involved. But in the end, it's the satisfaction that people feel with the agreement that is most important.

Where to start

Start by sitting down and mutually agreeing on the skill sets and other factors that will be required to make the venture successful in a specified period—say three years at the most. You'll be listing things like technical capability, selling, raising money, making contacts, running the operation, etc. Weight the factors. Do this together. If you disagree, talk it through until you agree. The conversation need not get emotional—you are understanding the business, its key success factors, and the skills you have available.

- Now take your list of weighted success factors and rate each of you on your ability to bring them to the business. Rate them on the same 0–10 scale.
- When you're finished, multiply these scores by the weighted factor and you'll have a mutually agreed upon measure of each person's relative contribution to the success of the business. And hopefully you'll have done it without any black eyes or injured egos.
- If you can't agree on what each of you is bringing to the business, you might want to reconsider whether you have the makings for a successful partnership to begin with.

Splitting the pie

Valuation and the resulting ownership is a stress-inducing topic. It can be legitimately thought of as fighting over a fixed pie—more for you is less for me. And, at some point in the future, *if* you are successful, real cash will change hands in line with these decisions such that *every* percentage point of ownership is connected to a material amount of money. However, even if greed were your *only* motivation (which we have yet to see) ownership percentage is *not* what you're trying to maximize. Cash is what you're trying to maximize. Sharing ownership wisely can create more cash than hoarding it. In new ventures, the pie is not fixed. You want to share ownership with talented people, partners, and providers of great resources.

✖🔧 PRACTICALLY SPEAKING: SHARING THE TREATS AMONG DOG FOOD INVESTORS

Castor & Pollux is an organic dog food company and a successful one. Founded by entrepreneurs with expertise in the

"Congratulations on becoming a partner—your share of company losses are £200,000."

How early stage investors learn about partners

Early stage investors learn about an entrepreneur's motivations before making an investment in many ways:

- **Referrals:** It's harder to fool people over time. Without referrals from people an investor trusts, it is very difficult to understand the core ability and motivation of entrepreneurs.

- **Interaction:** Meet time and again with the entrepreneurs to get a personal feel. Personal questions are fair game. Do you want to get rich? Do you want power and control? What kind of leader are you? How do you respond to disaster? How do you know?

- **Time:** While you are in a hurry when you're raising money, investors are not. Why hurry? It regularly takes 6 to 12 months to raise investment money, and over that timeframe they can see whether you're delivering on promises and remaining committed to the effort.

- **Committee:** Learn from the judgment of other angel investors, partners in venture capital firms, and other entrepreneurs.

Will the dogs eat the dog food? Testing your idea and getting it funded at the same time

Sometimes it's easier to grow your business with customers and suppliers than to raise investment capital. Why can't you just go sell what you're doing to buyers instead of raising money? You might find that you can do exactly that, lending great credibility to your business idea and to your own capabilities. A yes from a potential customer does not come easy. But a yes from an investor does not come easy either. And the yes from a customer is less likely to demand equity, and more likely to generate demand.

Real life: What else could Castor & Pollux have done for funding?

Imagine you are the founder of Castor & Pollux, looking for capital to expand an idea that is already growing. Think about the following questions and see how many alternative options you can come up with:

- Where might you find other potential sources of funding?

- What do you have to offer them?

- How would you approach them?

- What would they want from you?

pet food business, they chose to bring in a significant amount of angel investment to jump on what they saw as a great opportunity.

They doubled revenues for the first several years and continue to grow very quickly. Over the course of five years they moved, grew facilities, added people, changed packaging, increased marketing, and put that early capital to great use. It cost them about one-third of their business, board seats, and the requirement of sharing some control on major decisions.

They reached a point where early investors wanted to cash in their ownership. At the same time, the venture attracted later stage private investors willing to invest, bring additional expertise, and buy the ownership of those early investors at an attractive price. The entrepreneurs continue to own a significant portion of the venture, but it keeps shrinking.

Today, the entrepreneurial team owns much less then half of the business, yet they still hold substantial control of it within the bounds of a whole suite of

stakeholders, including new investors, original investors, lenders, customers, suppliers, and employees. Decisions about additional rounds of financing, new board members, new executives, strategic changes to the operation, and major capital expenditures are more explicitly group decisions. They would add, of course, that all of this takes place under the strict oversight of culinary-minded canines!

THE LANGUAGE OF VALUATION, TRANSLATED INTO CONTROL

With investors, valuation and ownership are more explicit than with partners. To start with, we need to be sure whether we are talking about the value of the venture before an investment or after an investment. Pre-money value is simply the value of the venture before the investor puts his or her cash into the venture. There is a corresponding post-money valuation, simply the pre-money valuation plus

BOARD QUESTIONS

	What you need to know about boards
Why do I need a board in the first place?	If you have a broad-reaching business concept and you want your business to mature, you should consider a board. You will not possess all the functional skills necessary to make sound judgments consistently. Nor, most probably, will you be able to afford that expertise and skills in the early stages. Having a board of advisors with balanced skills and experience will come in handy. The board can help you with financing and finding new customers. It will provide specific advice, offer wisdom of prior experience, keep you focused on agreed-upon strategy, and provide credibility to outside parties such as bankers and investors. And most important, it will be there to ensure you make fewer mistakes. Everyone needs to be accountable to someone, and as founder you will be accountable to the board. As one entrepreneur said, "I needed the board to save the company from myself."
Who should be on my board?	Initially, the board can be made up of insiders if you do not have outside investors. But it is better to have some members on the board who have complementary background skills to yours. So, if you have questions, instead of calling professionals such as attorneys and paying them US$250 an hour, you can pick up the phone and call your board member. You try to find people for your board who have been there and done it before.
When do I need the board—at what stage?	Consider having a board from inception. If not, you must have one by the time you want to raise outside capital. The board is there to help with current and strategic issues, but typical issues at different stages can look like the following, with board members focusing on needs at the relevant stage: **Stage → expertise/need** Seed → financial, legal, business development Emerging management → industry expertise, market, financial, legal, management Growth → similar to emerging, add in strategic Mature → strategic, market, financial, management
Do I need a board of advisors or a board of directors?	An advisory board works fine until you are in real business. But once you start bringing in cash, it is time to create a board of directors. The members should have specific responsibilities, be compensated, and they can also be fired. In choosing board members, setting these expectations up front is important. Your directors comprise your company's governing body and have fiduciary responsibilities for which they can be held legally accountable. Your advisors, by contrast, are high-level strategists—or mentors. For small companies, directors are generally shareholders and thus already have an incentive to spend their time on your company. Many companies might compensate advisors with a small token of stock, but most advisors are motivated not by money, but by the ability to help mentor an entrepreneur.
How do I find those people who can sit on my board?	Start with people you know and people who already care about and are deeply involved in your enterprise or industry. Do not take rejection personally. Good people have options, commitments, and not much spare time. When you find someone worthy, share your passion with him or her and candidly explore how s/he can add value to your organization. Appeal to someone who would like to help you. Self-selected stakeholders willing to make real commitments of time and interest are best. The key is to find those you want to work with and get them to want to work with you—not by "selling" them on the deal, but by persuading them enough so they sell themselves.
How do I know whether I have the right people?	Carl F. Frischkorn, a successful entrepreneur, angel investor, and board member with many young companies, talks about his three criteria for choosing which boards to participate in: *I have to like the CEO as a person. I need to believe that the person has good ethics and integrity. A person who would listen and also argue. If she wins the argument, then she wins, but if she didn't, she has to make a change. I think it's fantastic to stand up for what you believe in, but you also need to respond to feedback and then make the changes.* *I have to like the product, understand the concept, and think that the product has good market acceptance and growth opportunity.* *I have to think that I can add value being involved as an advisor.*

BOARD OPERATIONS

	What you need to do with your board
What are the duties of directors?	You should create job descriptions for members of the board before bringing them in. In general, the major responsibilities of a board are to: • participate in policy formulation and financial and strategic planning • serve as a sounding board to the CEO in major decisions • evaluate the performance of senior management • determine the compensation of senior management • ensure adequacy of financial controls and monitor compliance with laws and regulations • advise on succession planning.
How engaged should my board be?	Boards can have varying degrees of engagement. For some companies, boards are passive, functioning at the discretion of the CEO. They only ratify management's decisions. At the other extreme, some boards are operating boards, making all the key decisions, while the management is simply present to implement those decisions. A properly engaged board will provide insight, advice, and support to the CEO. It will oversee both your performance and your company's and add value to decisions by providing the necessary expertise. Good board members will not hesitate to pick up the phone and call people for you or call you on their own initiative when they come across information or possibilities—both positive and negative—for the survival and health of the business.
What is the best use of my time with the board?	Boards function best when they are tightly managed and have enough diversity of experience. Bring in people who are neither afraid to question your judgments, nor uncomfortable with your independence with regard to the final decision. And when you have a working board, communicate with them as much as you can. Hold four to ten meetings a year. Talk to them by phone whenever you are in doubt or need a certain expertise. Prior to every meeting, preview key issues with each director and provide a written agenda and information package at least a week in advance. Give your directors bad news quickly and be measured with good news. Taking care of key issues will ensure your board remains focused and comes to your assistance. Otherwise, you may start seeing your board meetings as a waste of time.
How do I compensate board members? What's in it for them?	Signing on is one thing, contributing to the board is another. So, you must keep your board members interested. With advisory boards, the problem is that you can never pay them what they're worth. One way of keeping them interested is to pamper them. Send them free company products, pay for dinner at the best places in town, and if possible arrange out-of-city meetings and pay for spouses to attend. The best way to keep them interested is by communicating regularly. What's in it for them? It is the pride in helping the youngster. To some of them, it will be like a second chance. If you have a formal board of directors, make sure they have some skin in the game. Use stock, warrants, options, and cash to keep their interest. Often, the entrepreneur will believe that board members serve because they like serving. But ultimately, all of us want to be paid for our time. If your advisory board transforms into a real board and you want it to work properly, set aside 3 percent to 10 percent of the company as a compensation for what they are doing. Do not assume that there is a standard package for compensation. People care about different things, and they often work for strange things. This is where it is important to spend whatever time it takes while recruiting board members and setting expectations up front. You are building a long-term relationship. Take the time to get to know each other and what you care about and why.
What are the other common conflicts that I should be aware of?	If the board is informal in structure and it is time to make a real board of directors, compensation issues may arise. The first conflict usually happens over valuation of the director's time and expectations. As founder, you will be working 365 days a year; your advisors will probably give 5 percent of their time. So when there is a question of sharing the pie, you may think they are asking too much. The solution is to be upfront about the issue. The second conflict usually comes if, as founder, you are unable to grow with the company. Running a company at the start-up stage is very different from running it when it is big and mature; it requires different skill sets. Conflict arises if you are unable to change and your board thinks you are unfit to be the CEO. The only solution is to learn to manage your company well. As long as you are making good decisions, your board members and investors will not want to take the company away from you. They would rather spend 5 percent of their time on the company and not be involved in day-to-day affairs. Remember, they have other businesses to run too.

Explained:

Dilution protection

Existing investors may try to protect themselves from dilution of ownership when new investors bring more cash into the company. The most straightforward anti-dilution protection is the right of first refusal, pre-emptive rights (also called "pro rata"). These establish the right of an investor to invest in the company before new investors, and they may be capped at the amount of investment that would keep their ownership percentage the same (i.e. if they own 20 percent, they have right of first refusal on whatever shares in the new round it would take to keep them at 20 percent, but they have no more). Sometimes they are not capped, meaning an investor has first rights to all future rounds. A special version of this is called a ratchet, which protects existing investors in the event of a "down round" (when the value of the firm drops over time) by maintaining their ownership percentage even if new investment is brought in at a lower valuation. Anti-dilution enables early investors to maintain control.

the amount of cash the investors put into the company, and ending ownership percentages are determined using post-money value as the denominator. For example, if an investor puts US$1 million into a venture with a pre-money value of US$2 million, they own US$1 million worth of a US$3 million business or one-third of the company (and remember, this doesn't mean they control one-third of everything). Investors may want to guarantee that they can always own their fraction of the business, and ask for anti-dilution protection.

A lot of time can be spent negotiating the pre-money valuation of a venture and the terms of the investment. This is understandable because the higher the pre-money valuation, the less dilutive the investment is to the current owners, but the less attractive the deal is to new investors. In that

regard, it's just like buying a house: A higher price is great for the sellers and worse for the buyers. But, in this case, the seller and the buyer have to cooperate after the fact, extensively. In fact, their ability and desire to cooperate effectively is part of what expands the pie, making consequences of valuation less clear cut than "higher is better" for the seller.

One concrete example of this is the consequences that high valuation has for future fundraising. An empirical fact: The average series A pre-money valuation for a venture taking on formal venture capital investment is approximately US$6 million. If an entrepreneur is able to raise angel investment at a valuation of US$12 million, it is significantly more difficult to raise that series A money from formal venture capitalists (VCs). This is the case for two reasons: 1) The angel investors

object because it results in dramatic dilution to their ownership percentage, and 2) the VCs object because, at times, the dynamic produced by such a dramatic drop in valuation really undermines the ability of the group to grow the pie in the future; it complicates things and can simply be an easy excuse to say no and move on.

You can Google a whole litany of advice around what the "right" pre-money valuation of a venture should be. These are mostly rules of thumb around how much a patent should be worth or what the value of having a completed product is, along with various other milestones that can serve as a guide for valuation. We won't summarize them here.

Within the conceptual bounds of valuation in later financing rounds, there are really two things that dictate valuation in early stage ventures. The venture needs X amount of cash, and the investor is only willing to invest if s/he can own Y of the venture. Different people independently determine these.

For example, an entrepreneur needs to raise US$500,000 to complete a prototype and win her first major customer. An angel investor prefers to invest in opportunities where he can own around one-third of the business, so long as he has a seat on the board of directors and a say in the hiring of executives. If they were to execute the transaction, the valuation is essentially deduced rather than negotiated: US$500,000 is one-third of US$1.5 million, thus the post-money is US$1.5 million and the pre-money is US$1 million.

Explained:

Liquidation preferences

Often, shareholders will establish a claim on who gets paid first. A 1× liquidation preference means that shareholders with that right gets the amount of their investment paid to them first and foremost in the occurrence of a liquidity event. For example, if they invested US$1 million and the business sells for US$10 million, US$1 million is paid to them before any sort of allocation of capital according to ownership percentages is made. A 2× preference would mean that the first US$2 million would go to them, and the remaining US$8 million would be shared among owners that participate in the general ownership of the venture. Liquidation preferences give some owners priority over other owners.

Explained:

Protective covenants

These are specific rules about what types of votes, and by whom, are made for specific decisions of the venture. Decisions about new board members, changes in the size of the board, new rounds of financing, executive compensation, stock option plans, major capital expenditures, and so on can be detailed in such a way that the voting rights on a particular topic are not represented by the ownership percentages overall.

This may lead the entrepreneur to say, "I don't want to sell my stock at that valuation—US$1 million is way too low." Thus, she might like to sell less stock at that valuation; maybe she'd only want to raise US$250,000. However, the angel investor would still want to own about one-third of the company. The entrepreneur may have to find a different angel investor to accomplish the goal of selling less stock because the investment isn't being determined by the valuation. It's often the other way around; the valuation is being determined by the separate preferences of the entrepreneur and the angel investor.

There is a lot written about valuation, and you should read it before you start thinking about a term sheet for raising venture investment.

TERM SHEETS: EVERYTHING IS NEGOTIABLE

If investors and entrepreneurs are able to come to an agreement, the specifics are written down on a term sheet. Not all terms sheets use all the elements we discuss here. Angel investor term sheets tend to be less complicated than formal VC term sheets. As the venture grows and goes through many funding rounds, different rights are often assigned to different series of preferred stock issuance, and to common stock. All the terms are subject to the golden rule: S/he who has the gold makes the

The view from above: How advisory boards are different from boards of directors

An advisory board is most useful in providing strategic ideas or feedback on increasing revenue and building your business, with the members not involved in the details of your company. You go to them, as you would to an old high school friend whom you don't see often, to catch up and pick their brains—for a view of your landscape from 20,000 feet.

The members of your board of directors, by contrast, are more like your parents, the people you go to when you are up against it and you need not so much advice, but guidance on a day-to-day basis about how to navigate choppy waters: a lawsuit, for example, or the sale of your company. These people give you the view of your business from 200 feet.

Hoffman (2003)

The yellow sari

In Bollywood movies, when the heroine wears a yellow sari it usually signifies that something big is about to happen in the plot of the movie. If there is a yellow sari moment in the entrepreneurship classroom, it has to do with learning how to use equity as a tool in building new ventures. Students confuse equity with (a) control—or the right to make and implement key decisions; (b) piece of the pie—rights to the returns earned; or (c) compensation—for inputs brought into the venture (such as ideas, technical knowhow, money, effort, reputation, etc.). Equity can, and of course should, be used as all of the above. But the important point is that it is *not* the same as any of these. Equity is like the trump card in a card game. It can substitute for any card in the deck. The key is to know when to use it as what. By assuming in advance that it is any one card, even the Ace of Spades, we may be jeopardizing our chances of winning the game. Furthermore, in the case of equity in a new venture as opposed to a trump card in a card game, we can play the trump card again and again and sometimes just temporarily lease or even pawn it with the possibility of redeeming it under circumstances we negotiate for. So mastering the use of equity is truly key to how the story of the new venture will turn out. Beware, therefore, of the yellow sari—whenever it shows up, the plot is about to change—and the fate of the new venture is literally at stake.

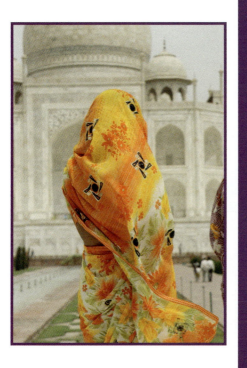

rules. When a venture must raise more cash or die, the negotiation power clearly lies in the hands of the incoming investors. All of these terms are then subject to re-negotiation at that point. Broadly speaking, good terms align the objectives of the investors and the entrepreneurs, while protecting the investors from entrepreneurial recklessness (it isn't the entrepreneur's money, so agency risks come into play) and protecting the entrepreneur from investor intrusiveness (because too many chefs spoil the broth).

There are hundreds of actual term sheets to be found floating around the internet or at universities, think tanks, law firms, etc. These term sheets can provide a black and white picture of how ownership is separate from control, and even how ownership can apply to different things. For example, ownership can change at different levels of upside, or downside, liquidity events, and even change over time. The details will pile up as your venture grows. Google away on these topics, and seek your own legal advice.

INVESTOR PERSPECTIVE: ANGELS

Angel investors often provide the seed capital for start-ups. They will invest less and earlier than VC firms. Typically, an angel investor will ask for between 20 percent and 50 percent of firm ownership. They may invest as little as US$1,000 and more than US$5 million.

Angel investors often feel that the valuation of a company is less than what the entrepreneur has proposed, and given the early and uncertain nature of the opportunity, it is hard to measure and even harder to figure out how to measure. Investors will work with the entrepreneurs' financial projections and use various valuation methods such as transactional value, market value, and return as a multiple of investment. The valuation methodology most frequently used is backing

What the investor sees in your venture

Venture investing is difficult and risky. Investors look at many deals and only invest in those on which they are incredibly bullish. In spite of this, they are wrong more often than they are right, and are more likely to lose money than make money on any venture investment. Angel investors lose money in nearly two-thirds of their investments. The wins have to cover all of the losses, and take into account the dilution in ownership over time.

You may believe you will sell the business for US$100 million in five years because the opportunity is incredible. An early stage investor can invest US$500,000 for one-third ownership, creating a US$33 million return in only five years. Seem obscene? You do the work, they make US$32.5 million.

Reality check. Most likely, you will return less than US$500,000 to that investor. Second, in order to grow the company to where you can sell it for US$100 million, you will raise additional capital, and the initial investor might see ownership percentage go from one-third to one-tenth, meaning that they would get US$10 million of the US$100 million exit, a very nice return, 20 times their investment, but nowhere near US$33 million. Reduce that by the risk of the entrepreneur not achieving targets, competitive entry, and difficulty of liquidity, and you see why the investor is slow to write a check.

Faces and wallets

Wallets always come with faces. So why not target faces instead of wallets? Luckily, faces often come with wallets too, so by starting with your means, particularly the means of who you know, you may generate good leads for investment. And having a relationship with people who invest in you will also make it easier for you to anticipate what kind of interaction your investors will want. And early stage investments are rarely at arm's length, so no matter what, you get the face with the wallet.

Summary: Ownership and control in term sheet terms

As you face a term sheet, think about trade-offs along the dimensions of ownership and control:

Ownership

- *Ratchet:* If there is a down round (valuation lower than the previous), early investors may protect against dilution, by adding a "ratchet" to their anti-dilution to adjust the price of their previous investments to new round.

- *Right of first refusal:* Major investors get the right to maintain ownership percentage on future financing.

- *Liquidation preferences:* Major investors get paid first in a liquidity event.

Control

- *Directors:* The ability to add a person to the board in conjunction with an investment.

- *Information rights:* Monthly or quarterly internal statements—and annually reviewed or audited statements.

- *Voting rights:* Preferred vote with common shares, except as required by law.

LAWYER QUESTIONS

	What you need to know about lawyers
Do I need a lawyer to incorporate?	Technically, no. A person can incorporate a business without the help of a lawyer. Check your government web sites for information; a simple incorporation (called an 'S corporation in the US') with one owner and no shareholders might take 20 minutes to register, with minimal fees applied. But it is always better to use professional help when you are not an expert. Good professional advice will save you from making mistakes that may prove costly down the line, especially if you anticipate having investors or selling your company later.
	There are even online services that take the place of live attorneys. They gather information from clients and automatically draft and customize the articles, bylaws, corporate minutes, stock certificates, and federal forms for each individual business. But because of the automation, it is sometimes difficult to completely customize. For example, creating specific bylaws within the Article of Incorporation is not possible using most of the online services.
How do I find a lawyer?	Ask the people you know and like—your professor, your friends or, someone who is doing business locally. Those people should be able to point you to one or two good lawyers. Find and talk to at least a couple of people before you decide on the person or company to go with.
What is the first meeting with a lawyer like? What do I say?	Usually lawyers will not charge you for the first meeting. This is the time to see whether that particular lawyer will be a good fit for you. Remember, the lawyer will also be trying to learn about you and decide whether s/he wants to do business with you. The first meeting involves bringing the lawyer up to speed on your business. What is the product? Who are the customers? What does the future of the business look like? And so forth.
	Have a set of questions ready for each lawyer. That way, you will be able to compare them before choosing. You should be asking the lawyer's opinion on: • what type of business entity you should choose given the business and its future vision • any other issues such as patents, copyrights, and other intellectual property rights (depending on the nature of the business, you may need other clearances).
What if I cannot afford to pay the lawyer? Do I offer him or her equity?	To the greatest extent possible, treat a lawyer as a professional service that you pay for. Good and understanding lawyers usually cut start-ups some slack because they think of working with you as an investment. They expect future returns—repeat business, referrals—when you grow.

Roadmap

Consider your own venture or one you know well:

- [ ] What do you need to have control rights over in order to make this venture succeed?

- [ ] Can you gain any level of influence or control over those needs without owning anything? You might be surprised how far you can get on this front.

- [ ] How will you use equity to align interests and encourage everyone to give their all? Who needs equity, and who doesn't, in order to accomplish that?

- [ ] What can you do for and with those stakeholders who don't want equity?

- [ ] What terms do you really care about if you are going to take an investment? Do you have to be in charge? Are you willing to sell the business? Are you willing to let others influence and possibly control major decisions facing this venture?

- [ ] Do you need a board of directors? Why? What value do you want to derive from that board? What will it take to build a board that you truly value? How will you attract and reward them (think beyond mere money).

into exit value. For example, if the company is expected to be worth US$50 million in five years, the company needs to raise a single round of US$1 million to reach that valuation and the investors will require a 10X cash-on-cash return upon exit, i.e. the investors' share must be worth US$10 million in five years. Thus, the investors would need to own 20 percent of the company, which implies a US$4 million pre-money valuation and US$5 million post-money valuation (this presumes no further dilutive capital is needed).

It is often said that because angels invest early and small, they miss out on the home runs. But based on our research, that appears not to be true. While the downside of an angel investor is less (from making smaller investments), the upside is as limitless as it is for the venture capitalist who must invest much larger amounts at later stages in the venture life. Because angels invest smaller amounts, they can make more investments and increase the chances of a home run.

TAKEAWAY: GOOD PARTNERSHIPS MAKE GOOD VENTURES

Regardless of whether your objective is to become obscenely wealthy or to create something of enduring value to society (or perhaps both), partnerships are a critical element of the formula. Structuring partnerships with investors, employees, board members, customers, and even lawyers demands a detailed understanding of the softer side—what each party values in the interaction. And it demands technical proficiency with structuring deals

So what?

Control does not equal ownership—you can get a whole lot of control without ownership, and control rights can be assigned very specifically to different aspects of what your venture is working toward.

Ownership enables alignment of incentives around the creation process.

along the dimensions of control and ownership. The key aspects that underpin negotiating any arrangement include determining and articulating the appropriate level of risk, the appropriate amount of control, and equitable provisions for ownership and liquidity.

It is important to realize that the spirit on both sides of the agreement is likely more important than the actual text of the agreement. As the venture, the environment, and the constellation of partnerships change, there is much opportunity for re-interpretation of the terms of the agreement, and it is useful to be able to fall back on a shared spirit. Further, if lawyers have to get involved to sort out differences in understandings of control or ownership, the likely outcome is that nobody wins, so it is good to be able to set as much shared foundation upfront as possible.

Bigger questions

- Who really owns the firm (customers, investors, management, society)?

- Where does control come from (how much is earned and how much is bestowed)?

- What is the role of the entrepreneur—to control or to own?

- What is the real cost of money?

CHAPTER 15

The question is not whether the unexpected will present itself in the new venture creation process.

The question is when and whether you will take advantage of it.

Optimists and pessimists

Both optimists and pessimists contribute to our society. The optimist invents the airplane and the pessimist invents the parachute.

G.B. Stern, novelist

A pessimist sees the difficulty in every opportunity; an optimist sees the opportunity in every difficulty.

Winston Churchill

The lemonade principle: Leverage surprise

AS WE SAW IN the story of ICEHOTEL (Chapter 13), contingencies can mark important turning points in the history of a venture. In the case of the ICEHOTEL, rain on ice sculptures was an unpleasant surprise. It wasn't what was meant to happen. But the ICEHOTEL story illustrates that contingencies—even negative ones—can be leveraged in positive ways. Instead of coping with the rain or trying to overcome it, Yngve Bergqvist did something a little less obvious: In his words, he "invented a new feeling"—instead of trying to preserve something against the forces of nature, he actually leveraged the natural process by letting the sculptures be destroyed and making something new in their place.

This response epitomizes the lemonade principle—the widespread bromide: "When life gives you lemons, make lemonade." It's the idea that in entrepreneurship as well as in other areas of life, you can often do well by acknowledging and appropriating the accidental events, meetings, and information that the environment serves up. Traditional entrepreneurship models suggest entrepreneurs should envision where they want to go, set goals, and do fairly extensive planning to reach them before they venture into a new business. However, while there are benefits of these activities, it is easy to overlook the costs. Pre-made plans tend to lead you to avoid surprises, try to overcome them, or adapt to them. In the meantime, by treating every surprise as a problem, you are missing out on the upside opportunity that surprises—even negative ones—potentially entail.

Instead of looking at the unexpected as a problem, it can be looked at as a building block—a resource—for a new venture. In every new venture, the entrepreneur knows some of the building blocks when s/he starts the venture but other building blocks are acquired along the way. In other words, some of the materials that the venture will be constructed from will only become known to the entrepreneur after the venture gets started. Expert entrepreneurs exploit contingencies as building blocks for their new ventures. For them, the unexpected event does not represent a loss of control over the situation; it is an opportunity to exercise control of an emerging situation by pointing it in a new direction.

In many ways, the lemonade principle lies at the heart of entrepreneurial expertise. It says that the unexpected is not a cost to a new venture; instead, it is a resource that may be turned into something valuable in entrepreneurial hands. Surprises may be few or many, come soon or take their time, and may be good or bad. But whatever form they take, whenever they come along, and however frequently they occur, they can be used as inputs into new ventures. Entrepreneurs can't predict surprises, and can't design them, but they can try to exploit them by incorporating them and rebuilding their venture around them as they go along.

EXAMPLES OF CONTINGENCIES IN NEW VENTURES

If you are reading this book, you probably know a story of how a contingency shaped an entrepreneur's new business enterprise. Famous stories abound of the role of the unexpected in entrepreneurship. We describe three of our favorites (with a bonus anecdote about Silly Putty), which should give you a feel for the range of contingencies that individuals leverage into ventures. As you read them, think about how they can be classified into groups—in the next section we'll talk more about what the underlying themes are.

PRACTICALLY SPEAKING: STAPLES

A terrific example of the role of contingency in the creation of new ventures can be found in the history of Staples, the discount office supplies superstore. Having recently lost his job working for a supermarket, Thomas Stemberg was formulating a business plan for a supermarket chain when he ran out of the printer ribbon for his Apple ImageWriter. It was the Thursday before the July 4 holiday weekend in the US, 1985. When he went to local stores to obtain a new printer ribbon he found that either they didn't have the ribbon he needed, or that the store had closed early for the holiday weekend. The simple information that printer ribbon was unobtainable was a trigger for Stemberg to have a new idea. In a later interview with CNN, he said, "It dawned on me that not only could small entrepreneurs not get stationery at the rate of bigger companies, sometimes they couldn't get it at all." Because he didn't have the printer ribbon, Stemberg couldn't finish his business plan for a supermarket chain over the weekend, but by then that issue was moot. Out of the contingency, he had created a new idea for a venture he wanted to start—a chain of office supply stores.

PRACTICALLY SPEAKING: J.R. SIMPLOT'S TAKE-OFF

Contingency often occurs in the form of unexpected people arriving on your doorstep. An example of this can be found in the history of J.R. Simplot, the potato magnate. Simplot built a business storing and sorting potatoes and onions during the Great Depression. Silver (1985) recounts that:

[I]n the spring of 1940, Jack Simplot decided to drive to Berkeley, California, to find out why an onion exporter there had run up a bill of US$8,400 for cull (or reject) onions without paying. . . . The girl in the office said that the boss wasn't in. J.R. said that was fine; he would wait until the man arrived.

Two hours later, at ten o'clock, a bearded old man walked in. Assuming this was his debtor, Simplot accosted him. But he turned out to be a man named Sokol, inquiring why he was not getting his due deliveries of onion flakes and powder. They sat together until noon, but still the exporter failed to arrive.

As the noon hour passed, Simplot was suddenly struck with an idea. He asked the bewhiskered old trader to a fateful lunch at the Berkeley Hotel. "You want onion powder and flakes," said J.R., "I've got onions. I'll dry 'em and make powder and flakes in Idaho."

Thus, through a contingent meeting with Sokol, Simplot found an opportunity to get into a new business. He went on to develop one of the largest agricultural businesses in the US.

PRACTICALLY SPEAKING: STEVE MARIOTTI'S FOUNDING OF NFTE

Sometimes contingent events come in rather unfortunate forms. In the case of Steve Mariotti, a mugging at the hands of six teenagers was the trigger event. In September 1981 Mariotti was walking in the Lower East Side of Manhattan when a group of youths surrounded him, slapped him, knocked him to the ground, and threatened to throw him into the East River. Their target: a US$10 bill he was carrying. Traumatized by the event, but determined to make something positive out of it, Mariotti decided to become a high school teacher in a New York City neighborhood in an effort to do what he could to improve the lives of young people in the inner cities by contributing to the education system. His experiences teaching high schoolers about making money led him to see the potential in entrepreneurship as a tool for changing people's lives, and he went on to found the NFTE (the National Foundation for Teaching Entrepreneurship), which is dedicated to educating kids about the possibilities for using entrepreneurship to better themselves.

Practically speaking

Silly Putty

Perhaps one of the best-known stories of a new venture founded on a contingency is Silly Putty. The substance was actually the result of a failed experiment to create synthetic rubber during World War Two in General Electric's New Haven laboratory. General Electric bounced the idea around for years in search of a practical use, but it wasn't until 1949 that Peter Hodgson, an unemployed advertising agent, encountered the compound as part of the entertainment at a party. Finding the stretchy material was an accident, but Hodgson did what he could with that contingent event. Unemployed and US$12,000 in debt, he saw potential opportunity and borrowed US$147 to produce a batch of the stuff. He renamed it Silly Putty and used his public relations skills to get it featured in Doubleday book stores, Neiman-Marcus and *The New Yorker* magazine. To everyone's amazement, sales took off. Peter Hodgson laughed all the way to the bank. When he died in 1976, his estate was worth US$140 million.

Photo provided courtesy of Crayola LLC, used with permission. © 2010 Crayola. Silly Putty® is a registered trademark of Crayola LLC.

UNDERSTANDING THE DIFFERENT KINDS OF CONTINGENCIES THAT CAN OCCUR

In general, contingency can be thought of as something that is a mere possibility that might or might not happen. Contingencies are, therefore, unnecessary things that can occur but also could not have occurred. In other words, there is no logical necessity for them to happen. Instead, they fall in the realm of pure chance or in that realm of things that happen without a specific known cause.

Contingencies come in many different shapes and sizes, so it is helpful to have a rudimentary way of thinking about how they can be categorized and how those categories might differ from one another. For instance, though the stories just told are all instances of contingency, in fact they are examples of three very different kinds of contingencies.

Unexpected meetings

One category of contingencies is accidental interactions with other people. Either you might meet a particular person by pure chance, or the content of your interaction with a person may be contingent. Both kinds of contingencies are illustrated by the Simplot story (see page 141), in which Simplot meets Sokol by accident, but also in which the two men strike up an unanticipated conversation about onion powder and flakes. Research in entrepreneurship suggests that meetings like the one between Simplot and Sokol are far more likely than you might think—for example, in one study of new technology at MIT, all eight of the entrepreneurs who tried to commercialize a particular invention were introduced to the new technology by someone directly involved in its development.

Unexpected events

Unexpected events are one of the major themes historians talk about, so much so that there is a new genre in the profession of counterfactual history—of wondering what might have been if such-and-such hadn't happened. Classic examples of the important role accorded to contingent events can be found in military history: Rain on the battlefield bogged down Napoleon's troops at Waterloo, allowing Wellington to carry the day; and a savage sea storm that scattered the Spanish Armada and saved Elizabethan England from invasion.

Steve Mariotti's mugging (page 142) serves as the classic contingent event,

SURPRISE AT WORK IN VENTURE CREATION

	Unexpected information	Unexpected meetings	Unexpected events
Positive (serendipitous)	Innis & Gunn (Chapter 7)	Simplot	Manon Chocolatier (Chapter 10)
Negative (Murphy's Law)	Staples	Easy Auto (Chapter 7)	NFTE

and a bad one at that. Other examples include the rain that melted the ice sculptures in the ICEHOTEL story (see Chapter 13), or the back injury Vidal Herrera accidentally sustained one day by lifting a 284-pound corpse (see Chapter 4).

Unexpected information

A third type of contingency is the unexpected arrival of new information. One example of this is unexpected information that changes your expectations about the "market." For example, when Honda entered the US motorcycle market in the 1960s, it thought it would be in the business of selling big motorcycles. In the meantime, its sales team rode mopeds for transportation around Los Angeles. It was an unexpected call one day from a Sears representative that informed Honda of the potential to sell mopeds in the US. Honda subsequently leveraged that

contingency into a significant market opportunity for the firm. New information might arrive in many different ways: in the Staples story (page 141), it was Thomas Stemberg's inability to find printer ribbon that generated critical information about the potential for an office supply chain in the US.

In the table below we show that you can further subdivide contingencies depending on whether your initial evaluation is positive or negative. When they initially look positive, people often refer to these contingencies as "serendipitous," i.e. good things that happened by accident. If at first glance they appear negative, people often refer to them as examples of "Murphy's Law," i.e. anything that can go wrong will go wrong. In the next section we will describe how you might think about leveraging contingencies regardless of whether they appear to be positive or negative.

LEVERAGING CONTINGENCY: THE PROCESS

In the examples we have used so far, it's important to realize that the

contingencies themselves did not automatically shape the future direction of the venture. Instead, what is important is how the entrepreneurs leveraged those contingencies—this is the core of the entrepreneurial behaviors we talk about in this chapter. Entrepreneurs are adept at seizing surprises in an instrumental fashion and figuring out ways to imaginatively utilize them to create new possibilities in the world.

There are several generic ways of thinking about how to handle contingencies. Two traditional ways of reacting to contingencies are to respond adaptively or to respond, what we might term, heroically.

- **Adaptive response** involves changing yourself to fit in with the contingency. For example, Thomas Stemberg (see page 141) could have taken the non-availability of printer ribbon to be a constraint that he would just have to cope with and resigned himself to printing his business plan the following weekend.
- **Heroic response** involves changing the world into a state that you prefer. Stemberg might have treated the non-availability of printer ribbon as an obstacle to overcome and—determined to print his business plan—he might have gone on an all-out campaign to find printer tape, spending the whole of the July 4 weekend combing every store within a 50-mile radius of his home until he found one that carried the printer tape he desired.
- **Entrepreneurial response** involves a different approach—

using contingencies as resources, as inputs into your entrepreneurial endeavors. Instead of adapting to or overcoming the contingencies the world throws at you, the challenge is to realize that contingencies are assets with which you may be able to do something creative. Whereas the adaptive response involves thinking "inside the box," and the heroic response involves thinking "outside the box," the entrepreneurial response is somewhat more subtle—it involves realizing that the "box" just changed, and then doing something to leverage the revised box in a new direction. Here, the colloquial "box" is seen as an input to the venture.

THE CONTINGENCY PATH TO NOVEL OUTCOMES

CONTINGENCIES
Information   Events
People

CHANGE YOUR MEANS
What you know   Who you are
Who you know

WHICH GIVES YOU NEW MEANS TO LEVERAGE
by asking yourself, "Now what can I do with my revised means?"

WHICH MAY GENERATE NOVEL OUTCOMES
i.e. new venture directions

Sometimes contingencies will obviously be good things; in these cases, the entrepreneur's job is to jump on them and try to milk them for all they are worth. But the most challenging contingencies are those that come in unfortunate or negative forms—such as the mugging of Steve Mariotti in New York City (see page 142). We focus on several of those here. As these examples show, it is almost always possible to leverage a contingency in some kind of positive way if you are creative enough about your reactions. Indeed, some of the most interesting entrepreneurial stories are just that because they are examples of how negative contingencies can be turned into positive forces in a person's entrepreneurial career. For example, Steve Mariotti's story powerfully illustrates that the critical point about contingencies is what entrepreneurs do with them.

This process of leveraging contingencies can be simplified into the contingency process diagram, which provides a toolbox for thinking through the contingency leveraging process:

The first element in the contingency process diagram is the contingency that occurs, which is the trigger for the process to begin. In the previous section we described how contingencies might be thought of as unnecessary people, events, or information that arrives on the entrepreneur's "doorstep."

The second element is seeing that a contingency usually changes your means. An entrepreneur's means (what I know, who I know, and who I am) are the defining point for the beginning of the entrepreneurial process. The contingencies we've described here tend to incrementally change those means: Meeting someone new changes "who you know" and new information and contingent events change "what you know" and perhaps "who you are." In fact, every individual person can more-or-less be thought of as partly constituted by a long list of contingencies that—in the long run—contribute to their personality, knowledge, and personal network. Think about your own lifetime, and all of the little events, people, and information that have contributed to your make-up. Contingencies play a significant role in forming most individuals' means. Therefore, when contingencies occur, entrepreneurs should consider how they alter their means, as a first step towards thinking through how contingencies might be leveragable.

The third element in the contingency leveraging process is forming a possible action in response. The general approach to leveraging contingencies that we outline here fits with some of the most important lessons learned from research on creative problem solving over the years. This research shows that, in general, there are two keys to being more creative when solving problems:

The first is the number of alternative solutions considered. In general, the more potential solutions you consider, the more likely you are to provide a creative solution to a given problem you face. For entrepreneurs, this means imagining lots of different things you might be able to do with a contingency that has happened to you. Very often there are immediate, obvious, spontaneous things to do, such as partnering with someone new you met (as in the case of Simplot meeting Sokol; see page 141). In other situations, there is no obvious thing to do, and the entrepreneur may take some time to imagine a variety of courses of action. For example, Steve Mariotti (see page 142) didn't have to make an instantaneous decision to become a high school teacher—that alternative emerged from his need to face his fears about being mugged.

The second general rule for improving creative problem solving is changing the way the problem is framed. For entrepreneurs, the typical way they do this is to invert the way a contingency presents itself: Instead of looking at it as a problem, they turn it on its head and look at it as a (badly disguised) opportunity. For example, Thomas Stemberg (see page 141) managed to see that the non-availability of printer ribbon was not a problem for printing his business plan, but instead signaled an opportunity to start an office supplies business. For Yngve Bergqvist (see Chapter 13) rain on the sculptures was an unpleasant surprise. But he turned that experience upside down by seeing the destruction of the ice sculptures not as a dreadful thing, but rather as an opportunity to redo the whole exercise over again year after year.

The final element described in the contingency process diagram is the novel outcome that may be generated. We say "may be generated" because, as with all creative processes, there is no

Practically speaking

Railtex

Like many of the stories we recount in this book, Railtex leans towards the mundane—after all, short-haul US railroading is not exactly the newest or most exciting business venture one could get into! The Railtex story starts in 1977, when Bruce Flohr put US$50,000 of his own money together with US$50,000 from investors to launch a railcar-leasing firm in San Antonio, Texas. Railcar leasing turned out not to be a particularly great idea: Five years later, the business was still not profitable and was struggling to stay afloat. The situation forced Flohr and his team to start doing consultancy work with small railroads as a way of pulling in some extra cash. The consulting work proved to be a stroke of luck: What they accidentally discovered was that small railroads were badly in need of competent management and marketing. This contingency proved to be a turning point for the firm. Instead of consulting for small railroads, Flohr started buying them, improving their operations, and growing them by marketing freight services to local businesses. Starting with San Diego & Imperial Valley Railroad, the firm went on to pick up dozens of short-haul lines, going public in 1993 and growing into the largest short-haul railroad operator in the US.

POSITIVE OR NEGATIVE, SURPRISE IS A RESOURCE

	Contingency	Changed means	New things to do	Novel outcomes
Staples	Unable to easily obtain office supplies	Knowledge of the non-availability of products for small businesses	Opportunity to sell office products for small businesses	Development of Staples retail chain
Simplot	Accidental meeting	Knowing someone with a specific need	Produce powdered onions using existing equipment	Major growth opportunity in dried fruits and vegetables
NFTE	Mugging by inner city youths	Personal fear	Actions to overcome personal fears	Become a high school teacher in a tough inner city neighborhood

guarantee that a novel, value-creating outcome is going to be forthcoming—just the possibility that this may occur. The key thing to understand is that contingency leveraging is about seizing the unique possibilities that may be created by the interaction between the entrepreneur—with all his or her unique attributes, prior experience, networks, personality traits, etc.—and a particular contingency. Different people will interact differently with different contingencies—so these interactions tend to be unique and unpredictable. Think about it. Something unexpected happens to you, and then you concoct an unexpected response—there is a double novelty in such interactions, which is precisely why they sometimes result in creative moments in the life history of entrepreneurial ventures.

In the table above we illustrate the contingency process flow we've described here by showing how the three stories we discussed earlier in this chapter turned contingencies into resources for their ventures.

PRACTICALLY SPEAKING: NANOSOLAR

Solar energy start-ups generate attention, but none like NanoSolar. With a charismatic CEO who is a veteran of several successful internet start-ups and a thin-film solar nanotechnology that promises both high efficiency and low cost, the firm's list of funders reads like a "who's who." Brand name venture capitalists Benchmark and Mohr Davidow share ownership with multinational firms such as EDF and Mitsui. Stanford University owns a piece of the firm, as do Google founders Sergey Brin and Larry Page. These and others have presented NanoSolar CEO Martin Roscheisen with half a billion dollars to bring them green energy and good returns from the warmth of the sun. Seems like a story with a guaranteed happy ending.

But even with such auspicious beginnings, surprises still rear up. And as with any other start-up, the game with every variety of surprise is to figure out how to use it to your advantage. One of the surprises Roscheisen encountered is the difficulty of bringing talent from abroad to NanoSolar's San Jose, California, headquarters. Many of the leading scientists and engineers in materials science and physics are not US citizens and are prevented from working in the US by the current tough immigration laws. For many firms, this might have presented a storm on the horizon. But rather than letting it turn to rain, NanoSolar managed to find a way of using the situation to their advantage by channeling specialists barred from Silicon Valley towards their operation in Luckenwalde, Germany. In doing this, the firm not only built an option for key talent, but it also created an entry point into the German solar power market, the largest in the world.

NanoSolar has also encountered positive surprises. New product development based on core research is an uncertain process. And in addition to disappointments along the way, NanoSolar has also been astute enough to latch onto technology surprises—advances that had previously been ignored or were hidden from sight by what has been routinely taken for granted among people working in the solar industry.

"One pleasant surprise was that a lot of very basic things simply haven't even been tried yet by anyone. Working in a space with low-hanging fruit definitely makes it easier to deliver on fundamental advances"

says NanoSolar's Roscheisen.

The firm has been able to turn these surprises into some of their 200 patents, has already started production and sale of its thin-film nanotechnology products, and posted its first profitable month in September 2008.

Looking ahead, NanoSolar will doubtless face many more surprises. For example, crude oil, which fuelled investments into alternative energy firms when it cost US$140/barrel, was at US$65/barrel in 2009. The surprise drop in price may force NanoSolar to reconsider its economic value proposition, target applications, customers, or its technology. This could point to disappointed investors, but it could also point the firm to new opportunities.

Like NanoSolar, the stories of many entrepreneurial firms are not fairy tales. They represent a series of thoughtful transformations when the founders face surprises. Surprises do not always spell disaster; some may offer new opportunities, and they can even offer the basis for a completely new firm. For starters—what's the opportunity if the sun doesn't shine?

NanoSolar application question:

How might NanoSolar respond to (relatively) cheap oil?

PRACTICALLY SPEAKING: HUNTING WITH THE PACK

Baloo Patel was born in Uganda in 1939, but the tracks to his entrepreneurial career had already been laid; laid by hand, in fact, by his ancestors who had been brought from India to work on the East African Railway. Starting out as a bank teller in Kenya, he soon moved to working in a tour operating company. Believing he could improve the business, he participated in a management buy-out of the operator, and with the stroke of a pen, became an entrepreneur.

With responsibility for the tour business, Patel started to imagine new services and new offerings. Clients enjoyed seeing the Kenyan landscape and wildlife from the ground, but might the air be even more dramatic? In 1981 he bought a plane and entered the aviation business. And in 1986 he bought a balloon and offered silent aerial excursions above wilderness treasures of the Masai Mara National Park. Business soared, and Patel used the proceeds to expand into real estate, printing, insurance, and mining.

With every step of expansion, Patel had the benefit of knowing the clients and the market, so he could be comfortable with demand, but he took the risk associated with buying hard assets. This risk was underscored in his printing venture with his cousin Nayan. In 2002 Patel observed that only about 300,000 physical phone lines supported Kenya's population of 35 million people. The cellular industry was poised to take off. He was going to benefit by printing pre-paid cellular phone cards. So he invested in specialized equipment for secure card printing. But the cellular phone operators in Kenya had existing suppliers, and they were wary of local providers. Patel's equipment lay still for years, until disruptions in Kenya's transportation system left the operators without foreign printed cards, putting Patel in business . . . finally.

The experience has added sophistication to how the two, now along with Patel's son Rohan, expanded the businesses. Wilderness Lodges, their high-end hospitality offering within the boundaries of Kenya's national parks, uses properties leased from the government. Their latest venture Sankara Hotels and Resorts, a hotel management company, will similarly hold no hard assets, but operate

contemporary five-star hotels for business travelers in Africa's key growing cities.

As you venture out into the savannah of entrepreneurship, it is worth thinking about who might share risk with you. Not only will these people or companies lower the amount of money you need to get going, they will also have an incentive to help you succeed. Perhaps the real entrepreneurial lesson from Kenya is that hunting is more effective when you're part of a pack than when you're running on your own.

Our new business, Sankara, is based on the Sanskrit word meaning "causer of tranquillity". Appropriately named, our goal is to develop refined hotels that offer functional yet tranquil guestrooms whilst simultaneously offering vibrant recreational and entertainment facilities that will become the centre of daily urban life. On a personal note, it has a special meaning for me; I find that the more I spread risk and reward with my partners, the more tranquil I am in running the business.

Baloo Patel

Big ideas: Unexpected responses that changed the world

In the course of this chapter, we have emphasized over and over again that the real source of value in contingencies is the novelty of the responses that entrepreneurs sometimes concoct when faced with them. The same principles that apply to entrepreneurial ventures also apply to creating value in society as a whole. A powerful example of this may be found in the story of Indian nationalist Mahatma Gandhi. While still in his twenties, Gandhi traveled to South Africa, seeking work as a lawyer. There, to his surprise, he experienced the full range of discrimination directed at Indians in South Africa. In a series of contingent events because of his race, he was thrown off trains, and stagecoaches, and beaten and barred from hotels. These experiences of racism deeply influenced Gandhi and, though he apparently never intended it when he went to South Africa, they led him to begin working as a social activist there. When the Transvaal government began forcing the registration of Indians in 1906, Gandhi concocted a novel response to the demand: Instead of advocating violent resistance, Gandhi turned the approach on its head and began promoting the method of non-violent protest for which he subsequently became famous. He urged Indians to burn their registration cards or refuse to register, actions that expressed the deeper novelty in Gandhi's approach, which involved defying the law and suffering the consequences for doing so. Public outcry over the harsh response of the South African government to peaceful Indian protests eventually forced the authorities to compromise. It was an important symbolic victory for Gandhi and his supporters and proof, once again, that unexpected responses can change the world.

MAKING SURPRISE WORK FOR YOU

There are several things you can do to improve the chances that leveragable contingencies happen to you. These are activities or ways of thinking that experienced entrepreneurs seem to have already internalized and often do more-or-less unconsciously and automatically.

Social networking

Information often arrives through people you know—your social network contacts—LinkedIn, Facebook, etc.—as we described in Chapter 13. Therefore, there is a non-trivial linkage between social network activity and position and access to new information. To the extent that more experienced entrepreneurs tend to have richer social networks, their network connections may expose them to information flows that make them more likely to encounter contingencies. This suggests that entrepreneurs may be able to engage in social networking behaviors that make it more likely that contingencies happen to them. Sony's "wandering chairman" brings this to a personal level. It was his wandering between different development teams that connected two disparate projects to create the speaker system for the Walkman. So as an entrepreneur you may be able to increase your exposure to contingencies by deliberately engaging in networking behaviors.

Openness to experiences

Access to contingencies may also be related to certain personality traits. These may play a role in receptiveness to contingencies and, therefore, the likelihood of leveraging them. Studies of entrepreneur psychology have found that in general entrepreneurs score higher on the variable "openness to experience" than comparable managers. Openness to experience is defined as someone who is intellectually curious and tends to seek new experiences. Such individuals may be more receptive to, and welcoming of, contingent events and information and thus more likely to view these events as opportunities for action. In a sense, these individuals display a taste for surprises. Therefore, another way to increase your exposure to contingencies is by deliberately cultivating your own taste for new things.

Opportunity framing

Some entrepreneurship research suggests that entrepreneurs are more likely to see the world in terms of the opportunities it presents rather than the attendant threats of changes in the world. This tendency is the opposite to the response of corporate managers, who are overwhelmingly more likely to see threats in any given scenario rather than opportunities. These different responses are probably related to the way entrepreneurs frame situations and, therefore, what information they tend to see as important in a situation. It's unclear what drives people to frame things differently, but one explanation may be that people differ in how they perceive the world and their place in it. If you view the world as being particularly difficult to shape, you are more likely to respond to contingencies by seeing them as a

Roadmap

Make a list of surprises you may find as you develop your venture. Imagine the negative and the positive and create some unique possible surprises.

- ■ How would you change your efforts in light of surprises like these?
- ■ Identify five things that have surprised you already, in relation to your current venture efforts:
- ■ How have these surprises helped you?
- ■ What did you do to leverage them?
- ■ Why do some of the surprises seem negative? Have the actual consequences of the surprise been as negative as the surprise itself?
- ■ How can you transform these surprises into positives every time? How can they be leveraged into new or different opportunities?

threat and trying to adapt yourself to them. Alternatively, if you view the world as open to transformation, you might see contingency as some kind of cue and opportunity for transforming things.

TAKEAWAY: HAVE CONFIDENCE IN YOUR OWN ABILITY TO MAKE A DIFFERENCE

Experience may be important here: Many entrepreneurs have "survival" stories that illustrate how even unfortunate contingencies are not only survivable in the short run, but also often actually led to the genesis of new business opportunities or were even the source of their long-run success. Thus, entrepreneurs who have successfully leveraged contingencies in the past justifiably have more confidence in their own agency and, therefore, may just have less anxiety about their ability to successfully face the unexpected in the future. The implication here is that yet another way to increase your exposure to contingencies is by cultivating your self-efficacy, recognizing and having confidence in your own agency in the world, i.e. in your ability to make a difference (however small that difference might be).

So what?

You will be surprised. There is no way around it. If you don't find a way to embrace and actually take advantage of this fact, you will constantly be swimming upstream.

Bigger questions

- [ ] Can you create surprises?
- [ ] Are there management styles that leverage contingencies?

© Mike Baldwin / Comered

"It's not enough to just show up. You have to have a business plan."

CHAPTER 16

Business plans have their time and place, though perhaps not in planning a business.

Business plans and business models: Make pitches

■ ■ ■

THE BUSINESS PLAN is one of the most "taught" aspects of entrepreneurship. As a work project, it provides a wonderful learning platform. The creation of a business plan requires that all the different functional areas relating to the venture be detailed: financial plans and budgets, assessments and assertions of market need, the four P's (price, product, promotion, and placement) of marketing, key talent needs of the venture, risk assessments, competitive details, and comparisons, and on and on.

This chapter will not teach you how to write a business plan. You can Google the topic and find all the outlines you need; there are whole books dedicated to the topic. One particularly classic article on this topic is entitled "How to Write a Great Business Plan" by Bill Sahlman (1997: 98). It offers some healthy skepticism and useful thoughts on the substantive essentials. This chapter is dedicated to the principle of substance over form in business plans.

Substance over form is essential because the business plan itself is largely a marketing tool, and we don't mean this in any pejorative sense. It is used to communicate perspective, insights, and guidance on how others might evaluate, categorize, and interface with your venture. And as with any marketing communication, you must know your audience and the objectives you want to accomplish with that communication. Audiences for business plans include virtually any resource provider to your organization—lenders, private investors, potential employees and board members, customers, upstream suppliers, downstream channel partners. With this diverse audience, the form of a business plan really depends on what you intend to do with it—how you plan to address the desires of your audience. Thus, we'll focus on substance, and you'll need to fine tune form.

Each audience has different information needs, and uses the substance of the business plan to different ends. Talk to them and find out what they really want to know and how they want to know it. Our suggestions in this chapter can help you get started, but we claim no encyclopedic knowledge on the needs and preferences of all of those audiences. All have shorthand rules/screens that help them process the information you provide much more quickly than you might think. They often have requirements involving minimum revenue levels, industry/technology/sector preferences, different risk factors they are willing to take on, team member details and relationships, or primary customers and marketing channels. In many instances you can learn the details of your audience's different "screens" and rule out many options right up front. Ask what different potential resource providers want and listen to them—some will fit, some won't. For example, most banks will not deal with new ventures, most venture capitalists won't deal with pre-revenue businesses, and most angel investors won't invest in ventures valued at more than US$5 million pre-money (often less). Ask and listen.

MANAGING RISK

Our starting premise: Business plans are not about selling the upside of your venture. Business plans are about sharing your mastery of the opportunity, which involves upside, downside, inside, outside, and blindside. One of the most under-addressed topics in business plans is risk management. No one wants to "spook" potential partners with frank discussions of negative possibilities while in the midst of selling the winning potential of their venture. Yet if we take to heart ideas about influencing and being influenced, staying committed to means more than goals, working with affordable loss, pre-committed partnership, and leveraging contingencies, then we must also take to heart the idea that things will go wrong. This is to say, things we wanted to happen sometimes don't actually happen. Murphy's Law applies:

> **Whatever can go wrong, will, and tends to do so at precisely the worst moment.**
> **Murphy**

If this is the game played by entrepreneurs, then the business planning and modeling that takes place must reinforce our ability to deal with problems, change, disappointment, and so on. Business plans that sell the upside with a mere nod to the risks are considered naive by good investors and useless by expert entrepreneurs. Yes, your graphs should

go "up and to the right," as Guy Kawasaki (a popular industry pundit and author) commonly jokes about the hockey stick revenue projections constantly created by entrepreneurs. But if you stop there, you will be unprepared to deal with the inevitable beatings that are coming your way. Additionally, if you only show "up and to the right" type information, you leave the risks to your audience's imagination and miss the opportunity to influence their assessment and learn from their honest feedback about those risks—naïve and useless.

We've seen countless business plans where the "worst-case scenario" is still a completely acceptable business, simply with lower sales growth, or where the short-term customers go away, but long-term you're still okay, or where the whole plan is simply an average of the best case and the worst case. Bad. And don't laugh, this is commonplace, and you'll likely do something similar unless you deliberately choose to do something better. Something better: Think through your Murphy's Law plan. Deal with the consequences of receiving a *no* from everywhere you currently hope to receive a *yes*. For example:

Yes:

- Yes, the technical milestone was just hit on time.
- Yes, the customer wants to set up a test and then scale out.
- Yes, we just hired the savvy and well-known marketing person we've been chasing.
- Yes, we just brought in an investor who brings a lot of expertise.

No:

- If you assume *no*, what will you do?
- Are there good fallback positions?
- Can you prioritize the pain from different failures?
- Can you take steps to shore up the highest priorities?
- Have you completely bet on one solution that could ruin you?
- Can you minimize the damage from any one particular no?
- In what ways have you kept things to an affordable loss in order to help minimize that damage?

Your Murphy's Law plan will not be entirely elegant. Sometimes, the answer to a problem is simply that you will have to work twice as hard to survive. Sometimes, the answer will be that you in fact have no response—and winning that particular *yes* is mission critical. Lose it and you lose. Okay. At least you see that. It should also mean that if you win it, then you should have really made a great step forward. Attract more resources with that win. Manage the expectations of investors, and demonstrate your expertise, by humbly considering these topics and ambitiously taking them on.

You won't share your Murphy's Law plan with everyone. Different details and versions of business plans have different audiences. It may be that you use it only with key leadership, board members, or potential employees in their last decision steps. It is up to you, but having worked out your thoughts on managing risk is genuinely useful for whatever form of business plan you choose to create.

BOTTLENECKS

Related to managing risk is identifying real bottlenecks. They aren't all operational, and they aren't all bad. Sometimes a little bottleneck is a very useful thing. Unknown bottlenecks don't fit into this category of "useful." You can learn a lot about bottlenecks from operational ideas in management.

What is going to be truly difficult about your venture? When? How will things change over time? Where will things get stuck? Where are they stuck right now?

Cash is quite often presumed to be *the* bottleneck for entrepreneurs. This is generally misguided. You must keep asking "why" questions: Why can I not get cash? Chase those causes, dig

a little de[...]
bottlenecks. [...]
you have to tak[...]

BUSINESS PLANS

Wrapping your arms arou[...] difficulties, problems, and risks [...] venture are consistently overlooked [...] business plans. Business models are rarely overlooked, but are consistently misunderstood and underspecified. While well-done business plans are primarily useful with potential resource providers, well-designed business models are primarily useful to guiding the entrepreneurial team in action.

There is no one pure definition of what a business plan is, so we'll proffer our own. A business plan consists of four components:

Research roots

Seat of the pants

Everyone says that before you launch a company, you've got to write a business plan. So how come so many Inc. 500 CEOs skipped that sober exercise? Research on founders of firms in the Inc. 500 determined that only 40 percent of the firms in that sample had created a business plan. And of those who had created a plan, 65 percent said they were doing something significantly different from their original idea. Remarkably, only 12 percent of the group reported doing formal market research before launching their firms (Bartlett, 2002).

These data are consistent with other research conducted by Amar Bhidé (2000) who investigated a broader sample of new ventures and found that 41 percent of the founders had no business plan at all, 26 percent had a rudimentary plan, and only 28 percent had a formal business plan.

In this regard, notable entrepreneurs that include Bill Gates, Sam Walton, and Jann Wenner are not unique. None of them started with a detailed business plan.

HE NUTS AND BOLTS OF VENTURING: EFFECTUATION IN ACTION

eper. Those are your real
As with managing risk,
e these on directly.

Business plan rules

- **Rule number 1:** A business plan is not any *one* of these components; the business plan is all of them. Under-specified business plans generally detail the revenue model and touch on differentiators, but they overlook the approach to operations and people/talent.
- **Rule number 2:** The map is not the terrain. A business plan is merely a map; it's not supposed to detail every micro nuance of what your venture is doing. It needs to focus on your key intended activities, on the primary drivers of your business success. If you can't be terse, you haven't yet made your map.

PRACTICALLY SPEAKING: THE CUBE WITHOUT A PLAN

Time to put away those champagne glasses, the 25th anniversary of Rubik's Cube mania is officially over. Hard to believe that the blockbuster toy that frustrated our childhood and sold almost a hundred million units between 1980 and 1983 is already an antique. But what was behind the product that created the first millionaire entrepreneur from the Communist Bloc?

The father of the Cube, Erno Rubik, was a sculptor, an architect, and a teacher of interior design. Spatial relationship problems were his business and realizing them in three dimensions was his specialty. In class, it was likely he would build a physical design in order to make a point—as he did with the Cube. Rubik's Cube was not originally intended to be a blockbuster, or even a toy. It was the presentation of a solution to a structural design problem of surfaces in three dimensions that could be manipulated in any direction.

Technical creations come along all the time. Making a market for them is the job of the entrepreneur. And without such explicit intentions, Rubik started the process by sharing his puzzle with his students and friends. Their attraction to it indicated opportunity. So, when Rubik met Tibor Laczi, a salesman from an Austrian computer company, Rubik was open to what happened next.

Laczi took Rubik's Cube to the Nuremberg Toy Fair where he met British toy specialist Tom Kremer. Kremer shared Laczi's attraction to the cube, and the pair negotiated an order for a million cubes with the Ideal Toy Company in New York. Rubik set up production in his native Hungary,

So, what is the role of business plans in building a venture effectually?

The very idea of a business plan may seem contradictory to an effectual approach to building new ventures. Yet the business plan is difficult to escape in a world of causal investors and the ubiquity of business plan contests. The difference between a causal business plan and the effectual business plan, therefore, is that in the effectual case, it is not a plan—it is merely a communication tool written over and over again as the venture develops and written differently for different stakeholders. Honesty demands that effectuators do their best in building predictive models but explicitly clarify that the aim is not to deliver on the plan but to do what it may take to co-create value for everyone involved.

to feed the escalating demand for his toy. But manufacturing high-quality consumer products behind the Iron Curtain in the early 1980s proved an insurmountable challenge. Ironically, the wild success of the cube, compounded with the expense of returned defective cubes, ultimately led to the collapse of Ideal Toy Company.

The interesting thing about entrepreneurship is that value created in the process finds many homes. Rubik himself came away with about US$3 million. Laczi did well. The Chinese factories that picked up the manufacturing that the Hungarians could not handle did well. The event organizers who held Rubik's Cube solution competitions did well. Retailers selling the product did well. So, even though Rubik himself is the obvious entrepreneur, the other players in the story contributed to the process, many benefited from it, and they are all entrepreneurs.

Fortunately, entrepreneurship is not a Rubik's Cube puzzle. There is only 1 correct answer and 43 quintillion wrong ones for Rubik's Cube. Perhaps

quite the reverse is true for an entrepreneur. Starting with what you know and using the partnerships you build may offer 43 quintillion possible paths to success. Rubik had no business plan. The chances of him being able to plan out, in advance, what happened with his cube are about 1 in 43 quintillion. And even if he had, nobody would have believed him until it was all history.

PRACTICALLY SPEAKING: gDiapers

gDiapers make completely biodegradable and flushable disposable baby diapers. Their business plan:

- **Revenue model:** They generate sales revenue by selling gDiapers products directly to grocery and apparel retail chains and direct to consumers from their website gdiapers.com. Retailers order crate-size shipments with return rights; consumers order starter and refill packs—about US$50 at a time.
- **Operating approach:** They focus on the design and marketing of their product and packaging, sourcing the components from focused suppliers, which ship finished boxed product to their main office.
- **People approach:** Critical talent needs to involve design, creative marketing in two different arenas (channel marketing and online marketing), and supply chain management. These skills are all

in-house skills, and they access additional talent around technical design issues through their supply chain partners.
- **Differentiators:** The key differentiation is the 100 percent eco-friendly disposable diaper with great style. It is one of a kind. They have also cultivated stellar relationships with a large group of remarkably passionate users online that help them manage channel opportunities and sell products online.

This is clearly just a summary of their business, a glimpse at the critical components gDiapers must master in order to be successful in their current endeavors. However, like a map, you can get a remarkably clear idea about the risk and opportunities facing this company. Business plans are design exercises, involving intentional design choices as well as emergent insights that result from working with different people. The business plan items (of revenue, operations, people, and differentiators) can be considered variables in the equation, and they can take different values as you play with the design. Business plan design involves imagining the alternatives and getting ideas for alternatives from potential partners. For example:

Revenue model
- selling store-branded product to chains
- selling through a wholesaler network; no direct relationships
- exclusively online distribution.

Operating approach
- full integration, design to product to marketing to sales

- exclusively use online marketing and order taking
- drop shipping only to retailers, no direct handling
- sourcing from similar operation in different country.

People approach
- online marketing in-house
- outside reseller network to retailers
- open sourced pants design (product exterior)
- technical expertise around the liner (product interior).

Differentiators
- custom pants designs online
- store branding to encourage channel adoption
- focus differently on "earth friendly"
- heavy on style and functionality
- position against cloth diapers rather than disposable.

The list of possibilities that could be here is immense, and is inherently creative. These are merely examples of other legitimate choices that could detail the gDiapers business plan, but don't. These choices about what are and aren't part of the plan are the critical ones. We hope the earlier parts

of this book will help you make these choices in ways that are coherent and actually connected to the preferences and aspirations of your potential customers, partners, and employees. Business models are the substance of business plans.

ATTRACTING RESOURCES THROUGH METAPHOR AND ANALOGY

Attracting resources to new ventures is rife with inherent contradictions. One of these is the simultaneous desire for the venture to be truly innovative yet provide evidence that it will work. New + proven = really tricky (oxymoronic really).

Well-designed and specified business plans help deal with this challenge. They allow you to legitimately use metaphors and analogies to other companies and industries as the evidence to go with your novelty. What industries and companies provide legitimate metaphor and analogy? The ones that share important dimensions of your business model.

What industries or companies would be relevant to gDiapers for learning?

- branded apparel (children's even more specifically)
- non-food products for sale in grocery retail (e.g. other baby products or video rental)
- design/marketing outfits (e.g. Nike)
- companies with a complicated mix of online and offline sales (e.g. Barnes & Noble or BMG)
- companies that use their suppliers for technical innovation (e.g. Dell)
- companies entirely positioned as eco friendly (e.g. seventh generation)
- obviously, other diaper companies (e.g. Huggies and Pampers).

Some of these are better metaphors, and provide more robust analogies than others provide. Certainly, you can imagine more. Come up with a set that you want to work with; let's call this your peer group. Now you can have some evidence to go with your novelty; now you can actually learn some things by looking really closely at this creative "peer group." Yes, it will add substance to your business plan, and yes, it can actually help you master your own opportunity more completely.

What evidence does your peer group provide that . . .

- Customers will adopt a product like this?
- Your venture can grow as fast as you want to show in your plan?
- Your particular business model choices are "state of the art?"
- Your business model is robust enough to endure mistakes?

If you were to tell the story of your peer group companies, what were their key *mistakes* as well as their key successes, and what do you take away as key learning points? If you've really done a good job of connecting the key components of your business model to those of the peer group companies, you'll be quite surprised by how much you can genuinely learn about your own business. Adjust your business model and strategy accordingly, and share some of this expertise in your business plan to combine some legitimate evidence with your novelty.

Traction trumps everything: How to win a business plan competition for gDiapers

Of course, there is no evidence quite as good as your own successes to prove that the novelty of your business venture is valuable. This evidence is commonly referred to as traction. Traction is what connects the power of a car engine to the road, actually resulting in the car moving forward (in this case you and your team are the horsepower). Every "yes" you win is a point of traction. Without traction, the effort you put into executing your business plan is simply spinning your wheels. No one wants to put resources (time, money, relationships, or talent) into perpetually spinning their wheels.

Business plan competitions are fun and interesting at times, and they can be outstanding learning experiences. The winners of these competitions consistently have genuine traction that differentiates their efforts from hypothetical business plans, and they demonstrate their potential for success—they aren't just spinning their wheels.

Conjecture
- We'll make disposable diapers you can flush down the toilet.
- We'll sell these diapers in Whole Foods.

Sound interesting?

Traction
- Watch as I flush this diaper down the toilet.

- The local grocery store paid us cash for the 1,000 diapers they sold last month.

You win.

Sometimes, you can't get traction until you've attracted certain resources. You might need an engineer to finalize the prototype. You might need cash to order 1,000 diapers for your first store test. Traction can at times be a serious chicken and egg problem. Remember affordable loss? You need to prioritize and pursue accomplishments, within your levels of affordable loss, which constitute traction. This is an art, and takes practice, but keeping this concept in mind will help you focus progress, and make sense of the small victories you accumulate as you proceed.

TRANSACTION ECONOMICS

This brings us to the overemphasized demand forecast in business plans. At this point, you actually have some ideas of what customers seem to want, you've learned a lot about other relevant companies and what they were able to accomplish over their development, and you've learned a lot about different markets you can sell into in terms of their overall market size and competitive mix. This all begs the question: What do you think you can accomplish with this opportunity over the next few years? It's obviously important, because it has a lot to do with your opinion of whether it's a good idea to attract more resources to the effort.

Different people have different opinions about top-down versus bottom-up forecasting. Top-down forecasting is simply estimating the overall size of the market, looking at what might be feasible in terms of market share and customer adoption, and doing the math. In our opinion, this sort of predictive work is highly problematic, and all too often leads to grossly high demand forecasts. Top-down forecasts are not terribly compelling, and lead to statements like this: We only need to get a 1 percent market share and we'll be really successful. These statements are nonsense and really undermine the credibility of entrepreneurs.

Bottom-up forecasts look at things in a more micro fashion. What customers can you actually reach this year, by name? How many customers can you currently keep in your sales process simultaneously? If you added four salespeople, what happens to that number? Can you name the list of prospects that you need to hit for each year you're forecasting in order to make those numbers real? What is the revenue from what you can actually produce right now? What are the bottlenecks keeping you from doubling your sales over the next 12 months? Can they be eliminated such that your sales forecast is legitimate? These types of forecasts are consistently lower and more credible, but many entrepreneurs don't feel that it gives justice to the true potential of their opportunity.

Here is the painful reality: Both of these types of forecasting typically lead to demand forecasts that simply don't get hit. Many investors, and all bankers, barely pay any attention to these forecasts made by entrepreneurs. Early stage investors will use them to

sort of broadly characterize the overall size potential of the venture—small, medium, large, if you will.

More important than either top-down or bottom-up forecasting is the more direct analysis relating to your business model. It's not the macroeconomics of the top-down approach, or the micro level of the bottom-up forecast; it is the transaction economics of your business model. Transaction economics are where managerial accountants excel. They are inherently less predictive, but help evaluate the robustness of your venture.

Key questions to understanding the contribution margin of a typical transaction

- What kind of marketing/sales investment is required to win a customer?
- What type of inventory will you have to build to attract sales?
- What drives your product costs? Are your gross margins fragile?
- What are the service requirements, potentially, after you make a sale?
- Over the course of a year or two, what kind of cash are you netting overall from your lead customers?
- How many customers do you need to land to break even?
- How many transactions are needed to break even?
- Are there business model changes that can materially change these transaction level economics?

If you can get clarity at this level of analysis, the needs facing your venture

will be significantly clearer, and it can actually inform your risk management ideas. Because this type of analysis involves less prediction (not zero prediction, just less prediction), it is less risky to use it in your decision-making. (Of course, keep in mind that garbage in equals garbage out. You have to do real work to identify your product costs, selling costs, and service costs, and validate your pricing.)

ESCALATION OF COMMITMENT

At this point, we must discuss escalation of commitment. A well-specified business plan, some interesting thoughts and strategies for dealing with real risk and surprise, and some emphasis on traction and gaining ground with customers, partners, employees, and investors can materially change how you choose to proceed as an entrepreneur. It can increase the emotional commitment you have to the work you've done thus far. This increased commitment to your plans, to the goals you now have in mind, and to delivering on the yeses you may have won from customers, partners, employees, and investors can pull you away from the principles of entrepreneurial expertise.

Your willingness to think of new ways to use your means, leverage contingency, stay connected to your affordable loss, and truly focus on pre-committed partnerships can disappear if you don't watch out. Timing is everything. As your venture develops, you will need to focus on goal driven activities more and more, on delivering what everyone has agreed to deliver, but you don't want to over-commit too early.

This is different from the notion of "lock in." Lock in involves material resource investments that constrain your ability to change strategies toward new opportunities. Escalation of commitment is the emotional side of this. Even in the absence of genuine lock-in problems, entrepreneurs often become less willing to change and pursue different opportunities that

reveal themselves through their work with customers, partners, employees, and investors.

Venture capital investors are a common example of this. Once Venture capital investors come into a

The rocket pitch

Entrepreneurs were originally challenged to reduce the description of their business to something someone could understand in an elevator ride, and it was called the "elevator pitch."

The world has gotten faster, and version two of that challenge is called the "rocket pitch." Imagine your business on a single slide, 30-point font, with a total of four or five bullets, in 30 seconds:

- Who are you pitching to?

- What are you saying?

- What is that person hearing?

- What is the one thing you want the person to walk away with?

- What you want them to do is describe it to the next person.

Remember that every pitch that fails gives you an idea for how to make the next one better. You should never make the same pitch twice as pitching is as much about your learning as it is about your gaining commitments.

venture, they've done so largely because they intend to execute on the vision, strategy, and opportunity championed by the entrepreneurs. With those new cash resources available, they go about executing in a much more focused and goal driven manner than they may have previously employed. Oftentimes, this is exactly what they needed and wanted to do. Other times, the opportunity changes, contingencies arise that could be taken advantage of, but the escalation of commitment to the current state of things prevents their ability to adjust.

We don't know the right way to resolve this tension. There is clearly value in focus sometimes, and clearly value in flexibility at other times. We do know that if you don't explicitly deal with escalation of commitment bias, you likely will not make a fully informed choice, and you can needlessly constrain your ability to succeed.

 **PRACTICALLY SPEAKING: THE WIND AND THE PLAN**

"New-age traveler" is a euphemism for a hippie, a house trucker, or even a vagrant. It's not the community typically associated with the next generation of business leaders. But then again, solutions to climate change and high-priced oil are not likely to come from typical business leaders. This may explain part of why Dale Vince, an ex-traveler himself, is among the most influential "green" entrepreneurs on the planet today.

Committed to a low-impact lifestyle, Vince's journey into business began with building small-scale windmills to serve his personal energy needs and limit his dependency on commercial power. One of the most complex pieces of the puzzle was reliably measuring the environment in order to identify a location that provides consistent wind to drive turbines. Not finding adequate solutions on the market, Vince also started crafting wind-monitoring towers in 1991 and, in 1992, founded Western Windpower. Though Vince has continued his own expedition, Western attracted large orders from clients like Scottish Power and is now Nexgen Wind, the UK's market leader in wind monitoring equipment.

Armed with more knowledge of wind measurement and power generation, Vince applied for permission to establish a wind farm in the UK and in 1992 gained approval. Just three years later, he founded Ecotricity (originally the Renewable Energy Company), offering the radical alternative of "green" electricity to both household and business customers. By the end of 2007 Vince's firm was operating 12 wind farms, representing 10 percent of England's wind energy, 46 GWh/year of renewable electricity, and savings of around 46,000 tonnes of CO_2 emissions a year, as compared with the same amount of "brown" energy. His accomplishments have been duly recognized. Vince has been presented with an OBE for services to the environment, a Queen's Award for Enterprise, and an Ashden Award for sustainable energy, and he made the list of the world's Top 100 Eco-Heroes. But this is really just the start of the story.

Fewer new-age travelers roam Europe today, and green energy is no longer a radical idea. With the external environment, Vince himself has changed. His networks, his knowledge, and even his assets have changed. And as is often evidenced with serial entrepreneurs, he is reconfiguring what he has in order to create his next opportunity. His current effort is a prototype electric sports car based on the Lotus Exige, which makes sense not only in light of Vince's relationship with sustainable energy, but also because Lotus is already an Ecotricity customer, building a wind-powered automobile factory in Norfolk, England.

And what lies ahead? Certainly, no specific business plan. A vegan, a keen advocate of organic farming, and still committed to a low-impact, self-sufficient life, Vince is currently experimenting with approaches to micro-generation at home. In fact, the more he does, the more he has to work with, and the more opportunities he has ahead of him. In addition to offering needed hope to our energy bills, this observation points to the real source of entrepreneurial opportunities. Less often are they blinding visions; instead, they are more often a whirlwind of the many things you already have, mixed together with unplanned changes and the needs of the environment.

Research roots

Business plans and new venture performance

Eager to understand the value of business planning, a team of researchers brought together all the prior work they could find that investigated the business planning-performance relationship. They found that planning is generally beneficial, but less so for newer firms and for firms in cultural environments highly desirous of avoiding uncertainty.

Brinckmann *et al*. (2010: 24)

The one thing I have learned is that you have to be flexible, you have to continually reappraise that which you hold to be true because things change internally and externally.

Dale Vince

A note on the standard form of business plans

Slide decks have risen to a status formerly held by lengthy business plans. Most often these days we see opportunities described in an executive summary of less than two pages accompanied by a somewhat brief slide deck. Generally, only the more formal requests from banks and somewhat later stage investors then put a longer formal business plan to use, after they've already begun to make judgments about you and your venture from those initial materials, their interactions with you, and referral information.

Slide decks provide an interesting window into the logic by which you understand your venture, as well as the logic that you believe "justifies" or "validates" your venture. Logic occupies a funny position between substance and form. At the highest level, we encourage you to look closely at that logic, and organize your slide decks accordingly. There are some patterns:

1. A: Look at our cool product.
    B: Look what it can do for these types of customers.
        C: Look how many of these customers there are.
            D. Look at what we're going to do to win them over.
                E. Look how talented we are.
                >> Therefore: provide commitments and resources to us.

2. A. Look at the massive size of this market.
    B. Look at this critical unmet need.
        C. Look at what our product can do to solve that problem.
            D. Look at how we will provide that solution to that massive market.
            E. Look who does business with us now.
                F. Look how talented we are.
                >> Therefore: provide commitments and resources to us.

3. A. Look at the customer/s we have won.
    B. Look what the customer wanted us to do.
        C. Look how we did it.
            D. Look how happy the customer is (value we created).
            E. Look at how many other customers could use this.
                F. Look how we will provide that solution to them.
                G. Look how talented we are.
                >> Therefore: provide commitments and resources to us.

Aside from the oversimplification, there is an artificial level of stability in those lines of reasoning, and for good reason. It may not be a good idea to show a line of reasoning like this:

A. Look at all the different things we can do.
    B. Lots of different people could value this for lots of different reasons.
        C. We're going to fish them and learn which ones value us right now.
            D. Then we'll do everything we can to make them happy.
                E. Then we'll find others we could also satisfy.
                F. By the way, look how talented we are.

Lines of reasoning like these are often the reality, the substance, and with closer relationships, they might be exactly what you want to communicate. It's not an unreasonable line of reasoning; the earlier chapters of this book are the theories, strategies, and tactics that underpin them. It's just that it may be less persuasive with resource providers because it may be non-committal and perceived as such. So what happens? You add a layer of stability to your plans that fits what you think that audience is interested in supporting, and that you also may be willing to support (because they may say yes!). The main point is this: Identify, test, and play with the logic of your venture and the slide decks you're using. Not all logical arguments are created equal, and different rhetorical uses of that logic might be more effective; you might try enthymeme, and focus differently on ethos, pathos and logos.

One other thought on slide decks. Each slide prompts one or two critical questions in the audience's mind. Useful slide decks deliberately prompt those questions (not explicitly necessarily, just deliberately) and then proceed to answer them on the very next slide. Anticipating (and motivating) the question then providing your best arguments to address it, straight away, is a very effective way of demonstrating your mastery of the opportunity and of the issues involved in your audiences' decisions. It can pre-empt anxiety, and actually motivate deeper questions and better learning for you as you pitch time and again to different audiences.

TAKEAWAY: WHETHER YOU PLAN OR NOT, TAKE ACTION

We hope you are both more confident in how to create a business plan if you want to, or to operate without one if you want to. Clearly, there are plenty of failed businesses both with and without business plans. And there are many successes with and without them as well.

Regardless of whether you have a plan, nothing takes the place of action—of accomplishing something with your venture. Whether it's closing a deal with a customer, shipping a product, or merely getting the sign up over the door, nothing happens in a new venture unless you do it. And doing it is what generates the traction that makes businesses happen, whether there is a business plan or not.

Aside from acting as a marketing tool for raising institutional investment, one of the best uses of a business plan

might be to help you take action. Not everyone needs the support of a plan in order to get going, but if it is something that helps you do so, then take advantage of it. Remember that, ultimately, the business plan is nothing more than a tool to help you get your venture going. If it is not helping you do that, then forget it. Forge ahead.

■ ■ ■

Bigger questions

- [ ] What things can you really plan?

- [ ] Is there something else that a business plan might provide—confidence to the entrepreneur?

So what?

Great business plans are different for the different purposes to which they are put to use. One size does not fit all. Above all, they need to be persuasive/compelling, not legalistic or focused on your divine predictions of the future. If you are doing it right, *you* will learn about your venture as you create different versions of your business plan.

New ventures start without a brand.

But all start with something even more central, potentially more useful, and free.

An identity.

Venture identity: Build brand

■ ■ ■

A S THE PROSPECTIVE owner, manager, founder, and first employee of a new venture, it is easy to look with awe at the world's greatest brands. Names like Apple, Coca-Cola, Toyota, and Nokia must give employees at these organizations an incredible advantage in the market. And here you are with nothing but an idea and a little inspiration (perhaps enhanced by the caffeine from that Coca-Cola).

The purpose of this chapter is to think about marketing a new venture, not from the perspective of the things you don't have (a recognizable brand, a large communications budget), but from the perspective of what you do have—an identity. An identity not only prepares you to start taking action without spending money, but also helps to set a foundation for what the brand will be as the venture grows,

for what the communications message will be from the very first day, and for deciding what product or service areas the firm might or might not operate in.

We should say at the outset that there is no single roadmap. Consider the following two examples. Cypress

Explained:

Venture identity

There are many opinions about what venture identity means. As we describe it:

Venture identity is the "persona" of a corporation, designed to be consistent with and facilitate the attainment of business objectives.

Venture identity is not a brand. Venture identity is not a logo. It is the philosophy, values, norms, and personality of the firm. The corporate brand and logo are parts of the venture's identity, but only parts of it.

Semiconductor, based in San Jose, California, makes programmable chips for custom computers that go into everything from automobiles to medical devices. Founder/CEO T.J. Rogers, named one of America's toughest bosses by *Fortune Magazine* in 1993, exercises with his direct reports at lunch. A recent strategy document downloaded from the internet starts with Cypress: We eat nails. Contrast that with the Vermont Teddy Bear Company, a folksy outfit known for people calmly sipping tea during meetings. What do the two companies have in common? Both are enormously successful. Both have a strong identity. And for both, the identity of the firm helps attract employees and partners as well as give the organization a foundation for what activities make sense for the business, and which ones don't. Yet their identities could not be further apart from each other. Clearly, there is no one right identity; the question is how to create and use your identity.

atic and often mundane internal and external actions that employees (or the sole employee) of the firm take every day. Simply taking action does not guarantee a desirable or coherent identity will emerge. To achieve that, you must do the following:

Faithfully reflect personality and values

Your firm's identity has to reflect your authentic, genuine personality. The same message goes to customers, partners, employees, media—any stakeholder who has contact with the company. Of course, when you have been successful at co-creating your venture with all the relevant stakeholders, this agreement emerges naturally. The goal is to succinctly understand, down to the level of individual words, the core principles of the company, principles that will help stakeholders relate to the value proposition of the firm. It has to be

unique, and it has to be genuine. HP, for example, has distilled it to a single word: "Invent." What will it be for you?

Act locally

Once you understand the persona of your venture (and this may be harder than you think), it is easy to see how your daily actions either reinforce it or undermine it. A major life sciences company with an identity built around safety made the decision to buy Volvos for its company-owned cars. That may not have been the most cost-effective decision, but it certainly is the one most consistent with their identity. Mark and Stacy Andrus (Chapter 12) employed their own product, pita chips, to do their marketing. Initially, they used the chips to keep people in line for sandwiches, and once they moved into the chip business full time, they used the chips as their primary promotional item.

YOU ARE THE IDENTITY; THE IDENTITY IS YOU

How identity is created

It will be of little surprise, after reading about "means" in Chapter 9, to learn that your means are directly connected with the identity of your venture. Never is this truer than when you are the sole employee of the venture, but it continues to be true as the venture grows. The reason is that your start-up's identity could not be created by the marketing department (even if you had one) in a vacuum. Rather, it is a reflection of the system-

"As our new company logo, I'm not quite sure it's sending out the right message."

Three thoughts on firm names

Should the firm name be the same as the product name?

There is no right answer. The logic for making the names the same is that stakeholders have a hard enough time learning a single new name, so why spend the effort teaching two? Companies like Oracle (the name of the firm, and of the firm's core database software product) illustrate the simplicity of this approach. Firms interested in creating a portfolio of products can be drawn to separating the two, and even focusing on the product brands above the company brand as firms like Proctor & Gamble illustrate.

Who is going to use your name, and is it suited to the different applications?

Think about all the different people who are going to use your name. If they speak a different language, what does your name mean in their language (recall that the Chevrolet Nova did not sell well in Mexico as the name means "doesn't go" in Spanish)? Consult the dictionary. If the press is a big part of your marketing, will they write you up in a comparison list with your competitors? If so, choose a name at the top of the alphabet. Will you speak your firm name to a lot of people? If so, it had better be spelled phonetically. Will your name go onto consumer packaging? If so, keep it short and think about the graphic elements of the letters (lots of curves—S, O, G—versus lots of angles—L, E, A). Will you do a lot of telephone business? A seven-character name can help you match it to a phone number in the US.

How can you assure that the firm name is unique?

This has gotten easier and harder all at the same time. Easier because you can Google the word you are hoping to use and see what comes up and check one of the Internet registration sites (www.register.com, for instance) very quickly to see whether and how the word is being used. Harder because everyone else can do this, and so there has been an explosion of site registrations and new company words created. If you want something unique, you are going to have to be creative, searching other languages, combining pieces of existing words, and even adding special characters to find something that is unique, and that you can own.

Be consistent

Every day presents opportunities that are not consistent with the corporate identity. Whether it's a new hire, a product innovation, a press release, or a partnership, managers need to hold the action up against the corporate identity. If it is not coherent, say no. One of the uses of a good corporate identity is that it helps managers figure out what the company is "not." In the 1970s Pierre Cardin had an identity tied with luxury. But Pierre Cardin has slipped a long way from the cover of Vogue, where it once was, to the discount stores where it is today. Pierre Cardin failed one corporate identity test at a time. Looking at new opportunities, partners, and customers from the perspective of the identity of your new venture can offer an efficient way of identifying those activities that are a good fit, as well as those that are not.

Think broadly

Identity is much more than a logo. Over the past ten years Apple Computer has consciously shifted its identity from that of a computing pioneer to the currently hip Apple (notice "Computer" is conspicuously absent), a provider of trendy lifestyle technology. In the process, their design firm, Mark Anderson Design, worked on literally hundreds of projects for the company to effect the shift. Some, such as letterhead, corporate signage, and product packaging, might be obvious. But others, like the annual report, press releases, and even the appearance of company offices, might not. Corporate identity is a message that benefits from reinforcement at every opportunity.

Another example is Starbucks Coffee Company. Brief text outlining the corporate identity is printed on the back of every "partner's" (employee's) business card. That way, all employees carry the corporate identity around with them wherever they go. They share it with every professional contact they meet. What a powerful and nearly costless way to communicate corporate identity with space that is otherwise blank.

Quixote: Applying identity

Personal identity is people's conception of themselves and how they relate or belong to broader social categories. Entrepreneurs often explain their actions and decisions in terms of their identities ("what kind of person I am") rather than their goals or preferences ("what I want and like"). Sometimes the identity has to do with being an entrepreneur, however idiosyncratic that might be; in other cases it comes from other areas of their lives—such as religious faith, political affiliations, childhood traumas, aesthetic pursuits, or even loyalties to favorite sports teams.

Identity often plays an important role in decisions, especially important life decisions, such as starting a new career in entrepreneurship.

Reasoning from identity works even when there is a lot of uncertainty about what the entrepreneur should do. Powerful examples of this come from great literature, such as the fable

of Don Quixote. In Quixote's case, knowing what a knight would do in any circumstance makes him very decisive even when possible consequences are extremely uncertain. His decision-making ability is deeply rooted in his sense of identity—in knowing who he is and what a person like him should do.

In other words, identity consists of having a strong affinity for particular ways of living and deciding, rather than for any particular consequences. Entrepreneurs in general appear to realize the value of creating and sustaining strong identities, which are helpful in the face of the high uncertainty they often face, when it is not otherwise clear what they should do. Identities may be fictive or real, freely chosen or socioculturally constructed, good or evil. Often, entrepreneurial identities are incrementally built in the course of building a venture— think for example of how the identities of Bill Gates or Steve Jobs developed during the course of their entrepreneurial careers.

> I know who I am and who I may be, if I choose.
> Miguel Cervantes Saavedra
> (1605–1616)

Questions

- Where does identity come from?

- How can I use identity as a foundation for marketing in a start-up?

- Is it expensive to build identity?

Terry Heckler: Creator of enduring brands

Terry Heckler, founder of Heckler Associates in Seattle, Washington, has helped create dozens of successful brands and corporate identities from scratch—ranging from Redhook Beer and Jansport Backpacks to Panera Bread and Starbucks, one of his earliest adventures into building a brand.

Heckler (2010) chronicles some of his adventures in some detail on his company's website.

Contrary to popular wisdom, Starbucks was not founded by Howard Schultz, who came in much later to become the driving force behind the growth of the company. The original Starbucks, a tiny shop in Seattle's Pike Place market that sold imported fine roasted coffee beans, was founded in 1971 by three friends, Gordon Bowker, Jerry Baldwin, and Zev Siegl, a writer, a literature teacher, and a history teacher, respectively.

All three founders were fans of Moby Dick and so wanted to name their

company Pequod, the name of Captain Ahab's ship in what in their opinion was the greatest American novel, *Moby Dick*. Heckler pointed out to them that nobody would ever buy a cup of Pequod and suggested instead the name Starbos—the name of a local mining camp in the Northwest during the 1800s. In fact, Heckler described his vision of "the quintessential moment of use" of the product—a miner's hand reaching for a green can of coffee inside the camp's tent in the beautiful cool and damp surroundings of Mount Rainier in the rainy Northwest. The three friends jumped on the name because it evoked the name Starbuck, first mate on the *Pequod*!

And so a great brand identity began its journey as a patchwork stitched together from the romantic dreams and values of its founders and roughly blessed by a young commercial artist who would go on to become a kingmaker in his own right. Heckler Associates has not only created successful brands for a number of new ventures that went on to embody strong corporate identities as the fledgling ventures grew into global brands, but also helped rebrand existing companies and create brand extensions as they expanded their horizons.

Take the case of the St. Louis Bread Company who hired Heckler Associates to redefine the brand, articulate its mission and values, and identify core attributes and differentials. Again, the Heckler vision of the quintessential moment of use can be observed in the logo and all design aspects associated with the name and the stores. The website describes the core of the identity as follows:

> **The central image of the logo was a painterly line illustration of a woman with flowing hair caressing a loaf of bread. She came to be known as "Mother Bread" and symbolized the core essence of the brand's differential. Interestingly, the process of making sourdough bread requires a small piece of the dough used to make the previous batch of bread dough. This starter piece is often called the "mother." Whenever Panera opens stores in a new region, a piece of the original starter that was created in the 1980s is lovingly carried to the new bakery to ensure that original** *Panera quality and character will rise again and again.*
> **(Panera, 2010)**

Jansport Backpacks has its own story too. The company was founded in the 1960s by Murray Pletz, who won a design competition sponsored by Alcoa for an aluminum flexible frame backpack, and his cousin Skip Yowell. Since neither of them knew how to sew, Murray induced his girlfriend, Jan Lewis, by offering not only to name the company after her, but also to marry her. When ski-maker K2 Corp bought the company in 1972 and tried to change its name, all the employees resigned. They wanted to work for Jansport and not for something called K2. When they were hiking on the Alps, it was Jan's name they wanted to point to on their customers' backs. K2 gave in and retained Jansport.

Heckler's philosophy of the quintessential moment of use is not a mystical one—it is utterly pragmatic and focused on the user as co-creator of the brand. Observe his blog on the very definition of "brand" (Heckler, 2010).

What's a brand?

If we're brand building, we better know what we're building. Here is how some smart brand builders define a brand . . .

1. "Branding supersedes logic. Accordingly, brands are primarily aspirational and exist to build emotional attachment to a product or company."—David Aaker, Professor

2. "Products are made in a factory, but brands are created in the mind. Simply put, a brand is a promise."—Walter Landor

3. "By definition, brand is whatever the consumer thinks of when he or she hears your company's name."—David F. D'Alessandro, Brand Warfare

4. "A brand is a fundamental promise, a name for your business strategy and what you're prepared to enforce. It's not what you say, but what you are or aspire to become."—Keith Rienhard, CEO, DDB Worldwide

5. ". . . branding is the promise you keep. . . . Brand is the intersection between core company (or product or service) strengths and what customers value."—Joseph Lepla, Lepla Parker Integrated Branding Quorum Books

6. Brand. (1) A name, usually a trademark of a manufacturer or product, or the product identified by its name. (2) Particular type of something, a distinctive type or kind of something.—Encarta

7. "A brand is a combination of features (what the product is), customer benefits (what needs and wants the product meets) and values (what the customer associates with the product). Brand is created when marketing adds value to a product, and in the process differentiates it from other products with similar features and benefits."—Timothy Mooney, Brand Strategies

8. "I am going to define a brand as an entity that satisfies all the following four conditions; (1) Something that has a buyer and a seller. (2) Something that has a differentiating name. (3) Something that is created rather than is naturally occurring. (4) Something that has positive and or negative opinions about it in consumers' minds for reasons other than its internal product characteristics."—Adam Morgan, Eating the Big Fish

9. "A brand is an intangible but critical component of what a company stands for. A consumer generally does not base a relationship with a product or a service, but he or she may have a relationship with a brand. In part, a brand is a set of promises. It implies trust, consistency, and a defined set of expectations."—Scott Davis, Brand Asset Management

10. . . . A brand is a concept that provides the thread of unification within a business that yields a consistently broader brand value experience. So many businesses are a series of disconnected silos under-leveraging their brand. They think of their brands as products rather than total experiences."—John Wong, Brand Imperatives

11. "Branding is something you do to cows. Branding is what you do when there's nothing original about your product."—Roy Disney quote from WSJ article 3.4.04

We could go on and on, but it gets to be the same thing over and over, "a brand is a promise". It sounds like a good sound bite. It doesn't help me much as a brand builder. A promise sets up some kind of a performance expectation. When I pick up an orange with the intention of taking a bite there is the promise it will taste like an orange. When I pick up an orange with a Sunkist logo on it, it also promises me it will taste like an orange. Of course, the Sunkist orange is signaling it's a branded orange but both the branded and unbranded oranges are presenting a promise. All kinds of generic unbranded entities make promises.

We think a brand can be anything someone is trying to own and make special. Ownership can be legal as well as just in people's minds. It could be a company, product, service, program, organization, group, person, sensory experience or ranch. You name it and someone has probably tried to make it a brand. We like this definition because it's simple and can deal with any branding situation. There are many different brand classifications, types and roles they can play. When brands are defined by equity qualifications or specific value variables people can quickly find themselves dealing rhetorically with what is or isn't a brand. We've been in situations where certain marketing people have told us, "It's only a brand if it has a consumer facing and revenues of a certain level."

(Heckler, 2008)

PRACTICALLY SPEAKING: DUCATI'S UNIVERSAL IDENTITY IN PICTURES

Ducati builds sleek Italian racing motorcycles—machines that are more often referred to as art than transportation. Though not exactly a start-up, Ducati is a niche player with a start-up-sized marketing budget in an industry that includes superpowers like Honda, Yamaha, and Kawasaki. Ducati has to be incredibly thoughtful and consistent in how it communicates. With a market share below 5 percent, the firm does not have the marketing budget of its Japanese competitors. Instead, Ducati has built, at a very low cost, an identity that appeals cohesively to the huge range of stakeholders it serves. The core values and personality of Ducati, the passion for racing, and Italian design, performance and speed come through in every small thing they do. In this practically speaking pictorial, consider not only how Ducati communicates its identity to each individual stakeholder, but also how it even uses one stakeholder to co-communicate with another, effectively building a community around the identity:

Ducati for new customers

Instead of hiring models, Ducati uses its own employees and customers for its advertising.

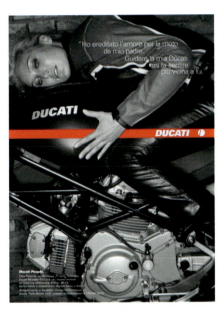

Ducati for employees

Using a photo from Ducati in the 1920s, the company reinforces its racing history by updating the photo with the new employees. And the Ducati parking lot is reserved for Ducati owners—anyone driving anything else must park farther away.

Ducati for existing customers

Every two years Ducati puts on a paid event called "World Ducati Week." The gathering draws tens of thousands of attendees who both participate and entertain (here the rock band Simple Minds play for free, as they are "Ducatista"—Ducati owners themselves).

Ducati for vintage bike owners

The company created a vintage motorcycle rally called the "Motogiro D'Italia" and a motorcycle museum to bring enthusiasts into the tribe. Both are supported by attendance fees and sponsors.

Ducati for press

Always interested in free press placements (PR), Ducati invites journalists to events. This journalist from the *Daily Telegraph* enjoyed the "Motogiro D'Italia" so much, he turned it into a front-page piece.

Ducati for suppliers

Critical to Ducati's bike delivery, the firm invites suppliers to attend special events at MotoGP and Superbike races, connecting partners with racing, customers, and with the company.

As you appreciate the consistency and thoroughness of this set of corporate identity building actions, think about how much money Ducati might have spent on any one of them. Corporate identity can offer a great advantage, but it doesn't have to be expensive to build.

IDENTITY ACTION PLAN

Generating a plan for how to create and communicate your corporate identity is a straightforward process.

Step 1: Articulate your corporate identity

The goal is to reduce the elements of corporate identity to a few key words. These reflect the unique philosophy, values, norms, and personality of the firm that will inspire customers, employees, and partners to want to work with the firm. This is not something you do on your own. It is something you do with all of your stakeholders, inside and outside the firm:

- Ask yourself why you started the venture.
- Ask your co-founders why they joined you in the venture.
- Ask your customers why they (would) buy from you.
- Ask your partners why they work with you.

Step 2: Assess your current actions

Are the things you do every day aligned with the identity you want to create and communicate? One easy way to start a personal assessment is by using your own "to do" list, or telephone call log. With your key identity ideas in mind, go through the list and underline actions that are consistent with the identity you defined, and cross out actions that are not. This should prepare you to generate ideas around questions such as:

- What current activities reinforce the elements of your corporate identity?
- Is there anything you do that conflicts with your corporate identity?
- What new activities might you initiate to communicate or reinforce your corporate identity?

Step 3: Put your corporate identity to work

Identity is a differentiator for your venture. At the start, it may be the *only* differentiator for your venture. You need to figure out how to use that uniqueness to help you accomplish your objectives. We have suggested some examples with corresponding questions. The list is by no means complete, but our hope is that it will serve to inspire thinking in your own context:

- **Obtain/retain customers.** Do your existing customers have a good community/collaborative way to share their enthusiasm for your identity with you?

- **Differentiate.** Is it clear to your stakeholders how your identity clearly distinguishes your offering from your competitors?

- **Build partnerships.** What new potential partners might be willing to help you achieve your objectives because they share your values and elements of your identity?

- **Improve visibility.** Are there members of the press and analyst community who relate to your identity and are willing to bring their passion to disseminating your message?

- **Add new products or markets.** In what new opportunity areas might your identity give you a competitive advantage?

TAKEAWAY: IDENTITY IS SOMETHING YOU CREATE EVERY DAY

As you move ahead, you will be able to continue to take greater and greater advantage of your corporate identity. Just keep in mind that corporate identity is something you create every day with the things you do, and should be an asset to you in overcoming most challenges you face.

Roadmap

- [ ] What are the elements of value in the identity you are creating?

- [ ] Can you distil them to a single word? At most five?

- [ ] What parts of your overall opportunity does this identity enable you to ignore? (And not just the obvious, choices that may actually be attractive but that might not fit.)

- [ ] Is your identity tied to a single product? Does that seem problematic?

- [ ] What other opportunities are suggested under the umbrella of that identity?

- [ ] What is it about your venture's identity that inspires you to come to work in the morning?

- [ ] What is it about your venture's identity that inspires your customers/suppliers/employees to work with you?

- [ ] What can you do to communicate and accentuate your identity in light of this?

Bigger question

Does a brand "cheat" its customers by charging for the premium?

So what?

A corporate identity is nothing more complex than a reflection of what you stand for on a daily basis. Shaping this identity, reinforcing it through actions, and communicating it effectively are central to the value you are creating.

Controlling the future is hard work, but it generates an outcome that is generally more desirable than chance.

The pilot-on-the-plane principle: Apply non-predictive control

∎ ∎ ∎

Throughout this book we have emphasized that one key to starting a successful venture is focusing on activities where you know your actions will result in outcomes you find attractive. These may not be the activities with the most upside, but they have to be ones within your control. For example:

- Taking action based on your means is more controllable (than actions based on means you don't have) because the resources you need are already in your hand.
- Evaluating actions based on whether the downside risk is acceptable (rather than on the upside being optimal) gives you more control over the risks you assume.

- Working with partners who are willing to make commitments with you gives you more control than predicting based on indirect market research.
- Being flexible and embracing surprises that come along gives you more control in an uncertain environment than trying to follow a pre-defined plan.

In this chapter we are going to pull together all these threads and show how they all draw on the central notion of control. We're going to explain why the desire for control is important, what exactly perceived control is, and describe the major methods entrepreneurs use to control the destiny of their ventures in uncertain environments. We'll also explain why control presents some major paradoxes in the entrepreneurial journey, and how successfully juggling these paradoxes is essential for those that wish to build wildly successful ventures.

As you read this chapter, remember that controllability is tremendously empowering in the context of starting a new venture. We already know from the earlier chapters that expert entrepreneurs focus on areas where they feel they can influence the outcome. We already know some of the decision heuristics that experts employ to effect control. In this chapter we will see how this underlying formula works.

WHY CONTROL?

The struggle for personal control is as old as humankind itself—it appears to be a primitive, innate desire in human beings. There is abundant evidence that most people are motivated to see themselves in control of the events in their lives, that they desire considerable control over their lives, and that such strivings for control are a human characteristic that spans across history and cultures. So, for today's control-strivings the venues, mechanisms, and instruments are different, but the issue is a perennial one. In fact, psychological research suggests that an enormous range of human behaviors relate to control-striving in some way and are intrinsically linked to healthy human functioning. For example, personal control is positively linked to the development of self-esteem and the reduction of stress, whereas loss of control increases the likelihood of feelings of helplessness and depression.

> Complete adaptation to environment means death. The essential point in all response is the desire to control environment.
>
> John Dewey

In other words, having a desire for control over your life doesn't make you a "control freak" (despite what your friends may say!); it's normal and healthy.

Many entrepreneurs instinctively recognize the importance of personal control: fundamentally, it's about "being my own boss." This enables entrepreneurs to work on the things they think are important, and that they are excited and motivated to do, and to control their own schedules, the pace of their job, and work when they feel like it. Many also attest that they feel differently about running a business that they own and control, that their mistakes and successes are their own, and that they value this aspect of being in control for their own sake. For them, the experience of personal control is closely associated with freedom, self-direction, autonomy.

The strength of a person's desire for control can be thought of as an element of his or her means: "Who you are." While everyone has some desire for control, people do vary on how strongly they desire control, and the strength of these desires also change with events over the course of their lifetime. For example, a high desire for control may motivate someone to become an entrepreneur, but the experience of working for

himself may strengthen this motive even further, leading him to utter the frequently heard remark that, "I could never work for anyone else again."

WHAT CONTROL IS AND ISN'T

While it makes sense that human beings, with their complex psychology, have a strong desire for control, there is a big difference between wanting control and the perception that you can control something. The perception of control involves an individual perceiving that to some extent his or

On the importance of control

People are highly sensitive to their world, particularly its causal texture. Although our efforts to specify the fine detail of this sensitivity—how it is acquired and represented and used to channel subsequent action—are ongoing, we nonetheless can say with confidence that people strive to appreciate what they can and cannot control. Whatever they learn is registered deeply and profoundly, influencing everything from physiological processes to world politics.

Peterson *et al.* (1995: 305)

her actions are causing something to happen. Very simply, the key here is the perception that there is a relationship between the individual's actions and a particular outcome. The individual's intervention has to make a difference in the outcome. In other words, the outcome is contingent to some extent on what the person does.

Perceptions of control are very important in understanding any kind of action, not just entrepreneurial action. People's motivation to participate in action depends on their perceptions of the controllability of a situation. When their perceptions of control approach zero, individuals aren't motivated to act. Your motivation to do something depends on your perception that there is some relationship between what you do and what happens. This is precisely what gives a person the motive to act in the first place.

However, it is important to realize that causing events to happen that offer no resistance requires no control per se. What characterizes control is that it involves making attempts to influence things that do offer some resistance. So, control involves something being contingent on not only what I do, but also on what others do. Your influence might be 1 percent or 99 percent, meaning that to some extent a phenomenon is contingent on your actions. Low control activities are those with cause–effect relationships that you can't influence much; high control activities are ones you have some significant influence over.

For the purposes of this chapter, we have carved up the space in which

action takes place based on how predictable the environment is, and the techniques used for control.

- **Effectual control techniques** mean preferring to work with elements where a significant contingency relationship exists between you and the element. An example would be pre-selling a prospective product to a client, where your actions significantly influence how the sale turns out, i.e. the management of the client relationship and the delivery of the promised product, which is in your hands. Obviously, not everything is controllable, but the entrepreneur focuses on what s/he can control.
- **Causal control techniques** mean preferring to work with elements where there is a low or no contingency relationship between you and the element. An example would be developing a business

Chew on this

The beauty of control-driven strategies is that you do not need full control—you only need *sufficient* control so you can move ahead to the next step and to the next stakeholder.

In fact, while novice entrepreneurs seek to find necessary conditions for success, experts master the art of making sufficient conditions.

plan on your prediction of the results of an election, i.e., "I'm going to invest in a construction company because the election will result in a large federal stimulus package that will spur demand for construction." You can't control the election results; precisely for this reason, you have to predict them, and then make a bet based on your prediction.

Control over inputs versus outcomes

Another set of ideas related to control, which we need to take into account, is control over inputs versus control over outcomes. For example, people often feel they could control their outcomes if only they had the "correct" inputs within their reach. Effectuators act based on inputs within their control on environments that they believe they can influence through their actions. But, of course, both of these can vary by individual actor as well as by whether s/he chooses to act causally or effectually.

When we combine these aspects of control techniques, we can observe the following four kinds of impetus to action:

Inaction: Learned helplessness
Perceiving both inputs and outcomes as unpredictable and outside of one's control can lead to a state that psychologists refer to as "learned helplessness." Learned helplessness occurs when individuals have their expectations repeatedly violated: they predict one thing, but the environment docs something different, and

no useful connections can be drawn about the relationship between inputs and outcomes. After a while, individuals feel helpless to take action, because their predictions are consistently wrong. They feel things are out of control. This is an important danger of using prediction in very uncertain circumstances. This is a situation outside the consideration set of an effectuator, as an effectuator would immediately take stock of means, begin with those, and move to block the third kind of impetus—high impetus to act.

Low impetus to act

When people do not believe they have the means required to achieve desired outcomes, they may not act, even if they believe they are capable of making a difference. They become susceptible to inertia induced by the *if-onlies:* If only I had the money; if only my personal circumstances were different; if only I had access to the technology; and so on. If they choose a causal approach under these circumstances, they face the prospect of chasing resources outside their control. In the case of an effectual approach, they need to be open to self-selected stakeholders. They can move toward action using either approach, but effectuation lowers the cost of the move by reducing resource requirements to affordable loss levels.

High impetus to act

When people are willing to work with things within their control, they are more likely to act even when they are unsure about how well they can influence outcomes. Again, affordable loss can be a powerful driver of action in this case, especially if actors are willing

to change their goals as stakeholders begin coming on board. If they choose to act causally, however, chances are their actions would involve elaborate planning and the necessity to place calculated bets in this quadrant. The environment is seen as highly predictable and independent of any person's or firm's actions. There is a danger of "analysis paralysis" in the causal case in this quadrant.

Compelling impetus to act

When both inputs and outcomes are perceived to be within one's control, action becomes virtually inescapable, be it based on a causal or effectual approach. Causal action here, of course, is likely to lead to predicted outcomes, while an effectual approach is more likely to lead to novel outcomes.

In sum, focusing on control strategies can have a positive impact on the likelihood of action, irrespective of whether the action chosen is based on a causal or effectual approach. Effectuation, however, leverages control in more ways and more directly than does a causal approach that requires predictability and upfront investments in planning and the pursuit of resources required to deliver on the plans.

> Immense power is acquired by assuring yourself in your secret reveries that you were born to control affairs.
> Andrew Carnegie

WORKING WITH AND WITHOUT CONTROL

	Working with inputs outside your control	Working with inputs within your control
Outcomes assumed to be within your control	**Low impetus to act** Causal = Need to change resources Effectual = Self-selected stakeholders	**Compelling impetus to act** Causal = Predicted outcomes Effectual = Novel outcomes
Outcomes assumed to be outside your control	**Inaction: learned helplessness**	**High impetus to act** Causal = Plan and make calculated bets Effectual = Be open to changing goals

Research roots

Self-efficacy

If there is one psychological trait that has consistently been shown to be correlated to people choosing to become entrepreneurs and to entrepreneurs who succeed in their ventures, it is self-efficacy. Albert Bandura (Bandura and Cervone, 1986: 92) of Stanford University defines the concept as follows:

Perceived self-efficacy is defined as people's beliefs about their capabilities to produce designated levels of performance that exercise influence over events that affect their lives. Self-efficacy beliefs determine how people feel, think, motivate themselves and behave. Such beliefs produce these diverse effects through four major processes. They include cognitive, motivational, affective and selection processes.

A strong sense of efficacy enhances human accomplishment and personal well-being in many ways. People with high assurance in their capabilities approach difficult tasks as challenges to be mastered rather than as threats to be avoided. Such an efficacious outlook fosters intrinsic interest and deep engrossment in activities. They set themselves challenging goals and maintain strong commitment to them. They heighten and sustain their efforts in the face of failure. They quickly recover their sense of efficacy after failures or setbacks. They attribute failure to insufficient effort or deficient knowledge and skills, which are acquirable. They approach threatening situations with assurance that they can exercise control over them. Such an efficacious outlook produces personal accomplishments, reduces stress and lowers vulnerability to depression.

In important ways, self-efficacy is the inverse of learned helplessness.

IS THERE MORE PERSONAL CONTROL NOW THAN IN THE PAST?

Changing social attitudes in the latter half of the twentieth century has definitely influenced individual perceptions of personal control. These perceptions are embedded in broader social belief systems, such as beliefs about individual freedom and choice, which have been legitimized by social movements in western democracies and political changes such as the collapse of communism in the former Soviet Union, and the spread of the free market system in China, India, and elsewhere.

So, perhaps more than any other time in civilized history, we live among political, social, and economic institutions that support individual rights to personal control.

CONTROL TECHNIQUES: THE *HOW* OF CONTROL

The starting point: Perceiving and selecting what is controllable

Part of learning how to successfully create new ventures is learning about where the more—and less—controllable elements are, and how to best leverage these elements. Prediction and control have different roles at different stages in the life of a venture, but our focus here is on the start-up and what can be controlled as it

launches into existence. There are a number of factors that can be used alone or in combination to assess the likelihood of the firm succeeding. Some of the factors can be directly controlled or managed by the firm, others can be influenced by the firm, and some are completely out of the firm's control.

The diagram on page 179 lists factors that institutional investors frequently use to determine the "investability" or viability of a venture. While it is by no means exhaustive, it represents a good starting point. Imagine that you are ready to launch into your own venture. Where do you start? What do you do on day one? Since you can't do everything at the same time, you will need to choose, to prioritize. Start with those actions over which you have the greatest degree of control. Ignore those you can't control.

At all times, be open to your perceptions being wrong. There are probably more courses of action within your control than you originally imagine. But even if your perceptions are not entirely accurate, just beginning with those actions you believe to be within your control is enough to get you jump-started toward the top right-hand quadrant in the "Working with and without control" figure we saw on page 176.

There's always another way

One reason for feeling a lack of control is perceiving that you don't have any other options—that it's this option or nothing. This means that you don't have any choice over which direction to go in. It is at such moments that the entrepreneur must remember that there is always another way of getting something done. Expert entrepreneurs would say instead: Having no alternatives usually means that you haven't brainstormed enough about what else you could do; it's therefore time to get creative and produce some new alternatives. Doing so will improve your perceptions of control over the situation at hand.

Use this summary to think about what you can control and what you would do first.

Elements that impact the likelihood of venture success

The way a firm undertakes its business includes a number of factors that are simply components of the overall business plan, such as defining the customer, market segment, distribution channel(s), vertical industry strategy, partnerships, and market position. Success within an entrepreneurial venture is not defined by the perfection to which these elements are resolved at a given point in time but rather by the ability of the organization to define, shape, and optimize each of these components as the industry, firm, market, and customers emerge/evolve. Think about how you will approach each.

Capital

More money provides a firm with more options. The interesting question around capital is not whether it predicts success, but whether there is a point of diminishing returns where the corporate value produced is less than the cost of acquiring it. Optimizing the number and size of funding tranches is an interesting problem. Think about how much cash you really need and what the alternatives are.

Competition

Almost by definition, entrepreneurs venture into new markets or attack existing markets with new technology, business models, or distribution strategies. As a result, failure due to competition is only symptomatic of a new venture that has difficulty refining or creating the differentiator(s) (technology, business model, or distribution strategy) that caused the new venture to form in the first place, or it suggests that the new venture is unable to execute. As you start your business, think about what makes you distinctive.

Customer pain: Aspirin or vitamin

It is reasonable to believe that both individuals and firms are inclined toward vitamins (products or services that enhance revenues or the standard of living) in good economic times and are inclined toward aspirin (products and services that help cut costs or address a specific need or problem) in bad economic times. As such, the ability of the team to understand the current economic climate and to match the positioning of the product or service appropriately is highly relevant to company success. Think about whether you want to offer a vitamin or an aspirin, or whether your offer can provide both.

Economy

Economic climate is highly relevant to the success of most new ventures as a good economy allows mediocre companies to succeed and helps good companies to flourish. After all, the rising tide lifts all boats. Unfortunately, neither prediction nor control is terribly good at managing the economy.

Execution

An entrepreneurial firm has virtually none of the brand, capital, infrastructure, and process assets of an established firm. As such, an entrepreneurial firm's ability to take action to create its own success is among its greatest differentiators and highly relevant to the likelihood of its success. As you look at execution think about the following:

- Are you focused on what you can do?
- Do you take the time to assess what you have done?

Existing investors

For venture-funded start-ups, the profile and reputation of the existing investors is relevant to the likelihood of success of the firm. First and foremost, the existing investors have determined the quantity of working capital that the firm has enjoyed to date. Within the investor community, the status of the initial investors can set a perceived ceiling for prospective investors that the firm can approach for future funding. Further, existing investors often make a range of introductions to other prospective investors for future funding. And existing institutional investors that manage larger funds are more likely to be able to participate in follow-on funding rounds for the firm, implying that existing investors have an impact on the likelihood of success of an entrepreneurial firm in several ways. Think about this before you sign on your first investors.

Existing customers

Existing customers are highly relevant to the success of an entrepreneurial venture as they provide three important inputs that serve to fuel company growth:

ELEMENTS THAT IMPACT ENTREPRENEURIAL VENTURE SUCCESS

◀ Less—Within the firm's control—More ▶

- revenue
- references
- attention from the press and analyst community.

It is generally assumed in the start-up community that the quality and the the quantity of referenceable customers are the two most important customer-related predictors of success. Following these, it is the revenue a firm is able to extract from its earliest customer(s).

Location

The physical location of the firm is relevant to the three success components of employees, funding, and customers:

- Until a company reaches a certain size, it is limited to recruiting a workforce that lives in reasonably close geographic proximity to the firm's headquarters.
- Funders prefer to finance companies that are geographically close to them.

- Business-to-business customers like to buy from companies that are geographically close to them.

In many situations, these success components may be at odds with each other. The interesting thing to think about is which of these variables is the most important to you and your situation.

Popularity of space with investors

It is important to know that the "herd" mentality that exists within the population of institutional venture capitalists can play to your advantage. As such, the popularity of a particular industry or sub-segment (life sciences, web video, alternative energy) will have high relevance to funding companies positioned there. Are you able to make your space attractive or make yourself attractive to the space?

Popularity of space with press

Buyers hate to be wrong. In that context, prospective customers want independent third-party reassurance that the products and services they are purchasing are relevant and popular and that the vendor they are considering purchasing from is a leader in the space. This perception is largely created through the press and analyst community and has relevance to the likelihood of success of an entrepreneurial venture. Do you have "champions" who can help you generate credibility?

Technology

There are a few instances where a successful company has been built strictly on new technology and the

"Wait a minute! This isn't your future... it's Ken Lay's future."

straight sale of that technology. These cases are the outliers. What is much more relevant to the likelihood of a venture's success is the ability to apply and adapt that technology to new markets, customers, and business models. Think about where your strengths lie.

Leader: The bottom line

The leader, usually the president or CEO of a start-up venture, drives the choices around advisors, culture, directors, and relationships with prospective investors directly. The attributes of the founder/leader of the start-up are, therefore, critical to its success. Be critical and objective about your strengths and weaknesses.

PRACTICALLY SPEAKING: HTI

One aspect of exercising control is deciding which elements you can and cannot control and working with those which you can influence. But there are also different ways in which you can exercise control over those elements and others. One way is creating partnerships to help you extend your reach. The HTI story is one example of building partnerships to shape the environment.

After a successful decade making industrial process equipment that treats liquid waste, such as the leachate from landfills, to protect the water table, Bob Salter made a major change. He decided to produce drinking water products for individual users. He was attracted to an opportunity where people choose to buy the product rather than being forced to through environmental regulation. But along with the change came technology risk, new distribution channels, and customers he had yet to serve. How could he justify an uncertain bet with Hydration Technologies Inc. (HTI; www.htiwater.com) when he already had a respectable business going?

Before Salter considered investing in a product for individual users, he already had a customer willing to make a financial commitment and that assured him of demand before he ever created a product. That customer was the US military.

Rather than shopping for potential users to explore a possible opportunity, Salter was only willing to "go" when a genuine customer seemed committed. Potential customers only lead to potential markets, and this uncertainty represents a big bet for a small company. But committed customers define real markets with tangible revenue. Salter says:

Two interesting things happen when you force yourself to get customers on board early. The first is that you might fail to get the commitments you want. But it's better to know sooner rather than later, and for a lot less money. And second, you might be surprised by the committed customers you actually find, and be led into even more attractive opportunities.

And surprised they were. After HTI developed an individual user product, not only have other defense customers joined in but HTI has moved into disaster relief projects and baby formula filtration that prevents disease and saves lives around the world.

Yet there is more to how entrepreneurs make investment decisions. How do you know if a customer is committed? When customers invest their own time and money, they have a vested interest in creating a market with you. In HTI's case, the US Army paid US$600,000 for initial product development. Naturally, they gained influence over what the final product would be, but Bob's financial bet was dramatically reduced. And the Army's initial purchase was approximately US$7 million.

Customers, suppliers, and partners that benefit from the value your new business can create are powerful sources of capital. They are more likely to offer favorable payment terms, cash up front for development, detailed purchase orders to borrow against, and even sell your products and services with theirs. By providing both capital and a market for your idea, they can effectively create your business. After all, one of the most useful strategies in controlling risk is gaining commitments from critical customers and partners as the basis for investing in an opportunity, rather than hoping for a pot of gold at the end of a big bet.

Control by intervening

Sometimes, situations that look like they absolutely require prediction tell you exactly what you need to know in order to gain some control in them.

Imagine, for a moment, that you want to start a business in the health and fitness industry by starting a weight-loss clinic. You observe that there is a big market in helping people lose weight but the fact is that nine out of ten people quickly regain that weight, ultimately making them unsatisfied with weight-loss clinics. Now, what are some of the ways you can use this data in your business?

- You could observe the nine out of ten probability of recidivism, decide that conventional weight-loss programs are a waste of time, and decide to start a venture in health foods instead.

- You could observe the nine out of ten probability of recidivism, and decide that weight-loss programs are an excellent business because customers inevitably will end up coming back, thus bringing you repeat business.

- You could observe the nine out of ten probability of recidivism, and decide that weight-loss programs offer an excellent opportunity to compete for business because all you have to do is decrease the recidivism rate slightly and your weight loss centers will be a runaway success with customers.

Now, what's the difference between the way prediction and control are used in these options? Simply, in the first two options the entrepreneur takes the information on the recidivism rate and uses it in a predictive way, to help him or her decide what kind of venture to get into; whereas in the final option that information is taken as a control lever, a point of intervention, a contingent-relationship that is potentially changeable if acted upon by the entrepreneur. Instead of taking the nine-out-of-ten ratio as given, the entrepreneur sees the nine-out-of-ten ratio as something that might be affected by the right knowledge and actions, and therefore a ratio that s/he might be able to get some control over in order to proactively influence the success of his or her venture.

The history of human action has proven time and time again the power of human beings to change the odds of events. Consider, for example, the odds of being crippled by polio. Globally, these odds are dramatically different now than they were 50 years ago owing to efforts made by the World Health Organization and individual country organizations to eradicate the disease. In other words, we have collectively changed the probability of a child getting polio.

The weight-loss clinic example is helpful because it challenges us to think about what might be controllable, and what is really not controllable. It also allows us to look at the relationship between prediction and control in a more "active" way. For controllers, understanding probabilities is valuable to the extent that you can find a way of affecting them, i.e. getting some control over them, rather than accepting you cannot control them.

> (Control is) . . . the characteristic of probability alterability. That is, if a participant could take steps to favorably alter the success rate in subsequent administrations of the task (not in the current administration), then the task is said to be characterized by control.
>
> (Goodie 2003: 598)

Knowledge of probabilities is thus used differently by controllers than by predictors. For controllers, probabilities are opportunities to manipulate events in the world by intervening somewhere; for predictors they are an opportunity to make a bet. While the predictor is working on the assumption that no one else will be successful in changing the probabilities, the entrepreneur is working on the assumption that other entrepreneurs out there are trying to find some way to change probabilities in order to increase the chance of success for their particular ventures.

Negotiated control with and through others (your stakeholders)

Why should you prefer to work directly with stakeholders rather than relying on market research data? Why do seasoned entrepreneurs say they prefer to do first-hand market research by going out and trying to sell a product, rather than gathering information about the potential market for it?

The answer to these questions is that working directly with stakeholders versus collecting market research data is fundamentally very different when it comes to controllability. Direct involvement with stakeholders is a more likely route for control than collecting market research data, for the following reasons:

- You control who you choose to interact with. Stakeholders select you, and you select them—the process is mutual. If you don't get along, you can decide to attempt to do business with someone else instead.
- Any relationship that is to some extent negotiable is better than one that is not because this relationship is more controllable. Negotiations happen in many different ways, including bargaining, haggling, manipulating, influencing, etc. These are methods of interacting with other human beings that involve some sharing of control and feel much more controllable than making bets based on predictions.
- You can be confident that your stakeholders desire one thing that you desire too—control. The fact that other people also desire control means that it makes sense to join forces with them and try to create a more controllable future together, rather than spend your time trying to predict what everyone else will do. A large part of the method of control relies on the fact that human beings generally prefer control rather than prediction, and are therefore willing to work with others to integrate their goals and plans.

It should be clear from the foregoing discussion that controlling with and through others requires an acceptance of an equal role for other people's desire for control. It involves the entrepreneur and stakeholders working together, to create a non-zero sum game, where everyone benefits by creating a shared future together as did Salter in HTI.

CONTROL PARADOXES

Now, we want to explain some important paradoxes about control in entrepreneurship. The crux of what you need to know is that control is a tool for helping you create and build a successful organization and market niche. The paradox therein is that to be successful in building these artifacts inevitably means that you will eventually have very little control over them! In the nearby figure we summarize some control paradoxes entrepreneurs experience, and then illustrate these with the example of Red Hat, a very successful software organization.

PRACTICALLY SPEAKING: HOW TO MAKE MONEY BY GIVING THINGS AWAY

In the software world, business models seem to change faster than designer fashions. Fifteen years ago, if an entrepreneur presented the idea of making money from giving away the firm's product or service, people would have laughed. Ten years ago, at the height of the internet boom, people scrambled

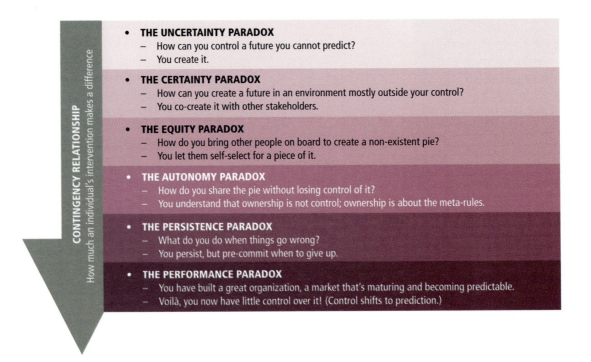

to invest in exactly that kind of business. Five years ago, in the wake of the dot-com crash, investors again wanted some connection between making something and getting paid for it. Amid all of these changes, Red Hat, based in the US in North Carolina, is still giving away software while at the same time netting a tidy profit.

The firm's story nicely illustrates the paradoxes of control that entrepreneurs experience:

The uncertainty paradox

How can you control a future you cannot predict? You create it.

In Red Hat's case, this was by inverting the advantages held by the established players in the software business. Red Hat was founded based on turning the development of software over to the user community using an "open source"

model. This tipped the traditional software model (such as Microsoft and Oracle) upside down. Now, the software code was no longer proprietary; instead, everyone could access it.

The creativity paradox

How can you create a future in an environment mostly outside your control? You co-create it with stakeholders.

In Red Hat's case, key stakeholders included the open source developer community, which enabled the firm's customers to do development and participate. In the words of Red Hat chairman Matthew Szulik, "Past and present Red Hat associates, along with members of the open source community and our customers and partners, picked up their brushes and dipped them into a paint palette of color to create this artwork called Red Hat."

The equity paradox

How do you bring other people on board to create a non-existent pie? You let them self-select for a piece of it.

Red Hat's programming team is complemented by a thousands-strong community of developers worldwide who enhance the software for free. The Red Hat community is comprised of self-selected stakeholders who create exactly the product they want. While anyone on the internet can download Red Hat software, the code is governed by a license that makes improvements publicly available.

The autonomy paradox

How do you share the pie without losing autonomy? You set the meta-rules.

Red Hat nurtures participation in the process of developing its software, but at the same time it sets the rules about what goes into versions of the software that it sells. The firm also controls and charges for customization of its software, special changes, packaging, and the consulting time for changes to meet individual client needs.

The persistence paradox

What do you do when things go wrong? You persist, but pre-commit when to give up.

When shares in the company crashed from US$300 a share to US$3 a share during the dot-com bust, Szulik and his family came under physical threat from some shareholders who believed that Szulik was personally responsible for the plummeting stock price. Did he persist too much?

The performance paradox

You have built a great organization that works well and a market that's maturing and becoming predictable. Voilà, you now have little control over it! (Control shifts to prediction.)

Red Hat now owns 80 percent of the market for enterprise Linux software. The firm has so many stakeholders, each with commitments to the Red Hat world, that autonomous control is now very hard. Any major changes the firm wants to make will require careful planning and use of prediction.

What is control?

To some extent, prediction will allow you a certain degree of control, as long as you are operating in a stable environment. But the type of control we discuss here is particularly useful in uncertain, entrepreneurial situations because it does not rely on the past to predict the future.

The control you exercise can be either exogenous (you shape the environment) or endogenous (you shape yourself).

Obviously, not everything is controllable, but the entrepreneur focuses on what elements s/he can control to create outcomes that s/he finds desirable.

Research roots

Overconfidence

Together with risk-taking preferences, there has been much research that has suggested overconfidence as an explanation for why some people become entrepreneurs. Overconfidence can refer to either overestimation of one's own performance, overestimation of performance relative to others, or overestimating the precision of one's beliefs. The basic idea is that people that are prone to being overconfident are more likely to start their own firms, whereas the underconfident will not. The general tendency among human beings to be overconfident has been used to explain why people become entrepreneurs despite the high frequency of entrepreneurial failure.

As usual, the truth turns out to be a little more complicated than initial inspection suggests. In a series of critical papers, researcher Don Moore has shown that, in fact, people both underestimate and overestimate their performance.

On difficult tasks, people overestimate their performance but simultaneously believe they are doing worse than others. Then, on easy tasks they underestimate their performance but think they are better than others. This suggests that the way a task is framed and perceived (as either "easy" or "hard") is intricately linked to manifestations of over and under confidence.

So which is it—easy or hard to start your own business? Whatever your starting point, it gets easier if you know the right techniques and with the more practice you get at doing it.

Summarized from Moore and Healy (2008: 502–17)

TAKEAWAY: CONTROL THE CONTROLLABLE

What you try to control depends on what you know about how controllable things are—or aren't. It is important to know both what you can control, or influence, and what you cannot. You can then tailor your strategies to the situation at hand:

- **Control** and influence what you can.
- **Predict** when it's more useful than control.
- **Heighten the controllability** of your situation by working as far as possible with factors you can influence and control. This reduces your dependence on prediction, and puts you on an overall firmer footing that is more controllable. It's about getting the mix right.

Implicitly or explicitly, entrepreneurs assume the power of human action at all levels and in all domains to control processes and outcomes. Effectuators see themselves not as risk takers defying long odds but as active agents who directly intervene in the world.

> One ship sails East,
> And another West,
> By the self-same winds that blow,
> Tis the set of the sails
> And not the gales,
> That tells the way we go.
> **Ella Wheeler Wilcox**

Roadmap

Imagine any new venture (an idea you have, a firm you admire):

- [ ] What would be the first thing you would do (remember that collecting information does not constitute doing anything)?

- [ ] Very likely, the things you would choose to do are things that will enable you to control some aspect of the venture, probably the area where you see the greatest uncertainty.

So what?

Action is what enables entrepreneurs to exert control on things that would be otherwise impossible to predict.

Bigger questions

Ultimately, is there anything that can't be controlled?

FOR YOUR INFORMATION, I AM ENGAGING THE ENERGY OF CHANGE AND COMPLEXITY TO CREATE THE FUTURE I DESIRE.

I am an entrepreneur now: How far can I go?

The chance for screw-ups increases exponentially with respect to the length of the boat, the distance sailed and the number of crew on board, which is precisely what makes big-boat ocean racing as complicated as it is exciting.

Paraphrased from *The Proving Ground* (Knecht, 2002), a factual account of the 1998 Sydney to Hobart race where 115 boats started and just 43 finished. Six sailors perished and 55 were rescued as the fleet was decimated by unforecast hurricane winds and 80-foot-high waves.

PART III

Make it big.

Make a difference.

Having successfully navigated the rocky waters sailed by new ventures, you face new challenges. Will you want to stay with your venture as it grows? Will your venture want you to stay as it grows? Though not surprising, the very heuristics that help you create new ventures, markets, and products are something of a liability in a larger firm serving a mature market where prediction prevails. This explains why so many entrepreneurs are concerned with scaling up and exiting. Exiting may be individual, or may involve selling the business. Either way, the founder entrepreneur who leads the firm into scale, such as Bill Gates at Microsoft, is something of an anomaly. Clearly, Gates was able to make the transition from employing heavy use of non-predictive strategy at the outset to effectively utilizing prediction as Microsoft grew. But most leave, are thrown out, or venture off to start a new business. The exact path has much to do with individual motivation, which is why we not only include a chapter on keeping large firms entrepreneurial, but another on social entrepreneurship. These represent two of the four main paths taken by serial entrepreneurs. The third involves starting again at the first chapter of the book. And the fourth involves long walks along a private tropical island. We felt that the fourth path needed little explanation here. The point is that successful entrepreneurs have dramatically expanded the means available to them. And so, while some may feel trapped having to run "their baby," the truth is that that the consideration set is not only broader than that, it is significantly broader than when they started "their baby" in the first place. So whatever you consider a better place to be, we hope to have an appropriate chapter for you.

When the ID badges show up, it's time for me to leave.
Cam Clarke, serial entrepreneur

Must large firms shed their entrepreneurial roots?

We don't think so.

CHAPTER 19

When the venture grows up

∎ ∎ ∎

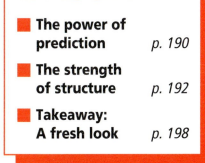

IN THIS CHAPTER:

■ **The power of prediction**   *p. 190*

■ **The strength of structure**   *p. 192*

■ **Takeaway: A fresh look**   *p. 198*

I T IS THE RELENTLESS business paradox. The entrepreneurial dream is to build a venture that becomes successful, enduring, and large. And yet executives from successful, enduring, large firms flock to business schools with the objective of somehow making their organizations and themselves entrepreneurial. There are enough large firms out there to reassure us that the entrepreneurial dream is possible. But will executives be forever unfulfilled in their quest?

It is important to acknowledge at the outset that the deck is stacked against large firms that aspire to be entrepreneurial. There are three natural and positive attributes of big companies and their people that directly conflict with approaches employed by expert entrepreneurs:

- **Prediction.** Firms become large typically because they are able to successfully create markets for their products or services. This success generates all sorts of positive reinforcement, like reliable revenue, a known brand, and a large client base. It also generates history. Successfully selling the same product year after year enables, encourages, and reinforces the use of prediction based on that history. Throughout the value chain, from raw material providers to distributors, the patterns generated from a history of success offer useful planning tools for further refining and expanding the business. Ironically, the reliance on prediction undermines managers' ability to pursue new opportunities, the

uncertain ones that enabled them to grow in the first place.

- **Structure.** Scale must be managed. When a start-up is selling only a few units, a single entrepreneur or a tight team can oversee the whole operation. But as the firm adds volume, moves into more geographies, supports more clients, works with more suppliers, and seeks to standardize delivery, the operation grows. As it grows, the organization develops into specialized units within a hierarchy or a matrix, building structure under a small number of decision-makers at the top. Structure separates decision-making from action taking—the tasks expert entrepreneurs perform quickly, concurrently, and iteratively.

- **Process.** Process is a word with both positive and negative connotations. It is a natural result of the successful growth of a new venture and an asset to a large firm. Not everyone can interact with everyone else, so there is a want and a need for rules, policies, and procedures that enable the structure to function smoothly. Yet many processes design newness—the source of opportunity —out of the system.

A potential entrepreneur reading this might look at these large firm attributes and be reassured of the very reasons for becoming an entrepreneur in the first place. But these are some of the mechanisms that enable firms to become large and successful. Surely, capitalizing on a market the firm worked to create cannot be undesirable. What the entrepreneur implicitly objects to is that these attributes do not generate novelty. They do not free the organization to create. And the reason for the entrepreneurial disdain of prediction, structure, and process is that these elements emerge in more mature environments, while entrepreneurs operate in the uncertain setting of venture, market, or product creation.

Our research has identified five specific differences between approaches for uncertainty versus maturity. Though we describe them as either/or for clarity, many situations have elements of both uncertainty and maturity, so you are likely to see both at work within the same company or even project.

Our objective is to take the best of expert entrepreneurial thinking and re-design prediction, structure, and process in a large firm setting to free parts of the organization to work on creating the next market, product, or service—creating the longer-term future of the large firm.

THE POWER OF PREDICTION

When we give a business problem to a series of expert entrepreneurs, one of the things we notice is how little they use prediction. In the course of creating new ventures and developing expertise, one of the heuristics expert entrepreneurs learn is not to rely on history for making decisions. Confident (wrongly or rightly) that they will change the environment where they operate, they focus instead on actions that will create a future where they will benefit.

Of course, entrepreneurs are not the only experts out there. There are expert doctors, chess players, taxi drivers, and even expert corporate executives. The same logic applies. Over the course of time (at least ten years) and practice, expert corporate managers learn heuristics that work well in a large firm environment. One of those heuristics is prediction.

> What we need is an entrepreneurial society in which innovation and entrepreneurship are normal, steady and continual.
>
> Peter F. Drucker

Institutionally, prediction is forced on corporate executives. From forecasts to budgets, from personal target objectives to measuring customer satisfaction, historical data is used as a basis for planning and for goal setting. And well it should be. It works. Plotting the sales growth over past years to predict sales this year in order to plan staffing levels and production gives a good and useful result. So the institutional mandate is reinforced by the fact that prediction is sufficiently useful, and it is what corporate executives learn.

Predictive choices

In fact, corporate executives learn prediction so well that it becomes the hammer they use in any situation, regardless of whether the problem is a nail or not. In an experiment, we presented senior corporate executives with a decision-making scenario. It started in a very mature industry— making strategic decisions for a fictitious refrigerator manufacturer named Frigus—over a series of periods (described as years). For half the executives, the company and the industry stayed mature over time. Little changed. The same competitors made the same products and the same consumers bought them. For the other half of the executives, the environment got uncertain. Competitors merged, new competitors entered, new technologies appeared, new consumer segments and new distribution channels arose. In both situations we measured the extent to which executives based their decisions on prediction. As you might expect, in the mature environment executives used prediction more and more as the scenario unfolded and they realized it was a useful tool. What you might not expect is that as soon as executives were presented with the uncertain situation, they chose actions based on prediction even more than their peers making the decisions in the mature environment. Despite the obvious disconnection between what had happened historically and what was happening, expert managers, unsure of what to do next, defaulted to what they learned through expertise.

Prediction solutions

Are corporate executives destined to deploy the hammer of prediction in any situation? No. Awareness helps. The understanding that prediction is but one of many possible tools actually helps. Enabling executives to see their own decision-making bias helps as well.

In addition, we analyzed two elements in our refrigeration company simulation that meaningfully impacted the

CONTRASTING PERSPECTIVES: EXECUTIVES AND ENTREPRENEURS LOOK AT OPPORTUNITY

	Large corporation	New venture environment
View of opportunities	Defined and narrow Corporate policies restrict options. Typically, only opportunities adjacent to or supporting the core business are considered.	Diverse and negotiable. Everything from product offering to target market is negotiable. Investors can consider investments unrelated by business area, size, customer, or nature of product.
Potential funders	Few and restricted. New opportunities often have a single point of approval. This limits both the ability to get a project started and to change the direction of a project as the opportunity unfolds.	Many and flexible. The diversity in the investor population gives entrepreneurs a market of potential funders.
Financial criteria	Impact the bottom line. For a US$20 billion company, a minimum meaningful impact might be US$1 billion, precluding consideration of smaller opportunities, and forcing the firm to make very few, very large bets.	Positive return. Investors invest in a small fraction of the business plans they review. Level of investment can be scaled to the size of the opportunity, so the range of "interesting" can be broad.
Outlook	Supportive and measured in quarters. Large public firms answer to the stock market, and inevitably manage toward quarterly earnings reports. Once funded, a project is typically supported unless faced with overwhelmingly negative results.	Iterative and measured in years. A venture capitalist-funded start-up might raise four to six investment "rounds" prior to liquidity. Each new investment requires that significant milestones were achieved with the last investment, and offers a checkpoint to adjust direction.
Value added	Offer infrastructure and build synergy. The large enterprise offers distribution, brand, manufacturing, and administrative support to the venture. These assets are typically helpful only after the opportunity has been created.	Offer a network and build a portfolio. An investor brings relationships that might generate customers, partnerships, or future investors to their portfolio firms.

ability of corporate executives to venture beyond prediction when faced with uncertainty. The first was how they viewed the situation. When they found the industry and competitive environment around the refrigeration company threatening, prediction was used even more strongly. But when viewed as an opportunity, executives were able to shift more quickly to approaches similar to those used by our expert entrepreneurs. The other factor comes back to expertise. Those executives who had experience in uncertain situations (new geographies, new products, new markets . . .) were also able to shift more quickly to non-predictive approaches when they saw prediction wasn't working. So helping corporate executives see opportunity and rotating them through job positions where they will face uncertainty seem like good approaches toward keeping people in large firms open to entrepreneurial heuristics.

THE STRENGTH OF STRUCTURE

How we think and how we organize are intimately connected. So it is natural that managers comfortable with prediction would build structures that reinforce and streamline repeating the same activities again and again. Consider the following situation:

There is a proposal for a new product on the top of the stack of papers on your desk. You left it there last night, knowing how important it is for the company to generate new opportunities. Before you even open it, questions enter your mind. How will you get this approved by the division

president? Are the numbers in the proposal big enough to get her attention? Are the numbers in the proposal so big the team can never achieve them? If it is approved, can the team execute fast enough to beat the competitors? If it fails, will you lose your job? If it is so successful it eats into the margin on the firm's existing profitable products, will you lose your job? Beside it sits a budget for a small marketing outlay on an existing product. Your gut tells you to pick up the marketing budget and ignore the new product idea for yet another day. Too many financial hurdles. Too much personal risk. Too much uncertainty. You reach, and . . .

Re-structuring structure

What is it about the organizational structure of a large firm that guides decisions like this one down the incremental path, refining existing products and discouraging the creation of new ones?

The new venture environment is simply friendlier to the process of opportunity creation. It is easy to see why leaders like Ross Perot left IBM to create Electronic Data Systems, and Steve Wozniak left HP to create Apple Computer, instead of developing those opportunities within a large firm. But by learning from the entrepreneurial environment, structure can be used to encourage, not inhibit, opportunity creation.

Entrepreneurial structure: The internal market

The new venture environment works as a market. Most large firms work as hierarchies. But imagine if the opportunity creation function within a large firm could be restructured to operate more like a market. Markets already exist within some companies. 3M uses a market-like allocation system for employee time; employees are given one day a week to work on whatever ideas they like. One of the many results is the Post-it note. Art Fry, a 3M employee, was working on this idea in his own time and, of course, the Post-it became one of 3M's biggest successes. Another example is Koch Industries, a large privately owned US corporation trading in oil and fertilizers. It practices "market-based management," which gives employees decision rights and performance-related pay. And in Silicon Valley, employees at highly successful Google can use 20 percent of their time to work on whatever projects they want.

The core idea is that a large corporation should represent a portfolio of differentiated opportunities that have some technology or market commonality. Ideas might originate anywhere and the objective is to create a structure to nurture them at an appropriate level so their full potential can be realized with minimal risk. An internal market functions on some or all of the following principles, derived from elements that make the new venture structure function:

- Open the market to all potential innovators. Offer time, freedom, or autonomy to people who have the drive to explore new opportunities. Provide structure so that anyone with an idea can submit a proposal for funding.
- Open the market to all potential investors. Anyone with profit and loss responsibility in the firm can apply to manage a fund. Investment returns are included in the profit/loss results of the investor's business unit. Fund sizes are set annually (at the most frequent). Decision-making for investing in new projects is distributed outside the CEO office, potentially even to outsiders—for example, individuals from the venture capital industry might be permitted to invest in internal projects.
- Encourage iterative opportunity development. The initial funder of the project is not permitted to exclusively provide follow-on funding. Other funders (internal and external) must participate. This has several implications. First, external funders such as venture capitalists, partners, or customers can help validate an opportunity. Second, internal funders have to be cooperative and quick to compete with external

Explained:

Threat rigidity

Researchers have shown that when faced with a situation people find threatening, people artificially limit the range of options available to them, typically to the approaches they have already been using—they become rigid in the face of the threat. However, when the situation is viewed as an opportunity, people see many more possible solution options and become much more creative with the possibilities.

Staw *et al.* (1981)

sources of funding for the best new opportunities. Third, it restrains "escalation of commitment" that initial funders can fall into—throwing good money at an opportunity that is clearly bad.
- Eliminate minimum investment sizes. Investments can be scalable based on the industry and the opportunity. This encourages people to fund projects that don't initially impact the bottom line and encourages people not to overfund early and uncertain projects, instead adding funding iteratively as the opportunity is proven.

- Make everything negotiable (within the philosophy and values of the company). Just like in venture capital, ownership, salary, amount of funding, nature of the business plan, milestones, and much more are all jointly agreed by funders and creators. Equity in opportunities can be bought and sold both in the internal and external markets at market rates. Intellectual property owned by the firm can be secured by the new opportunity team, and vice-versa.
- Support projects that compete with the core business. And even share company resources that might complement the new venture. Better for competition to come from inside than outside.
- Embrace failure. Offer employees the assurance that if they explore an idea and it fails, they won't be fired or penalized. Build a culture and a structure that uses failure as a mechanism for learning, not for weeding out employees.

Bringing many of these principles inside the firm, HP has established a close relationship with Silicon Valley venture firm Foundation Capital, learning both how to manage opportunities from venture capitalists, and exchanging ideas about future trends. And while it might be no surprise that Microsoft regularly meets with venture capitalists to shop opportunities too small for the software giant to bring to market, the trend is one that extends to companies in more traditional industries. Internal market elements drive new products at firms that include Coca-Cola and Citigroup and give energy to talent management at American Express.

Current research: The elements of the internal market

There are three core elements that can be used to make any company more market-like in the way it operates:

- **Autonomy:** Provide employees the freedom to pursue what they perceive to be interesting ideas.

- **Rewards:** If you create an innovation, you derive some benefit.

- **Psychological safety:** The assurance that if you have an idea, explore it, and it fails, you won't be fired or penalized for it.

In a recent study we looked at around 6,000 firms representing some 2.5 million employees. We found that these three elements—autonomy, reward, and psychological safety—are significantly related to innovation. But the element that stands out, where the relationship to innovation appears to be twice as significant, is psychological safety.

It seems the most important variable in the culture of an organization to promote innovation is to support employees and allow them to weather the storm of failure. People should feel safe to try out innovative, experimental ideas without fear of being penalized for it.

Looking again at the difference between a hierarchical organization and an internal market, this also has an impact on decision-making and the progression of ideas. The traditional hierarchical system is like a monopoly—if you come up with a good idea and your boss doesn't like it, it goes no further.

The real question here is how can companies institutionalize the idea of using failure as learning for the organization? After all, not every project will result in a positive financial outcome, but there will always be a positive knowledge outcome.

Different structure, different outcome

Let's return to new product proposal where we started. The firm runs an internal market, and you have a fund: a block of real money to invest in real opportunities. It is separate from your operating budget. Your peers also have funds of different sizes; they too may invest to create opportunities. In fact, you may be competing with one of them for a piece of ownership of the proposal on your desk. This fund is dear as you had to apply for it from treasury and you carry it on your unit's profit and loss. You will benefit both financially and professionally if you can turn it into something. Instead of a large research and development budget, it is a source of innovation for your business unit. Today, might you pick up the new product proposal rather than the small marketing outlay?

PRACTICALLY SPEAKING: THE GORE MARKET

Adventurers from New York to Nepal have long appreciated Gore-Tex. The material's seemingly paradoxical ability to keep the weather out while enabling perspiration to escape enables a wide range of functional and comfortable outerwear. And as the firm that delivered this innovation, W.L. Gore & Associates, has surpassed its 50th birthday, we celebrate by taking a closer look at how the company has stayed entrepreneurial for half a century.

W.L. "Bill" Gore started his career at DuPont in 1945 and joined a team finding applications for a novel polymer called polytetrafluoroethylene—Teflon to the rest of us. Bill experimented with the material as a tough, heat-resistant coating for wiring, an application that he felt offered great potential given the likely rise of the computer. Convinced of its technical merits, he tried unsuccessfully to convince DuPont to productize

Teflon-coated cable. Frustrated, in 1958 he created his own firm with his wife Vieve in their basement. WL Gore & Associates' cable product did create a market. Within ten years, the firm employed more than 200 people and Gore cable had been used on a mission to the moon.

Strong competition in the cable industry kept Bill and his son Bob focused on innovation. Continuing to work with Teflon, the pair figured out how to heat and stretch the material so it could be woven as fabric, and Gore-Tex was born. But even before that, Bill had started carefully crafting W.L. Gore & Associates' organization so that it could embrace innovation in the way his previous employer had not.

Employees of W.L. Gore are called Associates. In the non-hierarchical "lattice" structure, Gore empowered all his employees with the same level of authority. Leaders could only emerge if other associates committed to follow them, and associates had the choice of which projects to work on. The intent and outcome of the structure was to enable good new ideas to grow

organically at the discretion of the team. And the teams also had the support of Gore as he let them do just about anything that would not jeopardize the entire company.

Gore quantified optimal team size, and constructed his organization accordingly. He felt that when a team at a manufacturing facility exceeded 150 people, two things happened. First, the team lost a sense of cooperation, shifting decision responsibility from "we" (the team) to "they" (some anonymous faceless bureaucrat). Second, accomplishment per person started to decrease on teams exceeding 150. Consequently, when manufacturing teams exceeded 150 people, Gore split the operation into two.

The approach has worked. Today, W.L. Gore & Associates has created innovative products in areas you probably know, such as clothing and shoes, and in many more that range from guitar strings to dental floss, space suits to sutures. Gore is one of the 200 largest private firms in the US, and in 2007, for the tenth straight

year, the firm made *Fortune*'s annual list of the US "100 Best Companies to Work For."

Today, with more than US$2 billion in annual sales, 2,000 patents, and more than 8,000 employees worldwide, the company continues to defy the common expectation that large cannot also be entrepreneurial.

Gore application questions

- ☐ What are some potential pitfalls of the Gore model?
- ☐ How does the Gore model help us think about managing spin-offs?
- ☐ In what situations might the Gore model offer benefit?
- ☐ Which aspects of the Gore model seem most compelling to your business?

Staying entrepreneurial

W.L. Gore splits the firm every time the number of employees exceeds 150 in order to ensure that every "company" within Gore continues to operate entrepreneurially.

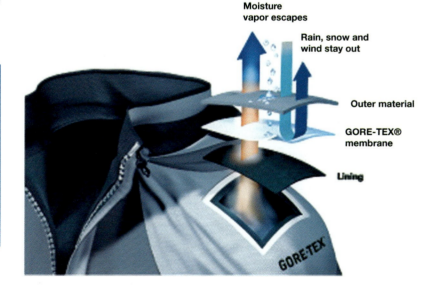

SAFETY IN FAILURE WITHIN LARGE ORGANIZATIONS—QUESTIONS AND ANSWERS

How should a professional negotiate a margin of failure with the boss?	The employee should consider expectations and affordable loss. Setting outrageous expectations for a new project or a new product may help get resources approved, but also makes it difficult to deal productively with any shortfall in the results. Be realistic with the boss. Second, and particularly with highly uncertain projects, evaluate the level of affordable loss, or the level of downside that the individual and the firm can tolerate associated with the opportunity. If managed effectively, failure will never get to a point where the project generates losses that the individual or the firm can't afford. This helps to make the post-mortem of failed projects less of an emotional exercise and something people can be objective about and can learn from.
Should the failures at work be discussed before or after they happen?	Failure should be discussed in advance in the context of where the pitfalls may lie (so they can be avoided or leveraged) and in terms of how much will be invested in the project. A project can still be considered successful as long as it stays within the predefined affordable limit—a key insight for being able to redefine losing as successful with a large organization. Also, every project deserves an "after-action review"—a chance to look at what the team liked and did not like about the project, what was learned from the project, and how to take that learning either into the organization and/or into the next iteration of the project.
How can a manager build safety within his or her team to increase innovation?	Walk the talk. Learn from his or her own failures. Share that learning with the team. Conduct "after-action reviews" with the team for all projects. Promote people who have been able to effectively learn from failure, and communicate those stories. This is clearly not something that can be put into a policy manual—it is an enacted part of a team or firm culture.

PRACTICALLY SPEAKING: THE POINT OF PROCESS

Despite the popular malignment of process, it has an intended function: to help organize, coordinate, and facilitate the actions of many individuals within a large organization. The problem is not the process, but the implementation of the process: what it is actually meant to accomplish. To provide a view into a different possible implementation of process, consider the story of an insurance software start-up named Guidewire. When John Seybold and his partners founded Guidewire Software in 2001, he knew little more about the insurance industry than an informed consumer. But as CTO of the upstart company, he also knew he and the team had to learn quickly if they were going to convince mainstream insurers to scrap their aging mainframes and adopt Guidewire's Java-based solutions.

Process objective: Flexibility

The team looked at the problem and made a decision. Above all, they would be flexible: flexible product, flexible business model, and flexible organization. They expected to gain insights every day from customers, partners, and competitors, and they wanted to be able to immediately benefit from everything they learned.

Process implementation: Sprint

Guidewire organized around small, nimble project teams. But here comes the twist. A project team's assignment only lasts a month. At the start of a month, each "sprint team" picks from the list of the most important tasks to be tackled. The team selects a leader for the month and devours the task.

At the end of the month, the team wraps up the project, reflects on its progress, reprioritizes, and picks a new task, and the process starts all over.

The key to keeping the whole organization moving toward success is the "master backlog" list of projects. As new ideas are generated and new requests come from customers, they are added to the backlog. No changes to priorities are made during a monthly sprint. But at the start of each new month, the organization reprioritizes the entire backlog and assigns only those tasks that top the list to the next month's sprint teams.

At the end of each month, each team has a specific deliverable: something that must be complete, tested, docu-mented, and ready for a customer. In fact, it is the customer who reviews the deliverable and decides whether to accept it or not. Doing this both forces the team to focus on creating something usable and complete, and also gives the customer a strong voice within the organization.

Every day, each sprint team meets for ten minutes in the morning at the whiteboard to discuss what they did yesterday and what they hope to accomplish today. Individual priorities and performance are as transparent as team performance. Completely transparent. At the end of each month, the teams examine the process to discuss what worked well, what did not work, and what they want to change when they reassemble for the next month's sprint.

Process outcome: Innovation

The success of the process can be demonstrated in the numerous industry awards and client references newcomer Guidewire has already garnered. But Seybold describes an unexpected benefit:

> When we first did this, I thought seeing the huge backlog and the small projects we finished in a month would discourage the team. But exactly the reverse happened. They said wow—we're in control and look at what we did. It was a real morale booster, and it has continued to be.

Guidewire has grown to over 400 people and counts more than 60 international insurers in its growing customer base. Large for a start-up, but still small compared with the insurance giants they sell to. Nonetheless, this process has continued to scale and work for Guidewire. By the way, if you are skeptical about this version of process within a large organization, you may smile to know that virtually all of Guidewire's large, conservative clients in the insurance industry use precisely this approach, learned from Guidewire, within their own teams that are implementing Guidewire's software.

Principles of process

Process generally does what it is designed to do. What Guidewire demonstrates is that it is possible to

Guidewire application questions

- ☐ How easy is it for you to terminate a dead-end project?

- ☐ Do you have a place for the customer in your organization?

- ☐ What kind of people will this kind of organization attract?

- ☐ Do you have a regular way to revise and optimize teams?

- ☐ Is your organization generating innovation at the rate you expect?

- ☐ Do your employees feel they make a visible and measurable contribution toward the success of your firm?

- ☐ Do you have the visibility you need in the innovation process in your organization?

design a process that enables, not inhibits innovation. As you think about your own organization, it is not necessary to do everything Guidewire has done. Elements of the process, such as monthly priority reviews or customer acceptance of deliverables, can be implemented in an organization without moving to small sprint teams. Also, an entire large organization does not need to have the same process. Teams, groups, cells, or divisions charged with entrepreneurially creating new opportunities might design their own process in the same way teams within insurance firms implementing Guidewire software decided to. Regardless of what the actual implementation looks like, it is liberating to consider how you might change the rules of the organization to encourage entrepreneurial action.

TAKEAWAY: A FRESH LOOK

Understanding expert entrepreneurial approaches and applying them to the large firm offers a new perspective on the questions that surround executives with the mandate of innovation and growth. Clearly, these approaches offer insight into managing new product projects and entering new markets. More subtly, they offer ideas on selecting, promoting, and training internal people inside a large firm as well as thinking on what might help entrepreneurs stay with the venture as it grows into a large firm. They have implications for the strategic planning process inside a large firm, in specific for acquisitions of start-ups and corporate venture funds. And they also inform research and development partnerships and overseeing technology licensing. Though the odds are against the large firm that aspires to be entrepreneurial, there are ways to overcome the three main structural barriers to acting entrepreneurially within a large organization. Perhaps the good and the great can be entrepreneurial as well!

Research roots

High-performance ventures create the most social value

In *The Illusions of Entrepreneurship*, Scott Shane (2008) surveys research on small business in order to highlight that the general public and economic policymakers tend to hold many misconceptions about entrepreneurship. One interesting misconception is the idea that new ventures are a public good because they generally create jobs. The truth is that a few new ventures that grow strongly are responsible for most of the job growth. This highlights what we have talked about in this book—that learning principles used by expert entrepreneurs who have demonstrated an ability to launch high-performance ventures that create new products and markets and new large firms is not only good for you but also good for society because it is the high-performance ventures that create the most social value.

Roadmap

- In your organization, at what number of employees does your "achievement per employee" level off (e.g. Gore)?

- How will you change selection and promotion of people inside a larger firm, in light of these ideas?

- If you were to create an "internal market" for opportunities, who would be your "buyers," who would be your sellers, and what would a transaction look like?

- Identify two research and development partnerships and/or two licensing relationships that already seem to be built upon these effectual ideas (they may have snuck in). Can you identify one more of each that you might run or re-design more effectually?

So what?

Large organizations are built to withstand entrepreneurial efforts involving the effectual principles laid out in this text. As a result, becoming more entrepreneurial as an organization requires more than hope and good intent, it requires specifically designed solutions to overcoming over-reliance on research, prediction, and big bets in the pursuit of new opportunities.

Bigger questions

- What might help entrepreneurs stay with the venture as it grows into a large firm (Bill Gates is exceptional; most founders leave or are forced out as the venture grows)?

- Is there an optimal size for any firm?

CHAPTER 20

What the scientific method did for nature, the entrepreneurial method can do for society.

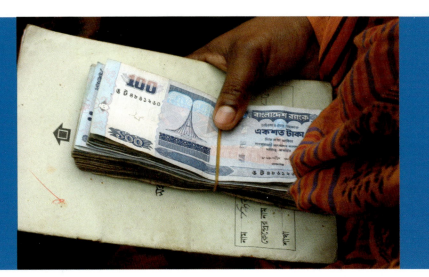

Entrepreneurship as a technology for social change

ERCY CORPS is an organization devoted to helping others in crisis: a worthy, though not unusual sounding, non-government organization (NGO), until you take a closer look. Mercy describes their mission as "helping turn crisis into opportunity for millions around the world." And when you notice that their staff is made up of engineers, financial analysts, project managers, public health experts, and logisticians, the news that the organization acquired a commercial bank (Mercy Corps acquired Andara Bank in Indonesia in 2008) starts to make sense. By blurring the lines that distinguish a charity from a business, Mercy Corps offers us one introduction to the idea of the social entrepreneur. Improving access to microfinance in Indonesia supports the organization's mission. Making money in the process does not detract from the organization's mission. Though this example is located in tropical Indonesia, it is a small step toward a revolution that may destroy the artificial and unnecessary distinction between a for-profit venture and a charity. And when you look around, revolutionaries can be found everywhere in the financial services industry, from Mohammed Yunus, creator of the Grameen Bank, to the team behind Kiva, a person-to-person micro-loan website.

This chapter is devoted to understanding the basis of a revolution, independent of geography or industry. As you read, consider how entrepreneurs resolve the question of doing

Birth of the social bank

When Mohammed Yunus, founder of Grameen Bank, realized he could afford to lend enough money for a whole village to rebuild its economy—the princely sum of US$27—he did just that. Only later, as he expanded his loans to multiple villages, did he bump against the cardinal rule of banking—loans without collateral ought to be deemed unbankable. The entire microfinance industry is now beginning to wake up to the notion of lending against cash flows as opposed to collateral—a point reinforced by Damian von Stauffenberg, the founder of Microrate—who emphasizes this as the key delineator between traditional lending and microfinance as well as the main differentiator between the best and the worst microfinance organizations in the industry.

what they ought against doing what they can, and how the principles we have explicated in this book work in the social sector.

PRACTICALLY SPEAKING: ONEWORLD HEALTH

The next time you pick up a prescription, take a look at the price of the product—not the portion you pay after insurance, but the actual price. Pharmaceuticals are expensive. And that translates into good business. Industry profits are in the 20 percent range, and with the aging population driving demand, today's global pharma sales are expected to more than double, reaching US$1.3 trillion, by the year 2020. For context, that is more than India's entire gross domestic product.

An opportunity of that scale attracts entrepreneurs by the score, but none

quite like Victoria Hale. She wants to make pharmaceuticals that don't make money. Yes, you read that correctly. Her firm, Institute for OneWorld Health, describes itself as a nonprofit pharmaceutical company. OneWorld is her solution to the problem facing people in countries like India who simply cannot afford many modern pharmaceutical treatments—clearly a worthwhile endeavor and it is worth understanding its foundation as well.

Hale comes from the industry. She has a PhD in pharmacology from the University of California San Francisco (one of the top medical schools in the US), and she has worked for both the US Food and Drug Administration and Genentech. Those experiences enabled her to see "opportunity" where others saw waste. Every day, patents on profitable pharmaceuticals expire, enabling anyone to produce and distribute the compound without paying a royalty. Every day, research and development projects are cancelled

because the resulting product could not find a profitable market. While useless to large pharma firms, these events could offer technology OneWorld could employ, at a price OneWorld and its customers could afford.

Also known as "black fever," kala-azar (formally visceral leishmaniasis) is a disease transmitted by sand flies. If left untreated, the resulting internal organ damage is nearly always fatal. Half a million new cases are estimated worldwide annually, largely in India, Bangladesh, and Nepal. Starting with an "off-patent" antibiotic, OneWorld assembled partners from the commercial, nonprofit, and government sectors to develop, test, and approve paromomycin—a compound capable of curing a black fever victim for less than US$10. Paromomycin distribution started in 2007 in India, and if Hale has her way, the compound could eradicate the disease completely.

Entrepreneurs are often described as "creative," but perhaps "creators" is a more apt term. Had Hale not dragged a solution from the dustbins of pharma and built partnerships to create a new business model that gets cheap remedies to "unprofitable" markets, it is unlikely that the need would be served today. In other words, while so many aspiring entrepreneurs search for opportunities just waiting to be discovered, real entrepreneurs roll up their sleeves to make them. And so new opportunities come to be that otherwise did not exist and so, of course, could not be found.

Hale's next foes are diarrheal disease, malaria, and Chagas disease. Her success against kala-azar offers her

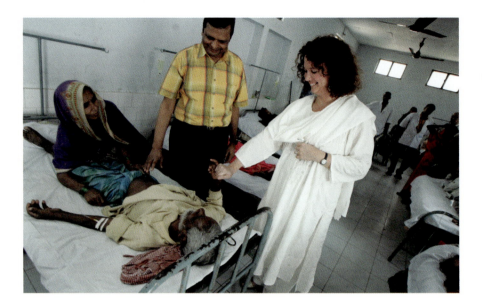

new means in these next challenges. She has new knowledge, new partners, and even new money. OneWorld has received more than US$100 million in grants from notables such as the Bill & Melinda Gates Foundation and the Lehman Brothers Foundation.

OneWorld application questions

- ■ Are there any industries that could not offer social benefit employing a Victoria Hale approach?

- ■ How might the for-profit pharma companies work more closely with OneWorld in a way that is productive for both?

- ■ What would a competitor of OneWorld look like?

OVERCOMING THE SEPARATION THESIS: MARRYING SOCIAL CHANGE AND PROFIT

What holds more individuals back from accomplishing what Hale and Yunus demonstrate can be done? How might we encourage people to break the separation between doing something productive and making a profit?

- **Change the tax code.** Perhaps the answer lies in making social enterprise more attractive at a regulatory level—reducing the tax burden on income from products or services provided by organizations that deliver social good. There is a wide range of implementations of different tax codes across countries and even local governments. But one theme is reasonably consistent: Taxation schemes clearly delineate between charity and for-profit enterprise. A graduated approach that appreciates the spectrum of different

business models might serve to encourage more firms to serve the common good by making a profit.

- **Take political action.** Separation is enforced at the political level, though perhaps needlessly. While one arm of the government is focused on bringing money in through taxation, a completely different arm is focused on pushing money out to socially beneficial programs that include welfare and health care. But what if these two bodies were to collaborate? And set up a scheme that allowed people like Hale and Yunus to take on the social needs of the community while at the same time generating a profit?

- **Teach and preach.** Educators have significant reach into the thinking of the educated population. There is certainly more opportunity to open the dialog about ways to break down the artificial separation between charity and profit. And while this can be accomplished with a Socratic dialog kind of an approach, or an evangelistic Billy Graham style, the opportunity exists.

- **Entrepreneurship.** But where are the revolutionaries? Will this problem see resolution from a top-down approach articulated by the first three alternatives? Not likely. Which is why we focus on the power of the entrepreneur. As a maker of new worlds, the entrepreneur has the freedom from historic assumptions, such as "doing something socially productive can't also make money." Why not do both? Because if there is an interest in doing both, then the real question is how.

THE "ENTREPRENEURIAL METHOD"

In order to gain insight into whether the separation thesis extends to actual entrepreneurs, we go back more than 200 years to the story of Josiah Wedgwood. As founder of the famed Wedgwood pottery works, he is associated with the accumulation of great wealth. But the manufacture and transportation of delicate pottery in those days was a challenging process. In addition to his Etruria pottery works, Wedgwood created a school to teach unskilled laborers the craft of fine painting. Wedgwood also undertook several major public works projects, digging the Trent and Mersey Canals that connected the River Trent with the River Mersey. In neither case was his motive solely altruistic. There were not enough skilled artisans to meet the demand for Wedgwood pottery. The roads were so uneven that much pottery was smashed before it was even delivered. Yet Wedgwood was able to deliver social good alongside profit from fine pottery. Before we ask the question of whether we really need social entrepreneurs at all, it is interesting to note that the Wedgwood fortune also funded Wedgwood's grandson Charles Darwin to embark on the voyage of the *Beagle*, a trip that would generate what scientists claim to be the most significant advancement in scientific thinking of the millennium.

Through the Wedgwood example, it is clear that for many entrepreneurs, there is no line between what for-profit ventures do and what social ventures do. Many entrepreneurs are simply both. And perhaps more important, what we find is that the same underlying method is at work in both cases.

Comparing The entrepreneurial method with the scientific method

The scientific method consists in the notion that the world can be systematically studied and understood in terms that do not include divine revelation or intervention (Sagan, 2002). It also incorporates the idea that the work of navigators, inventors, and craftsmen can be a model for scholars (Bacon, 1620). At the heart of the scientific method is the belief that Nature's potential can be harnessed for the achievement of human purposes—not the details of what exactly constitutes the method but the realization that such methods can and do exist.

The entrepreneurial method is analogous to the scientific method in the notion that societies can be systematically shaped and rebuilt without massive political movements or governmental regulations. It incorporates the idea that what actual entrepreneurs do can be a model for educators and policymakers. At the heart of the entrepreneurial method is the belief that human potential can be unleashed not only for the achievement of societal purposes, but also for imagining and fashioning new purposes for different groups of people at different points in time and space.

As eminent scientists have observed, even the social sciences have undergone a vast change in how they explain human behavior. It is no longer necessary to argue that people are pushed and pulled by their inner and outer environments. It is okay to model human behavior in terms of initiatives, active agency, and conscious choice. When Francis Bacon proposed that human beings can go beyond observing and passively predicting the inevitable course of nature to manipulating and controlling it, the reaction was one of shock and disbelief. After centuries of technological progress where millions of "ordinary" scientists have been educated to contribute to that project, we should be ready to embrace the idea that we can intervene positively in the transformation of our own social purposes and environments.

Bacon's enumeration of "experimentation" as a method of purposefully intervening in nature is a common technique of the scientific method and an essential part of all basic education today. So too, we hope, our explication of "effectuation" will become part of the mundane toolbox of entrepreneurial education—and entrepreneurship itself should become part of all basic education in the near future.

PRACTICALLY SPEAKING: HOW TO CHANGE THE WORLD

Imagine your dream is to change the world on a national or, better still, global scale. And the bureaucracy at your employer, the United States Federal Government, severely constrains what you can accomplish. What would you do?

Not many people would think of taking their own money and paying "salaries" to individuals in developing countries, even if these individuals might show promise in reforming their national environments. But that is exactly what Bill Drayton did when he launched Ashoka in India in 1980.

It is not just the founding of Ashoka that makes Bill Drayton an entrepreneur, but the "way" he did it—the process, the business model—and the fact that Ashoka literally is changing the world through social entrepreneurship. Let us examine Drayton's and Ashoka's journey, using the same principles we have applied to for-profit entrepreneurs. From the start, Drayton knew that he alone could not solve the world's social problems. But he had traveled extensively in India and Indonesia, and he did know that people existed who were already generating practical solutions to society's problems at a local level. These people and their ideas would provide him with resources—they would give him a place to start and he would give them a chance to disseminate what they had designed and learned.

When Drayton created Ashoka, he created the concept of an Ashoka fellow: someone with a new idea that has the potential for significant social impact, an idea he/she has proved locally and wants to roll out on a larger scale. Once selected, an Ashoka fellow is rewarded with training, a monthly living stipend (for three years), and networking opportunities.

Consider one of the first fellows, Fábio Luiz de Oliveira Rosa. Saddened by the exodus of farmers to cities in his native Brazil, Rosa developed a cheap way to bring electricity to poor, remote areas, allowing, for example, the irrigation of farmlands. For an investment of about US$400, rural farmers could then install a single-phase water pump system and drastically enhance their productivity, increase their incomes by an average of four times, and make farming a financially and socially attractive alternative to living in overpopulated cities. Seeing the potential, Ashoka named Rosa a fellow and helped him to persuade the Brazilian government to enable implementation by granting farmers loans for the upfront investment.

Starting with just US$50,000 (2009 budget: US$40 million), Ashoka has never risked failure on any single project. Quite to the contrary, the distributed approach of funding many local Ashoka fellows enables Drayton to spread the impact of the organization, and the risk, across 2,700 fellows from over 70 countries today. Consistent with how successful entrepreneurs manage risk, this approach lets individual failures become learning experiences, not venture termination points.

During the 30 years since Ashoka was founded, much has changed in the landscape of social enterprise.

For example, the Grameen Bank has proven a model of distributed small-scale investing which generates both returns and impact. Instead of viewing Grameen as competition, Ashoka has adopted its approach of "blueprint copying"—transferring best practice to a new problem or region, and it has also added micro-loans to the arsenal available to its fellows. And some of its fellows use micro-loans as part of their own arsenal of actions.

Each of the approaches described here has been observed in successful and entrepreneurial companies because they function equally well for profitable businesses as they do in the social sector. They have certainly worked for Ashoka. An early recipient of a MacArthur Fellowship (sometimes referred to as the "genius grant"), Drayton has received a National Public Service Award from the American Society of Public Administration and the National Academy of Public Administration, and he has also been recognized as one of America's Best 25 leaders by *US News & World Report* (Hsu, 2005).

Drayton says,

> **Our job is not to give people fish, it's not to teach them how to fish, it's to build new and better fishing industries.**

WHY DONATE WHEN WE CAN INVEST?

Why is it that we *invest* in Genzyme or Microsoft, but *donate* to Red Cross or Transparency International? Why is it that it takes 43 cents on a dollar for a good non-profit to raise a dollar when less than 5 cents gets the average banker that same dollar, and he or she lives much better than the average NGO official? Arguments fly back and forth that one subsidizes the other and that the former is less efficient and more fragmented than the other. And, of course, there's the same tired old pivot—that one is profitable and the other is not. We find it difficult to believe that investing in software is more profitable than investing in the creative fount from which such a thing as software originated in the first place. If a piece of code that moves around a bunch of electrical impulses can create wealth, it is absurd to think that the mind that creates that piece of code is less profitable—and societies that foster and develop such minds even less so. We seek answers elsewhere.

For millennia, human beings did not realize how to harness and use the energies locked up in steam or in the movement and structure of atoms—just as we today struggle to usefully harness the energy locked up in sun, wind, and corn. Similarly, we simply have not yet found the mechanisms that can unleash the potential to close the virtuous circle connecting healthy societies with healthy babies and wealthy futures. Once a society has grown the baby and the ensuing adult has produced goods and services of value, we have relatively efficient and useful ways of pricing them and distributing them to those who want them and are willing and able to pay for them. With the invention of credit, we even know how to identify some of these in advance and reap the benefits within reasonable time lags. But credit markets are relatively new in human history. There is considerable creative work ahead of us to expand them effectively to close the larger circle of human and social improvement. We do not believe this is a task better left to the revolutionary or to the policy-maker. Instead, we find tremendous scope in innovations already existent in today's credit markets. Moreover, these innovations can be transferred and transformed through entrepreneurial initiatives. The history of micro-credit, which started this chapter, attests to such a profitable transfer.

ENTREPRENEURS CREATE MARKETS—WHY NOT MARKETS IN HUMAN HOPE?

Throughout this book, we have described entrepreneurs as people who create firms, products, and markets. That entrepreneurs create markets is important because not only do markets provide the basis for economic growth (and profit), but they are also a vehicle for social change. It is with this view that it is clear that people creating social change do the same things that we associate with "for-profit" entrepreneurs. So everything thus far in the book is relevant to entrepreneurs regardless of whether the legal form of the venture is for-profit or not.

Consider the following questions: Why can't we buy futures contracts in Rwandan prosperity? Or options in environmental conservation in Brazil? Or equity in the emancipation of Afghan women? If we want to participate in the upside potential of biotechnology, we can buy Genzyme stock or shares in a biotech mutual fund with a couple of clicks of the mouse. But if we want to participate in the upside potential of literacy in the Congo delta, or even youth development in South Central Los Angeles, we have to research obscure charities, mail out checks, maybe fill out tax exemption forms, then cross our fingers and hope that our money will be put to some good use. We have no way of analyzing and selecting among competing models, monitoring our investments, trading them for liquidity, or cashing in on positive results.

Why is there a belief that investments in biotech can be profitable but investments in the eradication of human misery cannot? The latter are not even categorized as investments, but charity, to be financed through sacrifice without the expectation of a positive return. The irrepressibly cornucopian economist Julian Simon spent his life arguing that human beings are the ultimate resource. His

data runs deep and long, and his analyses are compellingly careful and explicit. If all economic value ultimately derives from human beings, shouldn't investments in the eradication of human misery be both viable and valuable?

Not all enterprises are investor owned—not even in the US

In the US as of 1990, there were roughly 1,700 consumer cooperatives with sales amounting to US$26 billion and representing 27 percent of all farm production expenditures (up from 23 percent in 1973.

Around the same time, nonprofits accounted for 64 percent of all hospital care, 56 percent of daycare for children and 20 percent of colleges and universities. In Japan, nonprofits account for almost 75 percent of higher education.

In France and Italy, there are thousands of employee-owned firms. And even in the US, both employee stock option plans and fully employee-owned firms are on the increase— take, for example, worker cooperatives in the plywood industry in the Northwest.

(Data from Hansmann, 2000)

As the examples in this chapter show, these questions are neither unrealistic nor unreasonable. Already there are efforts to create private equity markets in a variety of social sector projects. People are learning that there is value in human hope, and they are asking more and more questions about ways we might all benefit from the eradication of human misery. The answers to these questions will certainly require more struggle. But the struggle is worthy of all our creative efforts— especially those of us engaged in entrepreneurship and public financial markets.

EXAMPLES OF MARKETS IN HUMAN HOPE

In 2005 a massive earthquake struck the Kashmir region in the mountains of India and Pakistan. Eighty-seven thousand individuals perished in the quake and 3 million survivors needed to rebuild their lives. The international aid organizations rushed in with supplies and food. And they were joined by the entrepreneurs.

Marc Freudweiler is the founder of a Swiss derivatives trading firm named Derilab. Freudweiler saw both the humanitarian need to rebuild the Kashmir region and the economic benefit that would result. Kashmir had been a productive area before the quake. Repairing the infrastructure would enable the businesses destroyed by the quake to resume the creation of value. Freudweiler talked with people at the UNHCR (United Nations High Commission on Refugees), and the Kashmir Relief Note was born.

The Note was something completely novel: The idea that the public might invest in humanitarian relief and receive a return on their money. The specific outcome was a financial instrument that directs part of the investment into refugee relief and part of the investment into businesses that are likely to increase in value as the region returns to normalcy. Investors could direct funds to the crisis and could generate a return. Doing what we ought does not have to conflict with doing what we can.

TAKEAWAY: DOING WHAT WE OUGHT; DOING WHAT WE CAN

Hopefully, after reading this chapter, you come away with the appreciation that whether a firm is for-profit or not-for-profit, it is a design decision that's made by you. And that the same principles apply regardless. So, what are you going to do?

Change the world?

Make money?

Why choose?

Roadmap

Closing the value loop

When you find a cause that turns you on, or an injustice you want to correct, or a social problem you want to solve, think like a for-profit entrepreneur:

- ☐ Who are your key stakeholders?

- ☐ What is the value proposition for each of them?

- ☐ How can you create a product or service that the stakeholders would want to pay for?

- ☐ How can the beneficiaries of your product/service become your investors?

- ☐ How do you close the value loop through time so that the benefits pay for the costs, even as you make a decent living at it?

- ☐ In short, what is your business model?

Bigger questions

- ☐ How can we make government more entrepreneurial so it might be more supportive of some of these efforts?

- ☐ Unless you are taking gifts, why *not* be a for-profit venture?

So what?

Entrepreneurship generates sustainable solutions to social problems, while at the same time reducing the need to raise donations. By closing the value loop, you can raise investments and earn returns rather than beg people for money or coerce them through taxes.

Conclusion

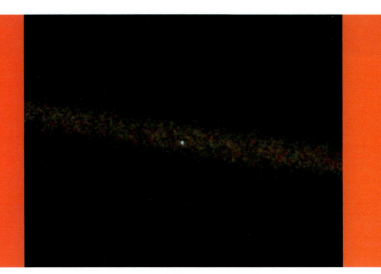

DEAR READER,

In the introduction to the book, we promised:

You will discover in this book that there is a science to entrepreneurship—a common logic we have observed in expert entrepreneurs across industries, geographies, and time . . . When you start a new venture—for-profit or not, individually or within existing organizations—you are not only trying to make a good living, you are engaged in expanding the horizon of valuable new economic opportunities. This book is designed to help you do that from start to finish. And in form and content, the book embodies the expert entrepreneurs' logic—bold, systematic, pragmatic, and at all times full of energy, mischief, and fun.

If you believe we have delivered on our promise, we would like to conclude by extracting a promise from you in return. After all, this is entrepreneurship—you have to pay with value for value delivered. So here goes:

The picture above is the only one of its kind. When the first (and only) human-made object to leave the solar system, the *Voyager* spacecraft, crossed into the vast space between us and the rest of the universe, it turned its camera to take a picture of earth from outside the solar system. Carl Sagan wrote about this picture in a moving way:

Look again at that dot. That's here, that's home, that's us. On it everyone you love, everyone you know, everyone you ever heard of, every human being who ever was, lived out their lives. The aggregate of our joy and suffering, thousands of confident religions, ideologies, and economic doctrines, every hunter and forager, every hero and coward, every creator and destroyer of civilization, every king and peasant, every young couple in love, every mother and father, hopeful child, inventor and explorer, every teacher of morals, every corrupt politician, every "superstar," every "supreme leader," every saint and sinner in the history of our species lived there—on a mote of dust suspended in a sunbeam.

. . . The Earth is the only world known so far to harbor life. There is nowhere else, at least in the near future, to which our species could migrate. Visit, yes. Settle, not yet. Like it or not, for the moment the Earth is where we make our stand.

In this book you have learned that you need not wait for the right technology or the proper resources or the massive machinery of governments or the feeble hope of the next election to rebuild your life and the world in which that life seeks to thrive. You can start today—with who you are, what you know, and who you know—and invest nothing but what you can afford to lose to begin building corridors through which your stakeholders can self-select into your valuable new venture. And together you can co-create a better world that neither you nor they can fully imagine at this point in time.

So get started on your (ad)venture and make your stand on this pale blue dot. And beyond. Bon voyage!

Directory of "practically speaking" sections by topic

Title	Country	Company	Green	Tech	Social	Bus client	Consumer	Means	Affordable loss	Partner	Contingency	Made v. found
—CHAPTER 1—												
Curry in a hurry	Global	Imaginary				●	●	●		●		●
Making a market out of a joke	USA	Pet Rock					●	●	●	●	●	●
—CHAPTER 2—												
Another person's treasure	USA	Agilyx	●	●		●		●	●			●
Turning a hobby into a business	USA	College Bed Lofts					●	●	●		●	●
Turning a passion into a business	USA	Kenny's Great Pies				●		●	●		●	●
Turning a disability into a business	Germany	Unsicht-Bar			●		●	●			●	●
One true media	USA	One True Media		●			●	●		●	●	●

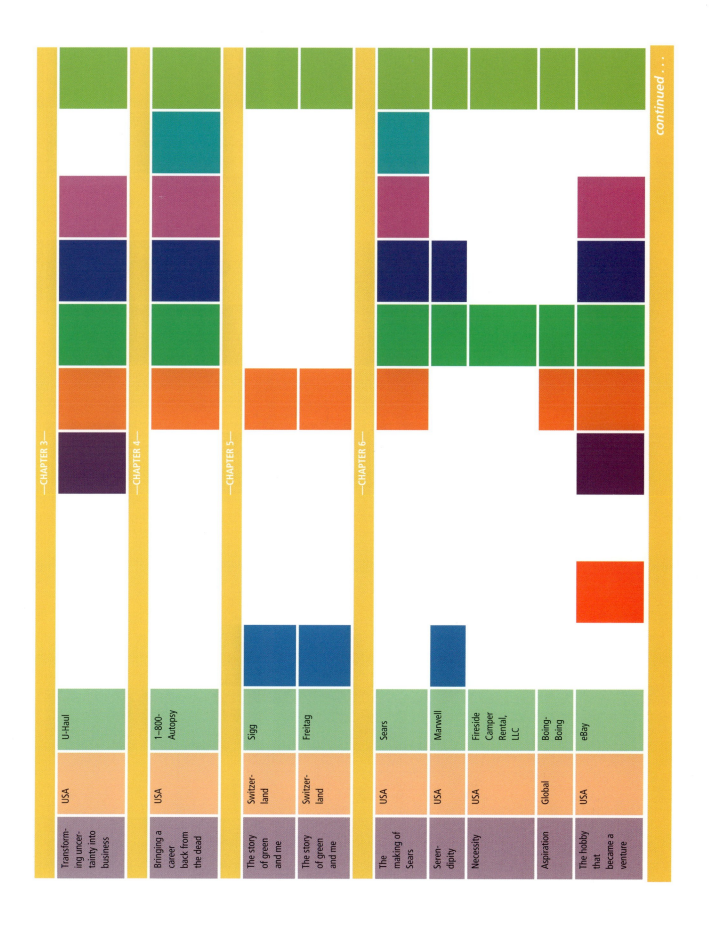

continued . . .

CHAPTER 3		CHAPTER 4		CHAPTER 5			CHAPTER 6				
	U-Haul		1-800-Autopsy		Sigg	Freitag		Sears	Marwell	Fireside Camper Rental, LLC	Boing-Boing	eBay
	USA		USA		Switzer-land	Switzer-land		USA	USA	USA	Global	USA
	Transform-ing uncer-tainty into business		Bringing a career back from the dead		The story of green and me	The story of green and me		The making of Sears	Seren-dipity	Necessity	Aspiration	The hobby that became a venture

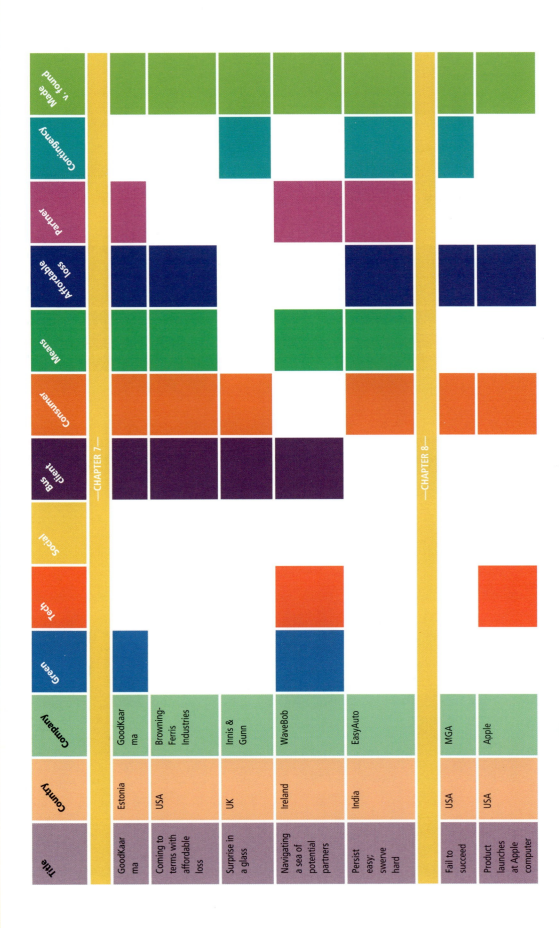

Title	Country	Company	Green	Tech	Social	Bus client	Consumer	Means	Affordable loss	Partner	Contingency	Made v. found
—CHAPTER 7—												
GoodKaarma	Estonia	GoodKaarma	●			●	●	●	●	●		●
Coming to terms with affordable loss	USA	Browning-Ferris Industries				●	●	●	●			●
Surprise in a glass	UK	Innis & Gunn				●	●		●		●	●
Navigating a sea of potential partners	Ireland	WaveBob	●	●		●		●		●		●
Persist easy; swerve hard	India	EasyAuto				●	●	●	●	●	●	●
—CHAPTER 8—												
Fail to succeed	USA	MGA					●		●		●	●
Product launches at Apple computer	USA	Apple		●			●		●		●	●

—CHAPTER 9—

—CHAPTER 10—

—CHAPTER 11—

—CHAPTER 12—

Case	Country	Topic
HERSHEY'S®	USA	Milton Hershey
Estée Lauder	USA	How Estée Lauder got into Saks
AquaStasis	USA	Means in a tank
Eco-Envelopes	USA	The big impact of small envelopes
SpaceShip One	USA	SpaceShip One
Dr. Fad	USA/Japan	Working with slack
Manon Chocolatier	Belgium	Chocolate magic
Nine Dragons	China	Dragon lady
Powerkiss	Finland	Charging ahead
Novozymes	Denmark	Biogeneration
Gardener's Eden	USA	Is a cost always a cost?
Stacy's Pita Chips	USA	Bootstrapping in action

continued . . .

Directory of "practically speaking" sections by topic

... continued

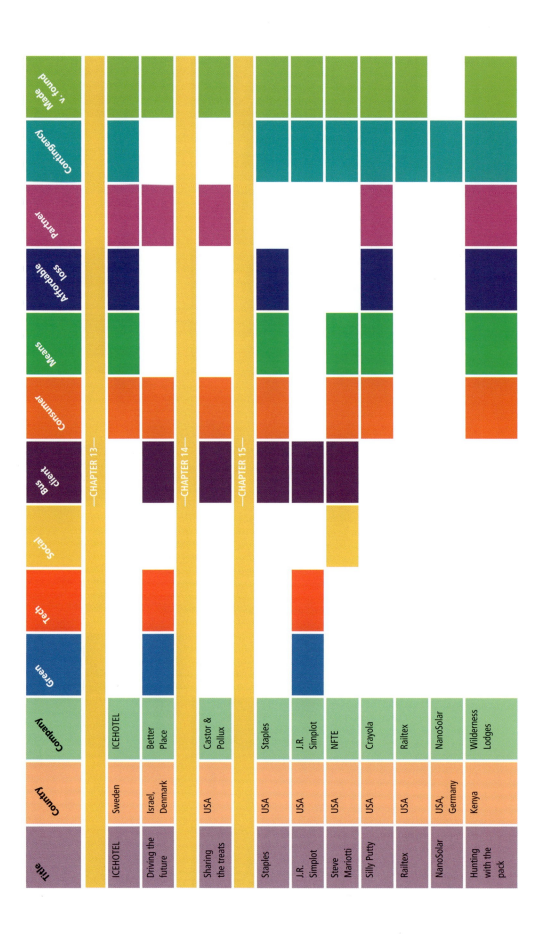

Title	Country	Company	Green	Tech	Social	Bus client	Consumer	Means	Affordable loss	Partner	Contingency	Made v. found
CHAPTER 13												
ICEHOTEL	Sweden	ICEHOTEL					✓	✓	✓	✓	✓	✓
Driving the future	Israel, Denmark	Better Place	✓	✓		✓	✓			✓		✓
CHAPTER 14												
Sharing the treats	USA	Castor & Pollux				✓	✓			✓		✓
CHAPTER 15												
Staples	USA	Staples				✓	✓	✓	✓		✓	✓
J.R. Simplot	USA	J.R. Simplot	✓	✓		✓					✓	✓
Steve Mariotti	USA	NFTE			✓	✓		✓			✓	✓
Silly Putty	USA	Crayola					✓	✓	✓	✓	✓	✓
Railtex	USA	Railtex									✓	✓
NanoSolar	USA, Germany	NanoSolar									✓	
Hunting with the pack	Kenya	Wilderness Lodges					✓	✓	✓	✓	✓	✓

Bibliography

Ch.	Author(s)	Reference
1	Carroll, Lewis	(1874) *The Hunting of the Snark*. London: Macmillan.
1	Bhidé, A.	(2000) *The Origin and Evolution of New Businesses*. Oxford University Press, USA.
1	Gompers, Paul and Josh Lerner	(2001) The venture capital revolution. *The Journal of Economic Perspectives*. Vol. 15, Iss. 2; p. 145 (24 pages).
1	Schumpeter, Joseph	(1934) *The Theory of Economic Development*. Cambridge: Harvard University Press. (New York: Oxford University Press, 1961.) First published in German, 1912.
2	Rogers, Everett	(2003) *Diffusion of Innovations* (5th ed.), New York: Free Press.
2	von Hippel, Eric	(1994) *The Sources of Innovation*. New York: Oxford University Press, USA.
3	Knight, Frank	(1921) *Risk, Uncertainty and Profit*. Boston, New York: Houghton Mifflin Company.
3	Christensen, Clayton M. and Joseph Bower	(1995) Disruptive Technologies: Catching the wave. *Harvard Business Review*. Vol. 73, Iss. 1; p. 43 (11 pages).
3	Christensen, Clayton M.	(1997) *The Innovator's Dilemma*. Boston: Harvard Business School Press.
3	Ellsberg, D.	(1961) Risk, Ambiguity, and the Savage Axioms. *Quarterly Journal of Economics*, 75, 643–669.
3	Smith, Adam	(1759) *The Theory of Moral Sentiments*. Millar, London.
3	Smith, Adam	(1776) *An Inquiry into the Nature and Causes of the Wealth of Nations*, W. Strahan and T. Cadell, London.
3	Kim, W. Chan and Renée Mauborgne	(2005) *Blue Ocean Strategy*. Boston: Harvard Business School Press.
4	Hurst, Erik and Annamaria Lusardi	(2004) Liquidity Constraints, Household Wealth, and Entrepreneurship. *The Journal of Political Economy*. Vol. 112, Iss. 2; p. 319 (29 pages).
4	Bhidé, A.	(2000) *The Origin and Evolution of New Businesses*. New York: Oxford University Press, USA.
4	Bartlett, Sara	(2002) Seat of the Pants. *Inc. Magazine*, October 15.
4	Dennis Jr.,William J.	(1998) *Wells Fargo/NFIB Series on Business Starts and Stops*. Available online at www.nfibonline.com.

4	Gianforte, G and Marcus Gibson	(2007) *Boostrapping Your Business: Start and Grow a Successful Company with Almost No Money.* Avon, MA: Adams Media.
5	Taleb, Nassim	(2007) *The Black Swan.* New York: Random House.
5	Tetlock, Philip	(2006) *Expert Political Judgment: How Good Is It? How Can We Know?* Princeton, NJ: Princeton University Press.
5	Busenitz, Lowell W. and Jay B. Barney	(1997) Differences between Entrepreneurs and Managers in Large Organizations: Biases and Heuristics in Strategic Decision-making. *Journal of Business Venturing.* Vol. 12, Iss. 1; p. 9 (22 pages).
5	Begley, Thomas M., Boyd, David P	(1987) Psychological Characteristics Associated with Performance in Entrepreneurial Firms and Smaller Businesses. *Journal of Business Venturing.* Vol. 2, Iss. 1; p. 79 (15 pages).
5	Taleb, Nassim Nicholas	(2007) You Can't Predict Who Will Change The World. www.forbes.com.
5	Drucker, Peter	(1985) *Innovation and Entrepreneurship.* London: Collins.
5	Rotter, Julian B.	(1954) *Social Learning and Clinical Psychology.* New York: Prentice-Hall.
5	Kelley, Harold	(1967) Attribution Theory in Social Psychology. *Nebraska Symposium on Motivation*, 15. pp. 192–238.
5	Heider, F.	(1958) *The Psychology of Interpersonal Relations.* New York: Wiley.
6	Benz, M. and B. Frey	(2008) *Being Independent is a Great Thing.* Working paper, Institute for Empirical Research in Economics.
7	Drucker, Peter	(1985) *Innovation and Entrepreneurship.* London: Collins.
7	Chandler, Gaylen N., Dawn R. DeTienne, Alexander McKelvie, Troy V. Mumford	(2010) Causation and Effectuation Processes: A Validation Study. *Journal of Business Venturing.* In press.
7	Fatjo, Tom and Keith Miller	(1981) *With No Fear of Failure: Recapturing Your Dreams through Creative Enterprise.* Word Books.
8	Headd, Brian	(2004) Redefining Business Success: Distinguishing Between Closure and Failure. *Journal Small Business Economics.* 1(1) 51–61.
8	US Small Business Administration	(2009) Frequently Asked Questions About Small Business Accessed online, April 23, 2010: http://www.sba.gov/ADVO/stats/sbfaq.txt.
8	Kirchhoff, B.A.	(1997) *Entrepreneurship Economics. In The Portable MBA in Entrepreneurship*, ed. W.D Bygrave. New York, NY: John Wiley & Sons, Inc.
8	Knaup, Amy E.	(2005) Survival and Longevity in the Business Employment Dynamics data. *Monthly Labor Review.* Washington: May 2005. Vol. 128, Iss. 5; p. 50 (7 pages).
8	McDougall, Andrew	(2008) Barclays reveals SME owners plan to stay in business longer than they'll be married. Barclay's Local Business Poll. Barclays Bank. Accessed online April 23, 2010: http://www.24-7pressrelease.com/press-release/barclays-reveals-sme-owners-plan-to-stay-in-business-longer-than-theyll-be-married-58172.php.

8	Communication from the Commission to the Council	(1998) Fostering Entrepreneurship in Europe: Priorities for the Future. Com (98) 222 final.
8	Sandage, Scott	(2006) *Born Losers: A History of Failure in America*. Boston: Harvard University Press.
8	Canfield, Jack and Mark Victor Hansen	(1993) *Chicken Soup for the Soul*. Florida: Heath Communications, Inc.
8	Petroski, Henry	(2006) *Success through Failure: The Paradox of Design*. Princeton, NJ: Princeton University Press.
8	Hershey Web Site	(2010) http://www.hersheys.com/discover/milton/ milton.asp (accessed 1 May 2010).
8	Twain, Mark	(1897) *Pudd'nhead Wilson's New Calendar, Following the Equator*. Hartford: American Publishing Company. p. 124.
8	Shepherd, Dean	(2003) Learning from Business Failure: Propositions of Grief Recovery for the Self-employed. *The Academy of Management Review*. Vol. 28, Iss. 2; p. 318.
8	Aldridge Foundation	(2009) Origins of an Entrepreneur. Aldridge Foundation. Available Online www. aldrigefoundation.com (accessed 20 April 2010).
8		(2008) *Fortune Magazine*. March.
Part II	Murray, William H.	(1951) *The Scottish Himalayan Expedition*. London: J.M. Dent & Sons Ltd.
9	Corcoran, Barbara and Bruce Littlefield	(2003) *Use What You've Got, and Other Business Lessons I Learned from My Mom*. New York: Portfolio Hardcover. p. 6.
9	Virgin Galactic Online	(2009) www.virgingalactic.com (accessed 20 April 2010).
9	Ronstadt, Robert	(1988) The Corridor Principle. *Journal of Business Venturing*, Volume 3, Issue 1, Winter 1988, Pages 31–40.
9	Milgram, Stanley	(1967) The Small World Problem. *Psychology Today* I (May): 61–67.
9	Hakuta, Ken	(1989) *How to Create Your Own Fad and Make a Million Dollars*. New York: Avon Books.
10	Schumpeter, Joseph A.	(1942) *Capitalism, Socialism and Democracy*. New York: Harper and Row.
10	Atkins, Robert	(1973) *Dr. Atkins Diet Revolution (The High Calorie Way to Stay Thin Forever)*. New York: Bantam.
10		TripAdvisor.com
10	Steven Gould and Elizabeth Vrba	(1982) Exaptation—A Missing Term in the Science of Form. *Paleobiology*, 8(1), 4–15.
10	Goldenberg, Jacob, David Mazursky and Sorin Solomon.	(1999) Toward Identifying the Inventive Templates of New Products: A Channeled Ideation Approach. *JMR, Journal of Marketing Research*. Vol. 36, Iss. 2; p. 200 (11 pages).

10	Schumpeter, Joseph A.	(1911) *Theory of Economic Development: An Inquiry into Profits, Capital, Credit, Interest, and the Business Cycle*. New Brunswick: Transaction Publishers.
11	Shackle, G. L. S.	(1966) *The Nature of Economic Thought*. Cambridge: Cambridge University Press, p. 765.
11	Thaler, Richard	(1985) Mental Accounting and Consumer Choice. *Marketing Science*. Vol. 4, Iss. 3; p. 199 (16 pages).
11	Thaler, Richard	(1999) Mental Accounting Matters. *Journal of Behavioral Decision Making*. Vol. 12, Iss. 3; p. 183.
12		Cite Wiki http://en.wikipedia.org/wiki/Bootstrapping
12	Joyce, James	(1922) *Ulysses*. Paris: Sylvia Beach.
13	Fischer, Eileen and Rebecca Rueber	(2009) An Investigation of the Implications for Effectuation of Social Media Adoption. Working paper.
13	Goodman, Nelson	(1983) *Fact Fiction and Forecast*. Cambridge, MA: Harvard University Press.
13	Vargo, Stephen and Robert Lusch	(2004) Evolving to a New Dominant Logic for Marketing. *Journal of Marketing*, 68 (1), 1–17.
13	Smith, Adam	(1798) *Lectures on Jurisprudence*. Oxford: Oxford University Press, pp. 493–4.
13	Cialdini, Robert	(2006) *Influence: The Psychology of Persuasion*. New York: Harper Paperbacks.
13	Schotter, Andrew	(2003) Decision Making with Naïve Advice, *American Economic Review*, 93.
13	Bhidé, Amar	(2008) *The Venturesome Economy: How Innovation Sustains Prosperity in a More Connected*. Princeton, NJ: Princeton University Press, p. 429.
14	Hoffman, Auren	(2003) *Business Week*
15	Silver, A. David	(1985) *Venture Capital—The Complete Guide for Investors*. New York: John Wiley.
16	Sahlman, Bill	(1997) How to Write a Great Business Plan. *Harvard Business Review*. Vol. 75, Iss. 4; p. 98 (11 pages).
16	Bartlett, Sara	(2002) Seat of the Pants. *Inc. Magazine*, October 15.
16	Bhidé, A.	(2000) *The Origin and Evolution of New Businesses*. New York: Oxford University Press.
16	Brinckmann, Jan, Dietmar Grichnik, and Diana Kapsa	(2010) Should Entrepreneurs Plan or just Storm the Castle? A Meta-analysis on Contextual Factors Impacting the Business Planning-performance Relationship in Small Firms, *Journal of Business Venturing*, Vol. 25, Iss. 1; p. 24.
17	Cervantes Saavedra, Miguel	(1605–1616) *El Quijote*. Madrid: Juan de la Cuesta.
17		(1993) *Fortune Magazine*
17	Panera	*(2010)* www.panera.com (Accessed online May 1, 2010)

17	Heckler, Terry	*(2010)* http://www.hecklerassociates.com/blog (Accessed online May 1, 2010)
18	Peterson, Christopher, Steven F. Maier and Martin E.P. Seligman	(1995) *Learned Helplessness: A Theory for the Age of Personal Control.* Oxford: Oxford University Press. p. 305.
18	Bandura, Albert and Cervone, Daniel	(1986) Differential Engagement of Self-Reactive Influences in Cognitive Motivation. *Organizational Behavior and Human Decision Processes*, Vol. 38, Iss. 1; p. 92 (22 pages)
18	Goodie, Adam S.	(2003) The Effects of Control on Betting: Paradoxical Betting on Items of High Confidence with Low Value. *Journal of Experimental Psychology: Learning, Memory, and Cognition*, Vol. 29(4), 598–610.
18	Moore, D.A. and P.J. Healy	(2008) The Trouble with Overconfidence. *Psychological Review*, 115(2): 502–517.
Part III	Knecht, G. Bruce	(2002) *The Proving Ground.* New York: Grand Central Publishing.
19	Shane, Scott	(2008) *Illusions of Entrepreneurship.* Hartford, CT: Yale University Press.
19	Staw, B.M., L.E. Sandelands and J.E. Dutton	(1981) Threat Rigidity Effects in Organizational Behavior: A Multilevel Analysis. *Administrative Science Quarterly*, 26: 501.
20	Sagan, Carl	(2002) *Cosmos.* Random House.
20	Bacon, Francis	(1620) *Novum Organum.*
20	Hsu, Caroline	(2005) Entrepreneur For Social Change. *US News and World Report.* November 31.
20	Simon, Julian	*(1998) The Ultimate Resource 2.* Princeton, NJ: Princeton University Press.
20	Hansmann, Henry	(2000) *The Ownership of Enterprise.* Cambridge, MA: Belknap Press of Harvard University Press.

Index